LOOK NOW, PAY LATER

LOOK NOW,
PAY LATER

The Rise of Network Broadcasting

Laurence Bergreen

DOUBLEDAY & COMPANY, INC.
GARDEN CITY, NEW YORK
1980

ISBN: 0-385-14465-2
Library of Congress Catalog Card Number 79-7859
Copyright © 1980 by Laurence Bergreen

To my wife and parents

Acknowledgments

The search for broadcasting history placed me in the debt of many generous people who were willing to share their knowledge and understanding of the industry with me.

I would like to place at the head of the list the Museum of Broadcasting in New York, where I was a member of the staff before undertaking this project. From Robert Saudek, president, and Mary Ahern, curator, I gained valuable insights into the industry's past and acquired a way of looking at programming as historical documentation. From the museum's painstakingly assembled and catalogued collection of programming, I was able to review the history of their output in all its genres.

Next, people who have played major roles in the development of the networks and could share their firsthand observations added an important dimension, one that goes beyond mute facts. I am grateful to the following for consenting to be interviewed by me: Norman Corwin, Michael Dann, Freeman Gosden, William S. Paley, Robert Sarnoff, Robert Saudek, Fred Silverman, Dr. Frank Stanton, David White, and Dr. Vladimir Zworykin.

Also of critical importance were the facilities of the CBS News Reference Library, where much of the research about the business aspects of network history took place. Marcia Ratcliff and Roberta Hadley were attentive and resourceful in guiding me through the twists and turns of industry development. I am also indebted to Vera Mayer, director, Information Services, at NBC, and to Al Pinsky, manager, Scientific Information Services, at RCA, for their assistance.

Leslie Slocum of the Television Information Office in New York and Catharine Heinz, director of the Broadcast Pioneers Library in Washington, D.C., steered me toward important documents, as did the staff of New York University's Elmer Holmes Bobst Library, where some of the manuscript was written. RCA Laboratories and the David Sarnoff Research Center in Princeton, N.J., have my thanks as well, along with the NATAS-UCLA Television Library in Los Angeles.

Bernice and Sidney Abrams, Jane Condon Bartels, Douglas Gibbons of the Museum of Broadcasting, Frederick Jacobi of WNET, Rosemary O'Brien, Gay Orde, Frida Schubert of RCA, and Jan Waring also provided invaluable assistance, as did ABC, CBS, NBC, WGBH, and the Museum of Modern Art.

Special thanks must go to Peter Lampack for his wise counsel and patience. Joseph Gonzalez, my editor at Doubleday, has contributed a great deal to the making of this book. His dedication and good judgment is in large part responsible for its initiation and completion.

Contents

". . . during the daily peak viewing periods, television in the main insulates us from the realities of the world in which we live. If this state of affairs continues, we may alter an advertising slogan to read: 'Look Now, Pay Later.'"

—Edward R. Murrow

Part I

SIBLING RIVALRY

1

High Hopes

In April 1927, when the National Broadcasting Company was hardly six months old and the notion of radio networks was just beginning to impinge on the American consciousness, the New York *Times* asked H. G. Wells to predict the future of broadcasting as part of a series of articles entitled "The Way the World Is Going." As a professional future-watcher, Wells had high hopes for the new medium: "We should hear the best we wished; Chaliapin and Melba would sing to us; President Coolidge and Mr. Baldwin would talk to us simply, earnestly, directly." Wells expected that "in a compact of ten minutes, Julian Huxley, for example, and Bernard Shaw would settle about Darwinism forever." Furthermore, "All sporting results before we went to bed would be included, the weather forecast, advice about our garden, the treatment of influenza and the exact time. One would live in a new world and ask in all the neighbors."

But Wells was sorely disappointed by what he actually found in the ether. Though he tried to write "impartial, impersonal, unsectarian, non-tendential, non-controversial, unprejudiced, kindly things" about radio, "like the stuff its authorities invite us to transmit," he was forced to conclude that the future of broadcasting was akin to the future of crossword puzzles, "a very trivial future, indeed." No genre of programming satisfied. The music was "tenth-rate." He ridiculed advertising and proclaimed radio drama "a new and useful art if only because it teaches us what life must be like for the blind." He predicted the only regular audience for a broadcasting service would consist largely of "very sedentary persons living in badly lighted houses or otherwise unable to read, who have never realized the possibilities of the gramophone and the pianola and who have no capacity nor opportunity for thought or conversation."

Given Wells's formidable reputation, his assessment touched off a transatlantic controversy, and several weeks later the *Times* ran a gaggle of angry replies written by those with vested interests in the new industry: Lee De Forest, inventor; A. Atwater Kent, radio manufacturer; and the vice-president and general manager of the Radio Corporation of America, one David Sarnoff. De Forest, a tireless promoter of radio, even to the point of operating his own station single-handedly, predicted, "the tastes and demands of the listening public are continually on the upgrade." He believed the "sort of trash which was acceptable two years ago would no longer be tolerated." And as to Wells's fond hope that broadcasting would fade away out of public indifference, De Forest replied, "No, 'H.G.,' radio is here to stay." Sounding very much like a present-day network executive defending his industry against charges that it reduces the audience to passive, inert beings subsisting on cynical and juvenile programming, the inventor countered with a paean to broadcasting's already sweeping influence: "For radio has worked and is now working too profound a change in our national culture, our musical tastes, ever to be cast aside. Obviously what you need, 'H.G.' is a new set and a good loudspeaker. Now I have in mind just such a combination!" History does not record "H.G.'s" response to De Forest's old-fashioned huckstering.

Sarnoff, the broadcasting entrepreneur *par excellence,* took an even more aggressive stand, consigning the respected author to the ranks of the "intellectually overfed or spiritually jaded." Sounding themes the networks echo today, Sarnoff said, "Radio still suffers from a certain amount of intellectual snobbery aimed at broadcasting. It is too universal, it is claimed by some, to be truly valuable; it serves too vast an audience to maintain a high standard of service." Already, in 1927, the lines were drawn. Highbrow versus lowbrow. Criticize radio and join the ranks of Sarnoff's "intellectual snobs" or indulge and participate in the decline of Western civilization. Sarnoff knew that broadcasting was not necessarily the best communications medium, but it could, in time, become the most widespread, and it was the size of radio's, and later television's, potential audience that would come to shape, indeed, obsess, almost all programming. "Any service transmitted to millions of homes must necessarily be based upon the greatest common denominator of public good," continued Sarnoff, who foresaw for broadcasting—and for his company—"a splendid destiny in the field of mass entertainment and edification."

By the time Sarnoff made his reply, "H.G." had tuned out. Nonetheless, the dismay Wells expressed at the reality of broadcasting, that peculiar mixture of awe and outrage, remains with us today. While Wells may have been done with broadcasting, one network, CBS, was not done with him. A decade after this controversy, Orson Welles's adaptation of H. G. Wells's science fiction story "The War of the Worlds" would, for a moment, suspend its author's judgments, in the process affording him a popularity he fully enjoyed. Broadcasting's influence had become so pervasive that not even its highly vocal detractor could escape it. It was on the way to becoming a national habit and, at times, an obsession.

At the time Wells and Sarnoff were sparring about the potential of the industry, broadcasting in both England and the United States was in the hands of monopolies aspiring to the unchallenged, government-sanctioned authority enjoyed, for example, by American Telephone and Telegraph. England had its young British Broadcasting Company and the United States had its National Broadcasting Company, an institution initiated and controlled by the Radio Corporation of America, which in turn had come into being at the behest of the Navy and President Woodrow Wilson. The vigorous, chaotic era of amateur experimentation had begun to give way to a centralized system as surely as country stores would give way to supermarkets or the horse and buggy to the automobile. Within a year, however, the American system underwent a profound alteration that would completely redefine its goals. Competition entered the scene as a group of ambitious but unfocused entrepreneurs banded together to form what would eventually become the Columbia Broadcasting System. After a period of financial turmoil, the new network, a frail operation, especially when compared to the vast resources of NBC, was acquired by the twenty-six-year-old scion of a cigar-manufacturing dynasty, William Paley. Under his direction, the little network prospered and mounted a serious and unexpected challenge to NBC.

The rivalry between these two companies has shaped almost everything to do with broadcasting in this country, from the system of transmission to the size and shape of the frequency spectrum and, most significant, the characteristics of the programming put forth by each. Very quickly, the rivals discovered that they were competing each day for the same audience. In the end, straight popularity would provide the only sure route to leadership. As a result, every programming decision was, and is, made with the goal of popularity in mind; even those unusual programs designed to appeal to minority tastes are not unaffected by the networks' rivalry. The nature of this competition, the history of which forms the subject of this book, determines what networks program every minute of every day. To understand the nature of the networks, it is therefore essential to understand the development of this competition. It is an often chaotic development, leaping ahead of government efforts to hold the networks in line. Government regulation has, in fact, served to foster and legitimize this competition over the years. Its role can be compared to that of an umpire making up rules as time goes along, and then trying to persuade two ferocious players to follow them.

"Broadcasting's bone structure was formed in the nineteen twenties, and has never since been fundamentally altered or improved upon," notes Robert Saudek, a veteran television producer and the president of the Museum of Broadcasting. Nowadays, broadcasting and networks seem synonymous. Nearly all television stations are affiliated with a network. Yet the networks themselves are nothing more than a system of distribution, one that came into being as a result of the technology and commercial atmosphere of the mid-nineteen twenties. Alternative methods of distributing programming have arisen in the past and will continue to do so, depending, as always, on the availability of new technology and new commercial strategies. This is the story of the rise and the early signs of decline of one such system, the fifty years of unchallenged network supremacy.

Curiously, the network system, at its inception, was never meant to be a commercial one, never designed to make much money. NBC's parent, the Radio Corporation of America, was primarily involved in the manufacture of transmitting and receiving equipment. It began a network both as a public service and as a way to entice potential listeners into buying RCA equipment. The RCA hierarchy professed, at the beginning at any rate, to disdain the vulgarity of commercial messages appearing on local programming around the country. Yet the financial rewards would, in the end, prove irresistible, even necessary for the networks to survive. When CBS appeared on the horizon, NBC suddenly had to reconsider whether it could rely on goodwill alone for its existence. And two years later, when the Depression struck, advertising, once scorned, became a necessity. "Goodwill" and "service" quickly became ideals to which the networks paid lip service when they could afford to and when these ideals enhanced the commercial aspects of their operation.

The chief architects of the networks were contrasting American archetypes. One was David Sarnoff, the impoverished Russian immigrant who rose from messenger boy to the top of RCA, and the other, William Paley, the wealthy heir who simply purchased his network.

By the time other networks appeared on the scene—the American Broadcasting Company in 1943 and the Public Broadcasting System in 1967—the nature of the game had long been established by these two men. ABC was, in fact, nothing more than a new incarnation of one of the two networks NBC operated and which the monopoly-suspicious Roosevelt administration had forced the broadcasting giant to sell off. In contrast, PBS represented a belated government effort to resurrect the ideal of a public-service network which the commercial networks had, over the years and in the heat of competition, gradually abandoned.

Over the course of fifty years of stratagem and counterstratagem, the networks, despite the appearance of change, have remained very much the same, even while technology and social needs have progressed. Television, the most radical alteration with which the networks had to contend and one which promised exhilarating new departures, was, in the end, subjected to the same old formulas that had always ruled the industry. The development of radio and television, in fact, was nearly simultaneous. In his 1927 castigation of Wells, Sarnoff took time to predict the imminence of television's arrival. And as early as 1923 Sarnoff was urging the commercial development of television, an innovation he eventually introduced with a combination of boundless confidence and strategic delay. Indeed, Sarnoff's sixty-five-year career with RCA and its antecedent, American Marconi, was based on the commercial exploitation of technological innovations. Sarnoff was an impresario of inventors. He could hasten the gestation of television when it suited his company's purpose or slow the progress of FM radio, when its introduction would, at a particular time, prove costly and awkward. In this scheme of things, NBC has traditionally been the lucrative, highly visible showpiece of RCA, though, in the last analysis, not as important to its parent company as manufacturing. This part of the business has proved to be a less spectacular but more reliable method of earning year-in, year-out profits and, occasionally, a useful ploy for turning the tables on the competition. Sarnoff revealed his philosophy of network broadcasting when he compared NBC to a pipeline. According to his analogy, the company merely laid the pipe, and that was enough. It was not responsible for what went through it.

Where Sarnoff seized the role of technological entrepreneur, Paley, during his fifty years as the head of CBS, has styled himself the showman, someone very much concerned with what was going through the pipe. Traditionally, broadcasting has been of primary importance to CBS, which for much of its history did not possess a manufacturing division or a rich supply of patent licenses equal to RCA's. As a result, programming assumed pride of place, and the emphasis imparted a gloss and vitality to the organization which contrasted sharply with the often sluggish machinations of its bigger, clumsier competitor. With no parent company on which to rely, Paley and his lieutenants, who were often refugees from advertising agencies, liked to boast that CBS was the largest advertising medium in the world. One of the first things young William Paley did when he came to New York to see about the failing network he had bought himself was to make the rounds of advertising agencies, testing prospects, picking up advice, setting a course for himself. Programming was merely a means to an end, since Paley's CBS, unlike NBC with its grandiose pretensions of offering BBC-like public service, was frankly in the business of selling audiences to advertisers. NBC quickly fell in step, of course, and over the years the networks have geared their programming with ever increasing precision to the needs of sponsors rather than audiences. The greater the size of an audience the network could deliver to a sponsor, the higher the advertising rate it could charge, and the larger the share of the advertising market it could command. More than any other entrepreneur in the nineteen twenties, Paley perceived the commercial possibilities of a chain of stations simultaneously broadcasting the same program to a national audience. To him a network could incidentally perform a service function, but primarily it was a business scheme, a tool of commerce, a way to distribute advertisers' messages.

These two men, Paley and Sarnoff, saw in the network principle two very different possibilities. Yet despite the differences between the two networks and the fact that they competed for the same advertising dollars, CBS and NBC also developed a symbiotic relationship. CBS depended on RCA-manufactured or RCA-licensed equipment, whereas NBC could point to its competitor whenever it came under attack as a monopoly. In the expedient world of network broadcasting, even rivals fulfilled functions for one another.

Network broadcasting represents a fusion of many fields of endeavor, pre-eminently technology, commerce, and art. The technology has always come first, lying dormant until deemed suitable for commercial exploitation. The art, needless to say, has been the most abused, the most primitive component of the system. While networks have given rise to a dizzying proliferation of clever business schemes, their artistic contributions have been rather meager, though not entirely absent. This account, accordingly, shall be concerned mainly with the development of the network system, the people who contrived it and made it work, and what they hoped to gain by their efforts. It is not, strictly speaking, a study of the vast arsenal of technology on which the networks are based, although it describes how the networks have exploited that technology. It is not a study of local stations, influential as some of them have been. It is not a study of programming, except in its role as a weapon, and only the most visible one, in the battle between networks. And, finally, it is not a history of the government agency which regulates the broadcasting industry, the Federal Communications Commission, except as it has affected the growth of the networks.

It *is*, however, about the networks themselves, how they have fed off programming, technology, local stations, and even government regulation. It is about a universe in which the entrepreneur is king, taking precedence not only over performers but also over inventors. It is about a broadcasting system that has, over the years, shown itself capable of prophecy and betrayal, of years of mediocrity and moments of inspiration. It is about a business of overwhelming vanity and brutality, a business with absolutely no memory, but one whose every action is dictated by its own, forgotten past. It is about an enterprise that has been both patron and nemesis for inventors and performers and a reason for being for advertising agencies. The story of the networks furnishes one more illustration of Gresham's law, that the bad tends to drive out the good, and Balzac's dictum, that behind every great fortune there is a crime. Yet the networks survive, indeed they prosper amid a mystical aura; they are a source of boundless scorn and fascination, a public trust and a private enterprise. They are, in the end, a significant part of the social history of the twentieth century.

2

Making Waves

TODAY, THE APPROACH TO THE CAREER OF DAVID SARNOFF, who died in 1971, is fraught with peril. The self-seeking realities of his business activities and the magnanimous, inspirational legends that have been extrapolated from them by several generations of company publicists are now so intertwined that one tends to reinforce the credibility of the other. The main repository for documents and memorabilia concerning the career of the chief proponent of nationwide networks is the David Sarnoff Library, located at the highly secure, immaculate David Sarnoff Research Center in Princeton, New Jersey. Perhaps it would be more accurate to describe this facility, which RCA built and dedicated to its chief in 1967, as a shrine, for here the presence of the General, as Sarnoff was usually called after he attained the rank of brigadier general during World War II, can be felt as surely as that of a giant of history. The shrine recalls Soviet museums dedicated to preserving the spirit of Lenin. Strolling on highly polished floors between rows of glass-covered display cases, the visitor expects to come upon the embalmed body of the General himself. It is here that one can find the fifty-six volumes of RCA vice-president E. E. Bucher's company history (unpublished), correspondence with presidents, and pull-out racks containing twenty-six honorary degrees and diplomas bestowed on a man who left school when he was fourteen.

According to the late Carl Dreher, a Sarnoff associate who began writing about the industry in the nineteen twenties, "What is *not* contained in the showcases and bookcases is as important as what is included. The innocent visitor beholds a carefully laundered reproduction of the man and his works." The author of the single comprehensive biography of David Sarnoff written to date happens to be the subject's first cousin, Eugene Lyons. Predictably, he is determined to put the best possible construction on all events.

Of chief importance among the historic bric-a-brac on display is a telegraph key. David Sarnoff was a virtuoso on the telegraph key at a time when it provided the primary means of telegraphic communication. His ability to tap out Morse code provided him with the opportunity to flee the poverty of his childhood and build a career in one of the reigning electronic communications establishments of his day, the American Marconi Company. Let us try to overlook the fact that the key is not the original, but a replica of the one he used on the night the S.S. *Titanic* sank.

The legend surrounding the key dates from 1912, a decade before radio entered most homes as a source of entertainment, a time when it was known as wireless and most commonly employed by the Navy for communicating with ships at sea. It is a mild April evening in New York. The twenty-one-year-old Sarnoff, a hot-shot wireless operator employed by American Marconi, is at his post, a station perched atop the Wanamaker department store. He is startled to hear amid the static that fills his earphones a distress call: "S.S. *Titanic* ran into iceberg. Sinking fast." Churning westward through the North Atlantic on her maiden voyage, the ship has struck an iceberg at full speed off Newfoundland. A few hours later, at 2:20 A.M. on the morning of April 15, the ship goes under, taking about 1,500 passengers along with it. In the meantime, the *Titanic*'s wireless operator, twenty-four-year-old Jack Phillips, sends out two distress calls, the old, "CQD" (come quick danger), and the new, "SOS." The signal reaches another ship, the S.S. *Carpathia,* which arrives at dawn and manages to rescue 866 passengers. The *Carpathia* telegraphs its list of survivors to the *Olympia,* which in turn alerts the Wanamaker station where Sarnoff listens intently.

What he hears is shocking. Among the *Titanic*'s passengers are some of the most eminent men and women of the times. For the next three days and nights, the young wireless operator records the names of those who have perished and those who survive. President Taft orders all other wireless stations to remain silent to allow operator Sarnoff to communicate without interruption. Reporters, friends, and relatives of those aboard the stricken vessel crowd around the wireless station, and they are horrified to learn that among those who have perished are John Jacob Astor, head of that prominent family, and Isidor Straus, the importer and department store magnate. At 2:18 A.M. on April 16, the Wanamaker station receives this message from the *Olympia*, then 1350 miles away: "*Carpathia* returning to New York with women and children numbering 866. Grave fears entertained for safety of the rest."

"I doubt if I felt at all during the seventy-two hours after the news came," Sarnoff later reminisced. "It was as if bedlam had been let loose. Telephones were whirring, extras being cried, crowds were gathering around newpaper bulletin boards." In the midst of this bedlam, Sarnoff is naturally indispensable. He maintains the sole link with the tragedy at sea. The world focuses its attention on him as concerned parties wait with bated breath for news of who has lived and who has drowned. There is no time for sleep. When Sarnoff requires a respite from the laborious task of noting down the dots and dashes and translating them into letters, he goes for a massage and a steam bath, then continues his mission at another Marconi wireless station, this time at Sea Gate, in Brooklyn. At last the toll is complete; the flow of messages ceases. Sarnoff at last rests, and when he awakes, he is worldfamous. "The *Titanic* disaster brought radio to the front," Sarnoff said, "and incidentally me."

So runs the Gospel according to David Sarnoff. Yet it is extremely doubtful that events happened precisely that way. In reality, the young telegraph operator played a minor role in the unfolding of the tragedy, yet Sarnoff did little to discourage the impression RCA promoted over the years that he had single-handedly tallied the death toll while an agonized world waited. Even his assessment of the incident, with its note of modesty, does not contradict the wilder claims of the legend. It is true that the sinking of the *Titanic* proved a boon to Sarnoff's employer, American Marconi. Congress subsequently passed a Radio Act requiring ships with more than fifty passengers to carry and use wireless equipment on the theory that if more ships had heard the *Titanic*'s distress calls, they would have sped to the site of the disaster and rescued even more passengers than the *Carpathia* had been able to. American Marconi welcomed a surge in business as a result of the law, and its stock shot from 55 to 225 over a two-day period. As for David Sarnoff, he did not become a hero to the public on the basis of relaying messages from the *Olympia*. His name does not appear in contemporaneous accounts of the disaster. Indeed, Dreher insists Sarnoff was not on duty at all because the Wanamaker station was closed at night. And when Sarnoff did come on duty, it is doubtful he maintained the sole link with the rescue vessel since the Wanamaker station, as an attention-getting installation atop a department store, was involved primarily in communicating with another installation, Wanamaker's in Philadelphia, rather than with ships at sea. It is more likely that Sarnoff copied the names of survivors which the *Carpathia* was engaged in relaying to another Marconi station, located at Siasconset, on the island of Nantucket.

Yet the incident was not entirely without value for the ambitious young employee of American Marconi. In his marathon at the Wanamaker station, Sarnoff, while not attracting renown outside the company, did come to the attention of his superiors, who took note of the dedicated young operator in their midst. As a result, he was catapulted out of the rank and file into management. Furthermore, Sarnoff learned valuable lessons from his sudden encounter with history which he was to apply throughout his career. In an industry dependent on intangible, highly technical electronic phenomena, he became acutely aware of the commercial value of fixing a distinct image in the public mind. And he discovered how events could be shaded or maneuvered to suit his purposes, to call attention to himself. By simply overseeing or being present during an event, he could claim credit for it. Such was the strategy he would repeatedly adopt later in his career as he went about promoting radio, television, and, finally, color television. In short, he had made himself a name and commenced his rise through the corporate hierarchy. Nonetheless, in the career of David Sarnoff, impressive though it was, things were seldom as obvious as they seemed.

Sarnoff was born to impoverished parents in the village of Uzlian, in southern Russia, in 1891. When his father went to America to seek his fortune, the young boy stayed behind with his great-uncle, a rabbi. In these surroundings, he was exposed to poverty but also to scholarship, especially the study of the Talmud and the rigorous learning associated with it. By the turn of the century, his father, a house painter, had saved enough money to send for his family, but the effort had severely taxed his health. Arriving in America, then, was a shock for the young Sarnoff, who was immediately enlisted to help support the afflicted family. In quick succession he held a variety of jobs, most significantly a paper route. "When I was selling papers in Hell's Kitchen," Sarnoff recalled, "the dread of remaining an *ahmorets* [uneducated person] was always under the surface of my consciousness. Often it came to the surface. It jelled in a determination to rise above my surroundings. Instead of selling newspapers, I thought, I shall one day write for them. I'll be a reporter, then an editor, maybe a publisher." Already the vague outlines of a vision were forming. While Sarnoff built his empire in another medium, he remained throughout his life a prodigious writer and speaker who relished, for example, the task of publicly answering H. G. Wells's condemnation of broadcasting.

Whatever his visions may have been, Sarnoff began in the new electronic communications industry by chance. In the course of looking for a position with a newspaper, he stumbled across a job as a messenger boy with the Commercial Cable Company at a salary of five dollars a week plus overtime. His childhood ended and his real working life had begun. At Commercial Cable, Sarnoff received his first exposure to telegraphy and began practicing on a dummy telegraph key in preparation for the day he planned to become an operator. He was on the way toward realizing his dream when he was fired for requesting three days off from work to sing in a synagogue choir during the Jewish holidays. But by September 1906 he found a better job for himself, this time as office boy at the headquarters of the Marconi Wireless Telephone Company of America, usually known as American Marconi, located at 27 William Street in lower Manhattan. Sarnoff was then sixteen years old.

The organization at which Sarnoff began his career in earnest was a prototype of RCA and subsequent electronic communications corporations. American Marconi represented an effort to exploit the commercial potential of one of the two new forms of electronic communications that had their origins in nineteenth-century scientific experiments and were now subject to intensive development. The first type involved cable or point-to-point communications and was given its first practical application by the American inventor Samuel F. B. Morse. By 1861 telegraph lines crisscrossed the nation. At last it had become possible for both ends of the continent to relay signals almost instantaneously, perhaps the most significant attribute of electronic communications. The next important step along this chain of development came in 1876, when Alexander Graham Bell demonstrated his telephone at the Philadelphia Centennial Exposition. Bell had discovered how to send along wires not just bursts of electricity, which shackled communications to the dots and dashes of Morse code, but the human voice itself. Now point-to-point electronic communications could come not only to a central station, but into the home. In time, responsibility for administering most cable-bound communications in the United States fell to the company Bell helped found, American Telephone and Telegraph.*

* Though broadcasting, or transmitting electronic signals through the air rather than through a cable, followed a separate line of development, the two systems were to overlap in ever more surprising ways. In the later nineteen twenties, when the networks began operating, they fed programs to affiliates through landlines leased from AT&T, and in fact became the

The second type of electronic transmission, whereby signals are relayed through the air, began with the German physicist Heinrich Hertz. In the process of testing the electromagnetic theories of Scottish physicist James Maxwell, Hertz showed that current can be projected into the air, where it takes the form of waves. This type of transmission was defined, in the manner of the horseless carriage, by what it was not: wireless transmission. Curiously, Hertz saw no great future for his discovery, but his name became part of the terminology of radio. (A hertz is a unit of electromagnetic frequency equal to one cycle per second.)

The next development in wireless transmission took place thanks to Guglielmo Marconi, a young Italian inventor who had been intrigued by Hertz's discovery. Marconi was just twenty when he invented a transmitter and receiver capable of relaying electronic signals through the air. To create the electric base for his system, Marconi passed a spark across a gap, thereby liberating electric impulses into the air; to recapture the signal in a wire, Marconi devised the antenna. Working on his father's estate in Perugia, Italy, the youthful recluse went about perfecting his invention, which amounted to the first workable wireless or radio transmitter. Furthermore, by installing a transmitter on board his yacht, Marconi pointed the way toward a useful and practical application for his invention: ship-to-shore communication. Though numerous inventors would eventually add crucial refinements to wireless transmission (above all, the ability to dispense with Morse code and transmit the human voice), it was Marconi who was chiefly responsible for liberating electronic transmission from the cable.

Unlike Hertz, Marconi not only predicted a great future for his invention but also was quite ready to cash in on it. After two years of experimentation, he moved to England, where the business climate seemed most suited to the exploitation of his invention, and a year later, in 1900, joined with a group of businessmen in forming a company that was to dominate the field of wireless communications for decades to come. In 1901, under the watchful gaze of both British and American governments, Marconi succeeded in transmitting the letter S across the Atlantic to his company's recently formed subsidiary, American Marconi. Remarkably astute in the matter of publicity, the inventor could rest assured that the strategic implications of his feat had been fully appreciated on both sides of the ocean.

Such were the origins of the company at which the young Sarnoff

---

company's biggest customer. Cable itself became an important adjunct to broadcasting in the nineteen sixties by offering television viewers better reception and more programming sources.

was employed and whose ways he rapidly learned. Since filing was one of his tasks, he took the opportunity to study letters and interoffice correspondence for both their content and their style. He also educated himself in the intricacies of the company's operation. Whenever the great man, Marconi, traveled to the New World to inspect the New York branch of his enterprise, Sarnoff endeavored to make himself useful. As a result, the young man found himself delivering flowers and candy to Marconi's numerous New York amours.

At the same time, Sarnoff pursued his dream of becoming a telegraph operator. The William Street headquarters of American Marconi maintained links with four shore stations: Sea Gate, in Brooklyn; Sagaponeck, located at the eastern end of Long Island; the Siasconset station on Nantucket; and the Cape Cod station. Sarnoff's practice with a dummy key eventually paid off when he was permitted to handle some of the inter-station traffic. In 1908 he received his first assignment as operator, at Siasconset, and just a year later he became manager of Sea Gate, a position which paid a respectable sixty-dollar-a-month salary. After a brief sojourn as a wireless operator on a seal-hunting trip, Sarnoff returned to New York, where he assumed a post as manager of the station atop the Wanamaker department store.

As we have seen, the publicity attendant on the *Titanic* disaster proved a windfall to the relatively unknown American Marconi. Having succeeded in calling attention to his company, and "incidentally" to himself, Sarnoff was rewarded with promotions that made his old dream of becoming a telegraph operator seem humble indeed. By the year's end, he had been appointed chief inspector of wireless installations on ships in New York Harbor. In short order, he became chief inspector on a national scale, then assistant traffic manager. Sarnoff further consolidated his position by lecturing executives on the technical aspects of the business with which he had such long-standing and rare rapport for a man in his early twenties. He also found the time to train aspiring operators, thus spreading his influence even further within the company.

This sudden alteration in Sarnoff's fortunes affected his thinking as well. No longer content to remain exclusively on the humbler, technical side of American Marconi, Sarnoff yearned to participate in the true center of power and profit located in the company's executive suite. He left the ranks of the inventors and engineers for those of the entrepreneurs. He had tasted power and gained a sense of the larger possibilities of the industry, and, incidentally, himself. Sarnoff knew he lacked the capability of devising an innovation equal to Marconi's and knew that having the best telegraphic "fist" in the company could

take him only so far. What was left to him then was to exploit the
fruits of the labors of Marconi and other, still unidentified inventors.
Over a meal he told an associate, "An engineer or a scientific experi-
menter is at the place where money is going out. The place to make
money is where money is coming in." Sarnoff's transition from employee to manager, from engineer to impresario, was essentially complete.

Sarnoff's influence was restricted to the limited universe of American Marconi. But Marconi was not the only inventor working in the
field of wireless communication, and his company not the only one siz-
ing up the chances for its commercial exploitation. Reginald Fessenden, a Canadian inventor who had come to the United States as a university professor to experiment with wireless transmission, speculated
on the possibility of replacing Marconi's dots and dashes with the
sound of the human voice, with music, and eventually with the full
range of human sonic experience. The secret of achieving this result,
Fessenden was quite sure, lay in the nature of the electricity used to
transmit the signal.

Fessenden had two kinds of current at his disposal: direct current,
in which electrons flow in a continuous stream, and alternating current, in which the electrons periodically reverse direction. By the turn
of the century, DC held sway; it had been the basis not only for Marconi's system but also for Edison's incandescent lamp, developed in
1879. Direct current was the kind of electricity the company Edison
helped to create, General Electric, hoped to sell to its customers. Rival
Westinghouse, on the other hand, became a proponent of AC, with
which Fessenden was experimenting. Nonetheless Fessenden found
patronage at GE, where another inventor, a recent Swedish immigrant
named Ernst Alexanderson, was already at work. Alexanderson was
one of the first of a new breed, the inventor working within the corporate framework. Whereas Marconi and especially Edison were lone inventors who eventually created companies to exploit their wares, Alexanderson and legions of engineers after him invented to order. In time
the company swamped the lone inventor, thereby setting up a tension
that was to persist throughout Sarnoff's career. Whether these com-
pany-sponsored inventors were truly innovators in the sense of an
Edison or a Marconi is questionable, but they were expert refiners.
Alexanderson set about designing a generator of alternating current
for Fessenden, to be located at Brant Rock, Massachusetts. Near the
end of 1906, wireless operators were astonished to hear, amid the conventional dots, dashes, and static, the sound of voices, music, poetry,
and song in their earphones. Fessenden had successfully replaced

Marconi's successive bursts of electric impulses with a continuous wave capable of carrying continuous sounds.

The experiments held vast implications for the nature of wireless transmission. The limitations of Morse code no longer stood in the way; radio, as the new means of electronic communication was coming to be called, suddenly had a future beyond naval applications and the limited sphere of American Marconi's activities. Not only could radio carry any kind of music or information, it could reach every receiver without a special hookup or cable. Soon wireless transmission came to be known as "broadcasting," a term derived from the broadcast or random-dispersion method of sowing seed. Fessenden's theories combined with Alexanderson's alternator meant that it was now possible to broadcast an unlimited variety of signals over enormous areas. The new medium was as free as the air, but its possible applications, while exhilarating in the abstract, were as yet dim, chaotic. From the vantage point of 1928, Sarnoff reflected on this turning point: "The mission of radio, it was thought, was the creation of a new system of telegraphic communications, and upon this basis marine and transoceanic services by radio were found in both Europe and the United States. The destiny of radio had been set. Then came the first faint sounds of the human voice." He sensed the beginning of the end for American Marconi and its ways of doing things. He asked himself how he could capitalize on the new industry that was sure to grow around the science of radio broadcasting. Though not yet in a position to demonstrate new applications, he followed the publicity-grabbing stunts of an inventor who was.

In January 1910, Lee De Forest, an engineer who had been graduated from the Sheffield School of Yale University, brought two microphones (actually converted telephone mouthpieces) into the Metropolitan Opera House and connected them to a transmitter on the roof of the building. On one night he arranged for a broadcast of *Tosca,* starring Enrico Caruso and on the following night, *Cavalleria Rusticana* and *I Pagliacci,* also featuring Caruso. Available receiving equipment did not match the magnitude of this venture. Only those lucky few with access to wireless equipment aboard ship or stationed at specially prepared receiving stations were able to hear the performances in their headphones. De Forest's feat was very likely the sweetest moment in an often bitter career which ran the gamut from inventing to broadcasting, investing, and quarreling with other inventors he thought were trespassing on his territory. As an inventor, De Forest achieved a record of solid accomplishments; as an entrepreneur, he engaged in an erratic assortment of experiments which other, cooler heads, like David Sarnoff, studied with great interest.

De Forest's work centered on the vacuum tube, then known as the glass bulb detector, which had been invented several years earlier, in 1904, by the English engineer John Fleming, who himself was building on an earlier discovery by Edison that a wire sealed in the bulb of an incandescent lamp would conduct electricity in only one direction. The deaf genius of Menlo Park perceived no immediate application for this phenomenon, which came to be known as the Edison effect, but Fleming set to work refining the device, making it the equivalent of a valve which could convert currents in the air to those that would operate earphones. De Forest added another element to Fleming's vacuum tube, a grid that caused it to deliver greatly increased amounts of energy, leading to a stronger, surer signal. De Forest called his invention the audion, patented it in 1906, and saw great things coming. Believing he had discovered the "Invisible Empire of the Air," he lost no time creating a company and commencing experimental broadcasts from a laboratory at Fourth Avenue and Nineteenth Street in Manhattan.

By 1916, De Forest operated what we would recognize as a broadcasting station. He relished playing the role of disc jockey and emcee, introducing speakers such as his mother-in-law (on women's rights), recorded music, live performances, and, most importantly, newspaper items about that year's presidential race between Woodrow Wilson and Charles Evans Hughes.

De Forest undertook this exhausting range of activities in the name of publicity. He did not expect to earn money from transmitting radio programs practically no one was capable of receiving, but by demonstrating the feasibility of broadcasting he hoped to secure corporate investment in his crucial invention, the audion. Broadcasting was simply a means of attracting attention to the hardware. De Forest's broadcast of election returns did merit attention from the New York *Times*, which reported that "amateur operators within a radius of 200 miles had been forewarned of the new information service, and it was estimated that several thousand of them received the news." The account also mentioned that many listeners were using "newly-manufactured wireless telephones," factory-built earphones, in other words. De Forest's experiments were known to everyone in the tiny radio industry, but news of the growing number of broadcasting enthusiasts eager for receiving equipment made Sarnoff's head spin. He was now a rising young executive in Marconi's sales division and at last in a position to capitalize on the rapid proliferation of technological developments. What could the company manufacture to sell to this potentially vast audience? What kind of equipment would they be needing and what would they pay for it? The inventors—among whom Fessenden,

Alexanderson, and De Forest were only the best known—had taken the new radio industry to the point where it was ripe for commercial exploitation. The technology had passed from the hands of the inventor to the company, which could, to Sarnoff's way of thinking, reap an enormous profit by selling it to the consumer. Accordingly, he concluded American Marconi could and should capitalize on the inevitable spread of broadcasting, even though the company was not in the business of manufacturing equipment for home use. He began writing memos about his ideas to his bosses.

To Edward J. Nally, Marconi's commercial manager, Sarnoff wrote in November 1916, just at the time De Forest was attracting widespread attention with his coverage of the Wilson-Hughes race:

> I have in mind a plan of development which would make radio a "household utility" in the same sense as the piano or phonograph. The idea is to bring music into the house by wireless. . . .
> The problem of transmitting music has already been solved in principle, and therefore all receivers attuned to the transmitting wavelength should be capable of receiving such music. The receiver can be designed in the form of a simple "Radio Music Box" and arranged for several different wavelengths, which should be changeable with the throwing of a single switch or pressing of a single button.
> The "Radio Music Box" can be supplied with amplifying tubes and a loudspeaking telephone, all of which can be neatly mounted in one box. . . . There should be no difficulty in receiving music perfectly when transmitted within a radius of 25 to 50 miles. Within such a radius, there reside hundreds of thousands of families. . . .

In this proposal Sarnoff attempted to synthesize the advances of the prominent inventors of the moment, each of whom naturally was inclined to be blind to any inventions beyond his own laboratory. Sarnoff took special pains to explain the developments that had taken place since American Marconi, which had once considered itself the last word in technical innovation, had gone into business. It should be noted that, though he was primarily concerned with formulating a device the company could manufacture, Sarnoff also speculated on the nature of the material that could be broadcast. He foresaw a limited number of wavelengths, or channels, and a great deal of music. He appears in the memo on the verge of suggesting that American Marconi follow De Forest's example and get into the broadcasting business as a means of stimulating equipment sales, but he did not dare go so far so fast. Sarnoff's message was that events were bypassing American Marconi, and on that score he was correct. The telegraph key, on which his career had been based, was swiftly becoming obsolete.

Hazy on programming, Sarnoff became quite specific about projected revenue from the sale of radio music boxes:

> . . . there are about 15 million families in the United States alone, and if only 1 million, or 7 percent of the total families, thought well of the idea, it would, at the figure mentioned [Sarnoff had proposed a price of $75 per unit] mean a gross business of about $75 million, which should yield considerable revenue.

This memo has been the object of considerable debate and controversy. Sarnoff proponents see in it proof that the twenty-five-year-old Marconi executive single-handedly dreamed up and launched a crusade on behalf of the radio, but in fact all the ideas he was proposing were in currency at the time, and had been for six years or so, ever since De Forest made his broadcast from the Metropolitan Opera in 1910. Sarnoff himself was sensitive about the originality—or lack of it—in the memo. In a 1968 collection of his writings entitled *Looking Ahead,* Sarnoff backdated the memo to September 30, 1915, probably to avoid the appearance that he was simply capitalizing on De Forest's experiments. Apparently ghosts were returning to haunt Sarnoff more than forty years after he followed so closely behind De Forest. Though the memo cannot be said to have originated the notion of regular broadcasting for home consumption, it does have the distinction of putting forth the electronic equivalent of the Model T, another device which most Americans could afford and which would, in time, begin to transform society. Like the automobile, whose rise it parallels, radio and subsequently television are umbrella terms covering a multitude of inventions grouped together for the convenience of mass manufacturing. There can be no single radio or television inventor any more than there can be a single inventor of the automobile; there are instead contributors to various lines of development, all leading to important components in the final product. Sometimes these contributors tread perilously close upon one another, as in De Forest's case, but it is the entrepreneur, the role Sarnoff now tried to fill, who determines the end result.

Sarnoff's memo, however, met with a stony response. American Marconi had no intention of entering the "Radio Music Box" market, for reasons that are not hard to understand. Who would pay seventy-five dollars for an instrument capable of receiving programs which were not yet being broadcast? American Marconi, furthermore, was in the business of equipping and operating wireless equipment for maritime purposes. In trying to cultivate a home market, Sarnoff was an anomaly. But he did not have long to brood over the discouraging reaction, because a new event was about to shake the entire wireless and radio industry, the First World War. On April 7, 1917, the day after the United States entered the war, the government shut down all non-essential broadcasting activities and expropriated whatever equipment it thought it might need. De Forest went off the air. The development of domestic radio broadcasting would now be at a standstill for an indefinite period of time, but at least Sarnoff did not have to fret over other aspiring pioneers getting the jump on him. Meanwhile, he took a forty-five-dollar-a-week job as commercial manager of American Marconi, now actively assisting the Navy in setting up a communications network, and married a young woman recently arrived from France, Lizette Hermant. Thereafter a joke circulated around the offices of American Marconi. "She spoke no English and I spoke no French," Sarnoff remarked, "so what else could we do?"

Though he had yet to achieve his new goal, i.e., the manufacture of a home radio, Sarnoff had, by the time the war arrived, come an extraordinary distance, especially in a business that was not partial to immigrants. He had come from Russia, speaking no English, and gone from messenger boy to telegraph operator to executive, and to accomplish this feat, he had adopted a feisty, competitive attitude. "I realized that I couldn't compete with gentiles in a gentile industry if I were merely as good as they were," he told an associate years later. "But if I were, say, twice as good, they couldn't hold me down. So I decided to be twice as good."

3

Cats' Whiskers

IN THE BEGINNING, THERE WAS CHAOS.

Sarnoff's determination to drag radio into the mainstream of big business ran counter to the experience of most Americans, to whom radio was a hobby, something to build, tinker with, and enjoy in the company of other enthusiasts. When the wartime ban on nonmilitary broadcasting was finally lifted on October 1, 1919, experimental stations, some licensed by the controlling organization of the day, the Bureau of Navigation, and some not, sprang up like mushrooms across the country. Since the notion of manufactured radios had gotten no further than Sarnoff's memos and others like it, most radio sets in use were home-built and did not use the vacuum tubes only an engineer could understand and a millionaire could afford. Instead, the key element of the amateur set was a crystal, commonly galena or silicon. The molecular structure of such crystals allowed them to capture electric impulses in the air, and if they were touched in just the right way by an extremely thin wire—known as a cat's whisker—they would pass on the signal to a pair of earphones. The crystal and cat's whisker thus performed the same task as De Forest's audion, much less efficiently but much more cheaply. This mechanism became the heart of the crystal set, the building of which was a widespread hobby by the end of the war. Instructions for the building of a crystal set were easy to come by in magazines or a Boy Scout manual, and the components cost just two dollars. With this kind of casual, home-built equipment, early radio was a radically different medium from what it is today. Active participation was required of the listener, who had not only to make the set but also to find the stations—the latter being an extremely tricky business. As opposed to staying with and enjoying one easy-to-receive local station, the challenge the crystal set enthusiast undertook was to tune in as many stations as possible. The inanimate crystal set seemed to be endowed with magical properties, truly able to pluck voices out of the ether. The excitement here was not so much in the actual programming as in hearing distant stations from other counties, other states. Operators of most transmitters were, like the crystal set owners and builders, enthusiasts who liked to use the airwaves to talk about their equipment. They were more akin to ham operators than commercial broadcasters, signing on and off as they pleased. Moreover, as amateurs, they had nothing to sell.

One station, however, soon broke out of the mold. The enterprise, backed by Westinghouse, was East Pittsburgh's KDKA, generally considered to be the first broadcasting station in the United States (i.e., the first to broadcast regularly scheduled programs). In 1915, a Westinghouse engineer, Dr. Frank Conrad, had built a small receiver to pick up time signals broadcast by the Naval Observatory. The following year, which also witnessed De Forest's broadcast of election returns, Conrad added a transmitter, which the Bureau of Navigation assigned the experimental call letters 8XK. The station was located in the second floor of the garage next to Conrad's home in Wilkinsburg, Pennsylvania. When the ban on nonmilitary broadcasting ended in 1919, Conrad began playing and transmitting phonograph music. Enough crystal sets had been built and were in use for Conrad to receive a large number of enthusiastic letters requesting a regularly scheduled service. Conrad obliged with two hours of music broadcast on Wednesday and Saturday evenings. Aware of the station's growing audience, local merchandisers groped for ways to exploit the commercial potential of the newest mass medium in town. Sponsored messages, or direct payment to the station in return for special programming favors, were, as yet, beyond the pale, but businesses discovered other ways of capitalizing on the instant publicity radio could provide. The Hamilton Music store, in Conrad's hometown, supplied the station with discs in return for an announcement telling listeners where they might purchase the recordings played; sales improved. The Joseph Horne Company, a Pittsburgh department store, went a step further. It began selling a ten-dollar Amateur Wireless Set, a precursor of Sarnoff's proposed radio music box, and to attract attention to the novelty, set up a receiver in its music department. H. P. Davis, a vice-president of Conrad's backer, Westinghouse, became convinced his company should also enter the market with a factory-built receiver. Soon a variety of new companies would be placing sets on the market, long before Sarnoff's device appeared. It was a case not necessarily of great minds running in the same direction, but of commercial minds hitting upon clever ways to exploit the obvious.

As Westinghouse became more seriously interested in broadcasting, it decided to erect a tiny station, a successor to the rig in Conrad's garage, in one of its East Pittsburgh plants. The new facility, a single room containing equipment and personnel, received a new license and call letters on October 27, 1920. The new letters were KDKA.*

Hoping to attract the same attention De Forest had received when he broadcast the returns of the Wilson-Hughes presidential race four years earlier, the newly licensed KDKA hastily made arrangements with the Pittsburgh *Post* to relay returns of the 1920 elections, which the paper would supply to the station over the phone. The number of listeners for the broadcast was estimated at about two thousand, but Westinghouse attracted priceless publicity for its new venture. Slowly and a bit awkwardly, the new medium discovered an advantage it had over newspapers: immediacy.

Throughout the early nineteen twenties, KDKA continued to discover new ways to expand its programming and studios. In warm weather engineers pitched a large tent alongside the original structure to serve as a studio for live musical broadcasts. The drapes worked well acoustically, and later became a standard feature of early indoor studios. Most of the live entertainment was supplied to the station free of charge. The station would obligingly send a car for the performer,

---

* The Commerce Department and subsequent government licensing authorities at first assigned all domestic broadcast stations a three-letter code beginning with *K*. As stations proliferated, the code expanded to four letters, and later those stations west of the Mississippi were assigned letters beginning with a *K* while Eastern stations had a *W* designation. Stations such as KDKA in Pittsburgh or KYW in Chicago remained exceptions to the new rule and retained their *K* designation even after the expansion. The popularity of KDKA helped to trigger a boom in station licensing. The Commerce Department licensed nearly a hundred new stations a month during the spring and summer of 1922, and various combinations of call letters were assigned for often whimsical reasons. The Detroit Police Department station was called KOP; the Chicago *Tribune* asked for the letters WGN for its station so that listeners would remember the slogan "World's greatest newspaper"; KFDR in Grand Coulee, Washington, wished to honor President Roosevelt; WTOP in Washington, D.C., hoped to remind listeners it was at the top of the dial; and KAGH of Crossett, Arkansas, was intended as an acronym for "Keep Arkansas Green Home." By 1923, six hundred stations were in operation.

perhaps a soprano on tour. Arriving at KDKA, she would find herself confronted with a studio which Robert Saudek, who began his career in broadcasting at KDKA, compared to "the inside of a burlap-lined casket. Burnt orange, a favorite decorator color in 1922, was chosen for the draped-silk meringues that billowed from the ceiling to disguise light bulbs. The door was very heavy. A sign on the wall framed the single word, SILENCE. A tall vase of gladioli stood in the corner. And in the center of this still room stood the working part, a microphone whose unruffled, impersonal, inscrutable self-confidence gave the whole place the feeling of an execution chamber."

Other KDKA programming highlights of this very early era included a speech by President Harding, the World Heavyweight Boxing championship bout, live from New Jersey (it was Dempsey v. Carpentier), the Davis Cup from Pennsylvania, and even the World Series from the Polo Grounds, where the Giants beat the Yankees. All these 1921 programs were firsts of their kind, and proved to be an extraordinary stimulus to the public demand for manufactured sets that Sarnoff had predicted five years before.

Along with the boom in stations came the boom in sets. In June 1921, Westinghouse introduced its first model, the Aeriola, Jr., priced at $25. The largest manufacturer of the day, however, or at least the one who claimed to be, was Powell Crosley, Jr., whose firm sold a single tube set for $14.50 and a Trirdyn Special for $75. By 1926, one fifth of all American homes were equipped with radio, and the audience became correspondingly vast. In contrast to the handful of listeners who heard KDKA's broadcast of the Harding-Cox election returns, approximately 20 million tuned in to hear Coolidge triumph in 1924. Newspapers began printing schedules of station programs as a way of attracting readers. The New York *Times* went so far as to carry the schedules of stations across the country, in order to prod the patient "DXer" (a listener attempting to receive as many stations as possible) into searching for WLS in Chicago, WSB Atlanta, and KPO San Francisco in the suddenly crowded ether.

When the Radio Licensing Act of 1912 was passed, most broadcasting occurred on the same frequency, 360 meters, which meant that signals commonly overlapped. Occasionally stations in the same locality would operate at alternating times of day, but in the boom era of pre-network broadcasting, such organized behavior was rare. More commonly stations adopted a silent night, an evening when the signal occupying the sole available frequency went off the air to allow DXers to pick up stations in other cities. To alleviate the crush, the hard-pressed Department of Commerce opened the 400-meter frequency for broadcasting in 1922. Stations on this frequency would have to meet certain standards, including transmitting at a relatively powerful level, 500 to 1,000 watts, and eliminating recorded music from their programming. The class B stations, gathered at the 400-meter frequency, became the most popular. Reception was clearer, programming more original, signal range wider. They came to represent a centralized approach to the chaotic business of radio and opened the way to further experiments with a chain of broadcasting. Meanwhile, the smaller, more locally oriented stations competed for space in the ether at the original 360-meter wavelength, and these stations, harder to tune in, more casual in operation, and less ambitious in programming came to resemble local and independent stations. Already, as early as 1922, a two-tier structure had begun to evolve, encouraged by the Department of Commerce's arbitrary limitation of available frequencies.

Broadcasting was still in the hands of amateurs and small businesses. Hotels and newspapers commonly operated radio stations as a way of attracting publicity, the hotel stations often broadcasting live music from the ballroom and the newspaper stations passing on headlines from the newsroom. The giant electronic corporations were active primarily on the receiving end, expecting to cash in on radio from the sale of sets. They were content to leave the erratic, expensive, and still primitive world of broadcasting to the more daring—that is, until AT&T entered the field. Things have never been quite the same since.

At first, the phone company envisioned an operation equivalent to an open-ended telephone. The company would maintain a station for members of the public, who would, upon payment of a toll, broadcast a message to an unsuspecting world, then yield the microphone to the next customer. AT&T called its system toll broadcasting, but the only component of this notion that survived was the concept of charging customers for use of the facilities. Eventually, of course, the "public" paying the toll would become advertisers. As a next step, the company, as early as February 1922, planned to link thirty-eight stations by telephone line, allowing them to carry the same programming simultaneously.

The company had stumbled upon the two basic conditions of modern networks: a chain of stations broadcasting the same program at the same time, and a charge for the use of the system. In August 1922, the phone company inaugurated its radio station, the famous WEAF, whose transmitters, located initially at 463 West Street in Manhattan, broadcast for a few hours a day on the tumultuous 360-meter wavelength. WEAF was in operation for only a matter of days before it broadcast what is generally considered to be the first paid commercial announcement. The Queensborough Corporation, a concern seeking to sell apartments in Jackson Heights, paid the station fifty dollars to allow one of its employees to step before the microphone and make a ten-minute-long flowery oration on the subject. The speech was apparently successful since the company followed up with more commercials. The net result of the first broadcast advertising campaign was several thousand dollars' worth of new business for the Queensborough Corporation.

That WEAF was serious about advertising became evident when, in November 1922, a former secretary of the Association of National Advertisers, George F. McClelland, became the station manager. The enthusiastic, charming, and gregarious McClelland held WEAF firmly to a commercial course and persuaded other companies to buy time for ten-minute talks. He was in business to make money, and he succeeded. By 1923, WEAF could show a profit of $150,000.

The WEAF experiment sent shock waves through the loyal community of enthusiastic amateurs and hobbyists, who bitterly resented the intrusion of big business in their field. To advertise or not to advertise became a hotly debated issue of the day. The trade paper *Printer's Ink,* after noting that half a million radio sets had been sold in the previous six months (this was still 1922, a banner year for the radio industry on a number of counts), delicately suggested that, "handled with tact and discretion, radio advertising might become effective and profitable; on the other hand, it may easily be handled in such a way as not only to defeat its own purposes, but also to react unfavorably upon advertising in general. It will not do to forget that the public's good-will toward advertising is an asset of incalculable importance." The analysis concluded, "Any attempt to make the radio an advertising medium, in the accepted sense of the term, would, we think, prove positively offensive to great numbers of people. The family circle is not a public place, and advertising has no business intruding there unless it is invited." Even the advertising community considered commercial announcements too intrusive to be effective. On the receiving end, amateurs displayed similar concern. *Radio Broadcast,* a handsome publication catering to the dedicated DXer, reminded listeners of the situation in 1922: "Driblets of advertising, most of it indirect so far, to be sure, but still unmistakable, are flitting through the ether every day. Concerts are seasoned here and there with a dash of advertising paprika." The monthly journal predicted that "more of this sort of thing may be expected, and once the avalanche gets a good start, nothing short of an act of Congress will suffice to stop it."

Congress was for the moment powerless to affect the industry's dizzyingly rapid progress. Commerce Department Secretary Herbert Hoover voiced great concern. "It is inconceivable that we should allow so great a possibility for service to be drowned in advertising chatter," he said, but his department merely licensed stations and did not attempt to control the content of their programming.

Despite a chorus of opposition, AT&T went its own way, contemplating the least offensive manner in which to insinuate advertising into the broadcasting milieu. The company was willing to risk public criticism because it foresaw extraordinary profits from the practice. A 1923 AT&T memo noted that WEAF cost $175,000 a year to operate and predicted that an "organized sales force" would show a probable revenue of $330,000 in a year. AT&T had further impetus to begin advertising because that was the only manner in which it appeared to be able to earn money out of broadcasting. Westinghouse's KDKA provided a service in the hope of stimulating that company's sales of radio sets, but AT&T was not yet planning to sell radios to the consumer. The only way it could get a return out of broadcasting was to adapt its telephone toll concept to the airwaves. From AT&T's point of view, advertising was a necessity. "To do anything else than make a complete sales effort is to invite failure," concluded the memo.

WEAF's toll broadcasting received a substantial boost when the station secured Department of Commerce permission to broadcast on the exclusive 400-meter band. Now WEAF was in the big time. Forbidden to use phonograph records, WEAF expanded into new studios for live performances, located at AT&T headquarters, 195 Broadway. The station also racked up an impressive series of remote broadcasts, primarily of sporting events. And always it benefited from AT&T's superb technical resources—the best in available equipment and technicians. Other stations had to make do with inferior lines leased from Western Union.

Since WEAF had to rely on live music, it became the radio showcase in New York for performers of all kinds. While this development served to increase the popularity of station and performers alike, it also introduced a new and troublesome concern, for the performers were no longer content with unpaid appearances. They clamored for what was known as "electric money." Musicians' and songwriters' unions portrayed radio as a threat rather than a source of free advertising. They pointed out that when it was announced that a concert given by the violinist Fritz Kreisler would be broadcast, half the tickets were returned. Record sales dipped. WEAF and other stations cleverly sidestepped both the musicians' claims and the public's distaste of advertising by adopting a form of indirect advertising. Companies wishing to use the airwaves to advertise did not sponsor messages, but gave their names to bands and orchestras which performed constantly on the air. Naturally, every mention of the band's name constituted a plug, not as effective as a direct sales pitch, perhaps, but not as provocative, either. In 1923, WEAF audiences heard the Browning King Orchestra (formerly Anna Byrne's Orchestra) and the A&P Gypsies. Other bands of the era included the Cliquot Club Eskimos, Ipana Troubadours, Champion Sparkers, the Eagle Neutrodyne Trio, and the Atwater-Kent Entertainers. Often more thought went into the names than into the music. Companies lending bands their name paid the station as much as four hundred dollars an hour for the privilege, in addition to the musicians' fees.

Then the enterprising WEAF hit on a new solution to the ticklish subject of sponsored entertainment. Why not charge a company for giving its name not just to a band but to an entire program? This was probably as close as the station could come to the alarming prospect of direct advertising without committing itself to a flagrantly commercial course. The willing "sponsor" was the National Carbon Company, manufacturers of Eveready batteries; the program, called "The Eveready Hour," thus became radio's first large-scale variety venture. Beginning in late 1923, the show presented a hodgepodge of talent: George Gershwin, Weber and Fields, the Flonzaley String Quartet, even D. W. Griffith, along with orchestras, bands, and dramatic readings, all of which drew on the formidable entertainment and artistic reservoir of talent available in New York.

In addition to presenting big-name performers, "The Eveready Hour" set other, less visible, but even more influential precedents. Though it broadcast the program from its studios, WEAF did not have a hand in organizing the program or in hiring the performers. It only supplied a service—use of its facilities—to the public, in this case National Carbon. Actually, National Carbon did not put the show together either, but hired the N. W. Ayer advertising agency to do the job. The agency created a stir by paying Will Rogers a thousand dollars to appear on the air. Big names, big talent, and big business had come to radio.

Most important, the program, though it originated in WEAF studios, was conveyed by AT&T landlines to stations around the country for simultaneous broadcast. WEEI in Boston, WEAR in Cleveland, and WGR in Buffalo, for example, formed part of a chain of stations linked together especially for the show, though they were otherwise independent of each other. Stations were delighted to join the chain, for it relieved them of the burden of furnishing programming for an hour and guaranteed them a sizable audience, attracted by the promise of stars.

For all intents and purposes, then, WEAF was serving by 1924 as the flagship station of a commercial radio network.

Though AT&T did not call its WEAF chain a network, the pattern

the networks would follow, when they were established three years
later, was set: a broadcasting station owned by a large communications company hired out its facilities to a company which in
turn engaged an advertising agency to package a program packed
with stars who would convey the company name to the largest possible audience. All this had come about hardly more than three years
after KDKA began regularly scheduled broadcasts in Pittsburgh, eight
years after Sarnoff advocated the manufacture of radios, sixteen years
after De Forest brought a microphone into the Metropolitan Opera
House, and just twenty-three years after Marconi contrived to broadcast the letter S across the Atlantic. All the building blocks of the network edifice were falling into place. From now on, new developments
would begin at the top and work their way down, wrenching the
fledgling industry out of the hands of enthusiastic amateurs and placing it at the disposal of government and big business.

4

E Pluribus Unum

To CONTEMPLATE THE CIRCUMSTANCES surrounding the creation of RCA and its network, NBC, is to mourn lost opportunities—the opportunity to establish the American equivalent of the BBC, to ensure programming standards at the network rather than the local level, to protect broadcasting services from a competitive mania—in short, to insulate the new network from influences everyone from amateur to advertiser professed to despise.

At the time RCA came into being, AT&T was well on the way to becoming the nation's primary broadcasting service. The phone company had in operation its flagship station, its network, and its sales team, and even planned to begin manufacturing radios. It sought to eliminate "amateur" transmitters it considered to be infringing on its patents. Sarnoff and American Marconi, in contrast, were in a temporary eclipse that had begun when the Navy took the company over during the First World War. What the future of the company would be, no one could say. AT&T was making Sarnoff's dreams come true, although he was unable to participate in their realization. But the picture began to brighten when President Wilson himself entrusted American Marconi with a mission that involved an old and familiar piece of equipment—the Alexanderson alternator.

At the end of the war, Britannia, base of Marconi's operations, ruled the airwaves, with America a poor second. Even American Marconi was merely a subsidiary of the British enterprise, which held the industry's essential patents. In contrast to this smooth-running telegraphic empire, the American interests were in disarray. Patents were divided among several companies, crippling their ability to develop or sell the technology of broadcasting. During the war, the Navy had circumvented the problem simply by ransacking the patent storehouse for whatever it needed, then indemnifying the company whose patent it had infringed upon. After the war, a stalemate ensued. It became virtually impossible to manufacture even the simplest vacuum tube without violating a patent.

This sorry state of affairs had come about because the patents had passed from the inventors themselves to corporations more concerned with hobbling a potential competitor than with developing new products. To take one prominent example: In 1912, when Lee De Forest was destitute, he began selling off rights to his audion patent to AT&T. There an engineer, H. P. Arnold, devised modifications of the audion. Over at rival General Electric, another engineer, Dr. Irving Langmuir, actually improved the audion to the point where it became a component of Alexanderson's alternator, the device that had helped make Fessenden's dream of broadcasting voices and music a reality. To complicate matters even further, American Marconi held the patent on the original two-element tube developed by Fleming, the foundation upon which De Forest had built his electronic edifice.

When the Federal Trade Commission finally investigated the matter in 1923, it came to the following conclusion: "The American Telephone and Telegraph Company could not manufacture such tubes for radio unless it acquired rights in the Fleming patent and cleared up the interferences of the Arnold application with the Langmuir application." The hairsplitting over patents extended even to the nature of the filaments employed in the tubes. Caught in the web of these infuriating dilemmas, the entire broadcasting industry, from set makers to stations, began to collapse under its own weight.

What attracted Wilson's attention to the situation was General Electric's intention of selling its Alexanderson alternator exclusively to *British* Marconi for the sum of $5,000,000. The deal had been negotiated back in 1915 by GE's general counsel, Owen D. Young, with the support of Marconi himself, who did not want the promising new transmitters to fall into the hands of a rival. While engaged in the creation of the League of Nations at Versailles in 1919, Wilson got wind of the scheme, and adamantly refused to allow Americans to sell the British still another device that would contribute to their telegraphic supremacy. In short order, the Assistant Secretary of the Navy, Franklin D. Roosevelt, wrote to Young requesting that he not consummate the deal until he had talked with the Navy. Wilson then asked Rear Admiral H. G. Bullard, at the time director of naval communications, to leave Versailles at once and return to the United States. There Bullard pleaded with Young to call off the deal. But, Young wanted to know, who would buy this contraption in which GE had already invested $1,500,000? Bullard replied that together they should form a new company, an entirely American venture, which could meet the British offer. Young was definitely interested.

The result of the government's manipulations and Young's formidable negotiating ability was the Radio Corporation of America, incorporated on October 17, 1919. The operative word in the corporate name was America, for everything about the new organization was designed with patriotic purposes in mind. Beyond this goal, the "new" company was little more than a reconstituted American Marconi, which had been on ice ever since the outbreak of the war. The new RCA was initially meant to continue American Marconi's functions in the field of wireless telegraphy. Broadcasting and radio manufacturing—activities which RCA would, in a few short years, come to dominate—were not actively contemplated at the time, except by David Sarnoff.

Having in effect seized the company, the Navy now turned it over to Young to purge of all foreign influences. The articles of incorporation specified that executives must be American citizens, that foreign interests could hold no more than 20 per cent of the stock, and that the Navy should maintain a presence on the board. Young became president in 1923, while the military was represented first by Bullard, then by Major General James G. Harboard, Pershing's former chief of staff. Most of the American Marconi personnel remained intact at the new RCA, including our hero David Sarnoff, who in quick succession went from commercial manager of the parent company to commercial manager and then general manager (at a yearly salary of fifteen thousand dollars) of the offshoot.

It was a curious way indeed to start a company. A military official, acting on a president's orders, played midwife to a newborn private company designed to serve a patriotic purpose. And the government, especially the Navy, continued to make its presence felt with a succession of high-ranking officials on the board of directors. When Sarnoff, in the wake of World War II, retained the title of General in civilian life, he was not just boasting, but rather capitalizing on a long-standing company tradition. Because RCA enjoyed this special government favor, it had many blessings at birth, the most important of which was access to patents.

The great stumbling block to patent power had been the telephone

company, which, as we have seen, aspired to monopolize national
broadcasting as it did telephone operations. But when Wilson and the
Navy contrived to set up a new rival outfit, RCA, AT&T knew it
would never succeed in controlling the nation's wireless communications, despite its precedent-setting successes with WEAF and
its ownership of many key patents. As a result, the company entered
into marathon negotiations with its rivals—GE, Westinghouse, and
oddly enough, the United Fruit Company, which had been operating a
wireless system to control its shipping in South America. Months of
torturous bargaining led in 1921 to the creation of a patent pool in
which all companies could share the patent rights of the others, including the newcomer, RCA. But its older, more established rivals did not
act entirely out of charitable impulses, for in return they received sizable blocks of stock in RCA: GE acquired 25.7 per cent, Westinghouse
20.6 per cent, AT&T 4.1 per cent, and United Fruit 3.7 per cent.

While the pool was being negotiated, and even afterward, patent
infringements became a fact of life as various companies both inside
and outside the patent pool sought bigger shares of the booming radio
business. To Sarnoff's frustration, his company was still not manufacturing radios, merely selling models made by its benefactors, GE and
Westinghouse. In addition, his boss was still Nally, the man who had
scorned his radio music box memo in 1916. And above Nally was
Young, seventeen years older than Sarnoff and clearly in control. Seizing on every opportunity to consolidate his position within the company, Sarnoff maneuvered for an opening, despite considerable opposition. "Unfortunately for those who sought to discredit Mr. Sarnoff
in the early days," recalls one RCA historian, "the young man made
good on the difficult or impossible assignments. . . . The very efforts
to unseat the general manager enabled him to demonstrate how
necessary he was to the organization, and left him more firmly in the
saddle."

An experienced infighter, Sarnoff persisted on behalf of the radio
music box, while all around him companies ranging from GE to Atwater Kent and Grebe were making fortunes overnight out of precisely the same idea. How long until the RCA brass saw the light?
Rather than pioneering the radio-set market, as Sarnoff in later years
liked to portray his role, he actually lagged far behind those two
hundred-plus companies who were already in the business. To prod
RCA into capturing a share of the market, he furnished an estimate of
the return the company could expect on sales of a seventy-five-dollar
model. He predicted 100,000 units would be sold the first year, 300,000
the next, and 600,000 in the third. Yet the company still balked, losing
precious initiative with each passing month. But by now Sarnoff was

so closely identified with the radio music box that he staked his position in the company on it; he would surely stand or fall by the success of his brainchild. Don't waste time worrying about patent infringements, he was saying, let's get our own model out and be done with it.

Sarnoff decided to test his idea with a dramatic stunt. Having learned the value of publicity in proving to the public and government alike the feasibility of broadcasting services at the time of the *Titanic* disaster, Sarnoff realized that he would require a new event on which he could capitalize. Luckily, late in 1920, RCA appropriated a token $2,000 for radio music development, and shortly thereafter his old nemesis Nally withdrew from company leadership. The road was now clear.

Coincidentally, Sarnoff had come to know Major Andrew J. White, editor of the magazine *Wireless Age,* an RCA publication. It seemed to Sarnoff that the magazine could serve as a useful publicity device for his scheme by carrying schedules and generating enthusiasm. An event which was sure to attract attention to broadcasting was the July 2, 1921, Dempsey-Carpentier fight at Boyle's Thirty Acres in New Jersey, the same fight broadcast by KDKA. With some trepidation Sarnoff approached White with his idea. Would the Major perhaps be interested in announcing the fight over the air? Indeed, the Major would be delighted. Emboldened, the ambitious young man helped himself to some company funds. As White later recalled, "Sarnoff, digging into his books as general manager, discovered twenty-five hundred dollars of RCA money in accumulated rentals of ship wireless equipment. 'Take it,' he said to me. Then he added cautiously, 'But don't spend a nickel more than fifteen hundred!'"

But their problems were only beginning. RCA had no transmitter with which to broadcast the event. Sarnoff tried to borrow one GE had just completed for the Navy, the world's largest, in fact, but, according to White, the Navy was "rather stiffnecked about lending it to some crazy amateurs." Undaunted, Sarnoff turned to the Assistant Secretary of the Navy, Franklin D. Roosevelt, who prevailed on his superiors to lend the equipment. With the help of a fight promoter, Sarnoff hooked up speakers in selected New York theaters to broadcast the blow-by-blow. All was in readiness. At the last moment, White did not get a chance to broadcast the fight. Too far from the microphone, he relayed events to an engineer, who in turn broadcast the results. An estimated 200,000 listeners gathered around crystal sets at home and congregated in the specially rigged theaters to hear an account of Dempsey knocking out Carpentier in the fourth round while Sarnoff and White watched at ringside. Dempsey's victory was one of a string, but Sarnoff's heralded a great new career. Even Nally was impressed. "You have made history," he cabled to the young comer. What Sarnoff had made hardly qualified as history; it was publicity. In the broadcasting environment, the one would often be mistaken for the other.

By now the sets of Crosley, Westinghouse, and Grebe were selling so well that the logic of putting a new one on the market was irresistible. Even if Sarnoff had never written a memo in his life on the subject, it was inevitable that RCA would have entered the fray, but as he did, he managed to capture the credit for the move, which proved to be gratifyingly profitable. Sales ran ahead even of Sarnoff's predictions: $11,000,000 in the first year of production, 1922, twice the amount the following year, and $50,000,000 in 1924. As a result, RCA suddenly had a new profit center and the complexion of the company changed rapidly. The pre-eminence of wireless telegraphy and military equipment gave way to products—sets and parts—for home use. Vestiges of American Marconi began disappearing, and RCA and its executives quickly gained esteem in the business community.

Yet despite its initial success, the company had come just halfway toward its eventual goal, at least as it existed in the mind of David Sarnoff. As the first issue of *Fortune* magazine noted from the vantage point of 1930, "The Radio Corporation of America, set up as a communications agency, found itself transformed by the erratic genius of electricity into a great amusement company."

Sarnoff's strategy was clever indeed, for if RCA could apply the government favor it enjoyed in matters military to the consumer market, it would have a decided edge over all other competitors, even the behemoth AT&T. Sarnoff followed that company's experiments with WEAF and, as he had done once before, speculated as to how his company could capitalize on the discoveries of a pioneer. "It seems to me that in seeking a solution to the broadcasting problem," he wrote in 1922, "we must recognize that the answer must be along national rather than local lines." Then he began to outline what we would recognize as a network, similar to the organization AT&T was attempting to build around WEAF. At the same time he articulated a prophetic theory of programming. "I think the principal elements of broadcasting service are entertainment, information, and education, with emphasis on the first feature—entertainment." He respectfully submitted for consideration and discussion the following plan:

> Let us organize a separate and distinct company, to be known as the Public Service Broadcasting Company or National Radio Broadcasting Company or American Radio Broadcasting, or some similar name.

This company to be controlled by the Radio Corporation of America, but its board of directors and officers to include members of the General Electric Company and the Westinghouse Company and possibly also a few fom the outside, prominent in national and civic affairs. The administrative and operating staff of this company to be composed of those considered best qualified to the broadcasting job.

Such company to acquire the existing broadcasting stations of the Westinghouse Company and General Electric Company, as well as the three stations to be erected by the Radio Corporation; to operate such stations, and build such additional broadcasting stations as may be determined upon in the future.

Sarnoff attached no glowing profit predictions to this proposal; the increase in revenue would show up in the rising number of RCA sets sold. In addition, Sarnoff had to move now, because AT&T appeared to be on the verge of swallowing up the industry whole as it commandeered available stations for its network. At the very least, RCA would do well to keep its options open.

On one point, Sarnoff sharply disagreed with the AT&T approach to a network. He could not see how the freest of entertainment, radio, would be compatible with advertising. "I am of the opinion that the greatest advantages of radio—its universality, and, generally speaking, its ability to reach everybody everywhere—in themselves limit, if not completely destroy, that element of control essential to any program calling for continued payment by the public." You can't charge the public coming and going, Sarnoff was saying; either sell them sets or advertise, but not both. "The cost of broadcasting must be borne by those who derive profits directly or indirectly from the business resulting from radio broadcasting. This means the manufacturers."

This time Sarnoff had the momentum with him. RCA nervously eyed AT&T's every move, now that the phone company was testing a radio set. "It would possibly put us out of business," Major General Harboard told Young in early 1924. Quickly, RCA went into broadcasting, at first in a small way, paying half the expenses of a radio station in New York, WJZ, located in Aeolian Hall on Forty-second Street. With the bluster characteristic of the industry, RCA called the tiny studio "Broadcast Central."

The phone company naturally refused to lease lines that RCA would need for occasional remote broadcasts or to maintain a chain. WJZ instead was forced to rely on Western Union's inferior equipment. And, hewing to Sarnoff's theory that it provide a free service stimulating radio sales, the station became a substantial drain, costing about $100,000 a year to operate. In contrast, AT&T's WEAF, which was more expensive a venture, showed a healthy profit. The difference, thanks to McClelland, was that WEAF made a practice of selling time.

And yet, despite healthy profits, there was something about this new broadcasting industry that went against AT&T's grain. It was such an open-ended endeavor; anyone could tune in free of charge. Sure, WEAF was making money, but there was still the question of what sort of programming to supply—news, sports, music, etc.—and how much of each.

In addition there was the problem of the patent pool. For five years, domestic broadcasting had existed on two disconnected levels: the amateur stratum, those jury-rigged transmitters and receivers strewn across the country, and the monopoly stratum in New York, the heart of which was the patent pool. In its present condition, the AT&T, GE, Westinghouse, and RCA monopoly amounted to an unnatural alliance of natural competitors. The patent pool made poor business sense, and the Federal Trade Commission threatened to investigate this apparent conspiracy in restraint of trade, rendered unlawful by the Sherman Antitrust Act of 1890.

With one monopoly under its belt and aspirations of adding another, AT&T was the most vulnerable to investigation. The WEAF staff, especially McClelland, may have perceived a glorious future for broadcasting, but the phone company did not share their enthusiasm. Feeling pressure from both the government and the business community, AT&T decided to abandon WEAF. In mid-1926, AT&T sold its network in miniature to none other than RCA for the hefty sum of $1,000,000: $200,000, plus $800,000 for goodwill. The latter came so dear in part because WEAF was one of the pre-eminent radio stations in the country. Furthermore, it could now boast its own clear channel, assigned by the Commerce Department at the 491.5-meter wavelength.

While the phone company appeared to be relinquishing a gold mine, the sale actually made sense to both parties, for each received benefits consonant with its long-range goals. The phone giant, for its part, won an important concession, one that would allow it to profit from the coming broadcasting boom. According to the purchase agreement, AT&T would have the sole right to supply RCA with the landlines needed to link stations around the country. If RCA could swing a broadcasting monopoly, then AT&T would surely enjoy a landline monopoly. This activity would be in keeping with the latter company's primary commitment, point-to-point communications.

On the other hand, RCA, thanks to government co-operation, saw its way clear to becoming the AT&T of broadcasting. Thanks to David Sarnoff, RCA had the vision to perceive a glorious future for broadcasting. Unlike his counterparts at AT&T, Sarnoff was willing to deal with the hurly-burly of organizing stations around the country, and he was quickly developing ideas about programming to link them. Both approaches came together in his concept of a national network, a way to reconcile the amateurs in the field with the monopoly in New York. Scattered and often unrelated events taking place in laboratories around the country, in Washington, D.C., and at countless radio stations rapidly fell into step. Increasingly, a system would come to dominate individuals, and inventors would recede in importance, elbowed out of the limelight by entrepreneurs and businessmen. Until this turning point—1926—each development had come about as a result of enthusiasm over a new discovery, say, the audion. Only then did inventors think about exploiting their hard-won breakthroughs. In the main they were impelled by a genuine desire to expand the possibilities of electronic communication, by the excitement of discovery. There had been high drama in the laboratories of De Forest and on Marconi's estate in Perugia.

But now the technology of radio—after less than a quarter century of development—was essentially complete. Deployment and exploitation of technology were the next goals, and with them, in an intensely capitalistic environment, competition came to dominate the actions of all parties. In the end, competition would serve as the spur, indeed the source of all future developments and refinements. Virtually every post-1926 move took place in this competitive framework, even those appearing to be noncommercial, *pro bono* activities.

Owing to the fortunate circumstances of its birth, and now in possession of an important radio station, RCA stood first in line to exploit the airwaves. Following Sarnoff's guidelines, RCA organized its new National Broadcasting Company, incorporated September 6, 1926. The network was entirely owned by its parent company. Actually, NBC became two networks, one centering around flagship station WEAF and the other around flagship station WJZ. AT&T, as planned, linked WJZ in a network with WBZ, then of Springfield, Massachusetts, KDKA in Pittsburgh, and KYW in Chicago; and it connected WEAF to WSB, Atlanta, WHAS, Louisville, Kentucky, WMC, Memphis, and WSM, Nashville. Engineers plotted the station-to-station hookups with colored pencils, red for the WEAF chain, blue for the WJZ chain. The two colors came to stand as a shorthand for the two networks, the Red and the Blue. By the year's end, the Red network had grown to twenty-five stations and the Blue to sixteen. NBC also formed supplementary Orange, Green, and Gold networks in the West.

As a consequence of maintaining two flagship stations, NBC acquired a dual heritage. The Red and the Blue exhibited remarkably

different personalities from the start. The Blue adhered to the old
service concept, espoused by Sarnoff himself, of a philanthropic venture dedicated to public service and education. To promote this
image, NBC established a highly touted advisory council including
such notables as Edward Alderman, president of the University of
Virginia, Walter Damrosch, conductor of the New York Symphony Society Orchestra, William Green, president of the American Federation
of Labor, Charles Evans Hughes, the former presidential candidate,
and Julius Rosenwald, president of Sears, Roebuck. "As late as 1930
you were told that if NBC ever made money," ran an early retrospec-
tive, "that money would go right back into the improvement of
broadcasting. For NBC was the guardian of radio, the Great Red and
Blue Father, a 'service organization' interested in the dissemination of
culture to the masses."

The Red, in contrast, inherited AT&T's aggressively commercial approach. McClelland remained with the company and continued selling
time. This clever arrangement enabled NBC to reconcile many
conflicts. On the one hand, it could offer a magnanimous public service. On the other, it could make money through advertising revenue.
By creating not one but two competing networks (though of course
they were both owned by the same entity), NBC could portray itself
as something other than a monopoly. Ultimately, though, NBC's heart
would come to reside with the Red network, the commercial operation.
Even at this early phase, the commitment to the two philosophies was
unequal.

NBC launched its Red network with an attention-grabbing hoopla
which further belied its blatantly commercial aims. In the fall of 1926,
RCA ran impressive, full-page ads to explain to the public NBC's mission. Describing the purchase of WEAF from AT&T, the RCA ad,
signed by Young and Harboard, declared that the company was going
into the broadcasting business because "any use of radio transmission
which causes the public to feel the quality is not the highest, that the
use of the radio is not the broadest and best use in the public interest,
that it is used for political advantage or selfish power, will be detri-
mental to the public interest in radio, and therefore to the Radio Corporation of America." The ad also asserted that RCA "is not in any
sense seeking a monopoly of the air." As time went on, both claims
would become ever more suspect, not only in the minds of critics, but
to Congress and the Justice Department. So much for the smoke
screen of high purpose. NBC turned rapidly to its primary purpose,
mass entertainment, with WEAF's gala inaugural program, broadcast
on November 15, 1926, over twenty-four stations. The site of the fes-
tivities was the Grand Ballroom of the Waldorf-Astoria Hotel. To the

surprise of the audience, the soprano Mary Garden sang ditties like "Annie Laurie" and "Open Thy Blue Eyes" from her Chicago apartment. In another remote segment, Will Rogers, backstage at a theater in Independence, Kansas, where he was giving a performance that evening, broadcast a talk entitled "Fifteen Minutes with a Diplomat," concerning his recent travels in Europe, the West, and the visit with President Coolidge.

It is worth noting that RCA's service-oriented Blue network enjoyed no such lavish premiere.

The question on every tongue was, Who's paying for all of this? NBC revealed the bash had set them back a formidable $50,000, half of which went for artists' fees. Clearly, this was no way to run a network and stay in business. Then came one of those morning-after capitulations that would become so characteristic of network publicity. "An official of the company," reported the New York *Times* on November 17, "said it was expected to make advertising ultimately pay the entire expenses of elaborate programs to come."

In September 1927, NBC established formal rates, offering coverage in fifteen cities for a $3,770 charge per hour between 7 and 11 P.M. on the Red network. The Blue afforded the sponsor nine cities for $2,800 per hour; day rates on both networks were only half as much. For a brief, suspenseful period, the advertising came in a trickle, with Colgate-Palmolive, General Foods, and General Motors in the vanguard. Eventually the industry would produce a massive barrage of quasi-scientific studies to convince potential advertisers of the effectiveness of broadcast advertising.

With the establishment of NBC and the glossy Red network in particular RCA took a turn that no one would have predicted at the time of its inception just six years before. The company had parlayed the instant authority the government had conferred upon it into a leading role in the domestic entertainment industry, a role far removed from its original purpose of competing with the British for control of world telegraphic communications. The unexpected shift was, of course, the handiwork of David Sarnoff, who had been advocating such a course for RCA's previous incarnation, American Marconi, for over a decade, but even he did not foresee the extent to which his pet project would become commercialized.

NBC came onto the scene with a minimum of government encumbrance. Beyond WEAF's clear channel, it required little from the Commerce Department. Then in July 1926 a court declared that the department did not even have the authority to regulate broadcasting. This state of affairs, which lasted until the passage of a Radio Act in 1927, meant that the government was powerless to direct one of the most important bonanzas in American history since the Oklahoma Land Rush. During this period, newborn NBC grew by leaps and bounds and the foundations were laid for the debut of CBS. How different the networks would have been had they come under careful scrutiny at their inception is anyone's guess. Instead, they prospered in a no-man's-land upon which the government has never seriously encroached. In most other nations, broadcasting became a government-administered monopoly. Free enterprise gained something of a foothold in foreign broadcasting only at a much later date, in part through the influence of the American example. The freewheeling, laissez-faire atmosphere in which the American networks grew up, and the fierce competitiveness fostered by that freedom, quickly became the distinctive national trait of American broadcasting.

Watching the situation with concern, Hoover called for some authority to regulate a potential abuse of advertising. "If the President's speech is nothing but meat between the sandwich of advertising for patent medicines," he said, "who will want the sandwich?" He oversaw the hastily completed Radio Act of 1927, which provided for a Federal Radio Commission to license stations and loosely regulate the industry. Its goal in essence was to keep broadcasting firmly in the hands of private enterprise, yet free of advertising dominance. Self-regulation rather than government interference was the main idea. Though government agencies would through the years try to claim more power over the industry, there was, in practice, little they could do but curtail flagrant abuses. Whenever the government tried to alter the course of network development, the results had a way of boomeranging, as we shall see. A little power could be worse than none at all.

So it was that the government lost the opportunity to direct the growth of the commercial networks, lost the opportunity to ensure a full-scale network commitment to public service, and lost the opportunity of playing a significant role in broadcasting beyond that of regulator. The initiative was now firmly with RCA and Sarnoff.

But, as AT&T had suspected, broadcasting was a wide open field. Only a year after its debut, NBC found itself in competition with a rival network, one that was, in contrast to RCA's labyrinthine structure, simplicity itself. At thirty-seven, Sarnoff could no longer be considered the boy wonder of the industry. That description now belonged to the twenty-seven-year-old heir of a cigar fortune, William Paley. Unlike Sarnoff, who was caught between two contrasting broadcasting philosophies, this young man had no compunction about making as much money as possible out of his network.

5

Shoestring

IF THE BEGINNINGS OF RCA could be compared to grand opera enacted by a cast of famous principals, then the earliest days of the Columbia Broadcasting System, which was to become its chief rival, had something of the character of a silent slapstick movie which promised to last no more than a reel or two. The innocence and desperation of the initial plan put forth by the men who began the company had all the doubtful and raffish appeal of a get-rich-quick scheme. They were amateurs trying to hit the big time, out-of-towners among the city slicks. If RCA built from the very top down, CBS rose from grass roots. The new network was to be the populist answer to RCA's government-sanctioned monopoly. It was also something of a con, put together by three very different men trying to cash in on the radio boom.

In the beginning, there was just a man observing the enthusiasm generated at the 1926 convention of the National Association of Broadcasters held at the Astor Hotel in New York. The man was George Coats, a promoter and sometime salesman of paving machinery. In the course of his stay at the Astor, he talked with the electronic enthusiasts and caught the radio fever. He even addressed the convention, urging its members to form a new artist management bureau. From a promoter's point of view, the embryonic industry seemed like a natural. Because he lacked the assets of the lofty NBC, Coats decided to restrict his interest to the commercial side of the broadcasting business, about which precious little had been done. To enter the field, Coats would require no patents, no licenses, no hardware of any kind, nothing more than a smile, a handshake, and a driving desire to sell commercial time on the airwaves. What Coats was trying to do, according to one early account, was sell "an invisible commodity to fictitious beings called corporations for the purpose of influencing an audience that no one can see. It is a business, you might say, that begins nowhere and ends nowhere."

Meanwhile, the second man, Arthur Judson, wanted to find a way to get the musicians he managed into radio. He considered broadcasting to be the salvation of music, and NBC his potentially greatest customer. He went to see David Sarnoff, then in the process of completing his blueprint for NBC. "Sarnoff read the plan with great interest," Judson recalled, "and it was my understanding that if it was within his power when he got his chain organized—which he was then doing —he would certainly put me in charge of the programs and of supplying artists." But the cozy arrangement never came to pass. RCA, blessed with a formidable monopoly, did not want to give the impression of taking control of still another aspect of the business, music management. Furthermore, following WEAF's precedent, the company already had an unstated policy of not paying musicians itself but letting companies buying time bear the burden. While waiting for Sarnoff to make good on his promise, Judson met up with Coats, whose fantasies for capitalizing on the ether coincided nicely with his. The two returned to their potential patron, demanding to know what he had for them. Sarnoff, having had time to consider all the answers, replied, "Nothing."

"Then we will organize our own chain," countered Judson. The RCA general manager, conscious of the vast resources upon which NBC had been built, laughed out loud.

"You can't do it," he told the hapless promoters. "I just signed a contract to take one million dollars' worth of long lines from the telephone company. In any event, you couldn't get any wires even if you had a broadcasting station. It can't be done." He was telling them, in effect, two things: one, that NBC had a monopoly on AT&T's vital services, and two, that they were rank amateurs. Undaunted, the two men decided to forge ahead despite Sarnoff's challenge. Judson and Coats "decided that if we were going to be shut out of the only chain in the broadcasting business then we would have to challenge the NBC monopoly." They realized that a network was, in essence, nothing more than a flagship or "key" station linked by AT&T's telephone lines to other stations around the country. Surely that arrangement would not be so hard to duplicate.

In January 1927, Coats and Judson formed their rival enterprise, United Independent Broadcasters, the "independent" component intentionally challenging what they perceived as the RCA–NBC monopoly. They took in several partners, most prominently Major Andrew White, the radio-magazine editor whom Sarnoff had drafted into the role of announcer. Though the Major was getting on in years, he was still someone to be reckoned with and could confer legitimacy on the operation. After assisting Sarnoff with his breakthrough broadcast of the Dempsey-Carpentier fight, White had gone on to a vice-presidency with the company, but the thought of founding a network turned his gray head. Why, all they would need were some stations, long lines, and money. But United Independent would prove singularly inept at acquiring all three. It was no wonder that it earned from *Fortune* the accolade "that miserable radio adventure, that mere shoestring."

First, Coats went on the road to line up affiliates. He returned to New York with an impressive roster of sixteen stations. They had agreed to broadcast ten hours of the network's programming a week, in return for payment of $50 an hour. It was an offer no station, struggling to fill up its daily schedule with everything from talking piano players to whistling concerts, could afford to refuse. The $500 a week would be a princely sum. Then reality crept in. How in the name of Heinrich Hertz was United Independent going to come up with $8,700 a week to pay its affiliates?

For his part, the Major had also been active, arranging to lease the studios of WOR at 1440 Broadway as the key station. He had even set a date for the network's debut in September 1927. So far the network had signed up affiliates it could not afford to pay to transmit programming from studios it had merely leased. In addition, there was the problem of long lines, for which United Independent would have to wait at least three years, according to AT&T estimates. Perhaps Sarnoff had been correct after all. But the enterprising Coats went on the road again, this time to Washington, D.C. The suspicion of bribery at this point is strong. Coats told Judson he had an anonymous contact in the government who could expedite matters with AT&T. "If you give him two checks," the promoter explained, "one for $1,000 and the other for $10,000, he will guarantee that you get the wires."

That solved half the problem, but where would they find the money? At this juncture, Judson made his contribution, prevailing on an heiress, Mrs. Christian Fleischmann Holmes, to invest in United Independent as a sporting proposition. At the last minute Judson was able to supply Coats with the needed funds, without bothering to inquire as to where they were going. Finances in this period were

handled in an extremely casual manner, with more reliance placed on
memory than on books. Even counting on their fingers, the intrepid
United Independent promoters required some financial legerdemain,
for their operating expenses alone came to $100,000 a month. The
good Mrs. Holmes eventually invested nearly 30,000 fast-disappearing
dollars.

To fill the ever growing financial gap, the partners began to search
for a corporate sponsor, an equivalent to NBC's parent company RCA.
They approached the Victor Talking Machine Company, makers of
phonographs, but Sarnoff had been there first. Victor would be sold to
RCA. Adolph Zukor, chief of the Paramount film studios, was intrigued by the venture, and offered to invest in it if the company
would change its name to the Paramount Broadcasting System. The
deal did not work out this time, but Zukor kept his eye on the new
network. For the time being, United Independent only went so far as
to take offices in the Paramount Building. Finally, the Major found his
way to a company almost as desperate as his, the Columbia Phonograph Company, which was suffering losses at the hands of radio. Columbia's head, Louis Sterling, took over the network for $163,000 and
introduced a certain organizational formality, establishing the Columbia Phonograph Broadcasting System as the network's operating company. However, he retained the right to cancel on a month's notice.
Sterling expected losses during those first few months, but not ones as
heavy as those actually incurred. By the time of its debut on September 18, 1927, the fledgling network had sold only a single hour to an
advertiser.

To introduce the Columbia Phonograph Broadcasting System to the
world, the network planned an ambitious program built around the
Deems Taylor opera *The King's Henchman,* with a libretto by Edna
St. Vincent Millay. From his office in the Paramount Building, the
Major sent a general order to affiliates telling them how they could
recognize the moment when they were to switch from local to network programming: "You will hear the orchestra or some musical instrument melt into the strains of 'Hail, Columbia'—then the announcer's voice saying something to this effect: 'This is the . . . hour
on the Columbia Chain, a program which is coming to you from the
New York studio.'" The network had a staff by now, sixteen in all, including a sales department of two and a versatile man by the name
of Harry Browne who served as program director, continuity writer,
banjo player, actor, and resident announcer. Stations in those days, besides being unwilling to pay musicians, were also fearful of announcers' becoming too popular and thus kept them anonymous. Accordingly, Browne would be known to his audience only as the Voice

of Columbia. In the music department, though, the network was, if anything, oversupplied. This tiny organization maintained thirty-eight musicians, including a twenty-two-piece "symphonic" orchestra conducted by Howard Barlow and a sixteen-piece dance ensemble under the baton of Don Voorhees. Subdivisions included Red Nichols and His Five Pennies and a trombone group named Miff Mole and His Moles. There were also a soprano, a contralto, and a male quartet. The presence of all this music, of course, showed the influence of Arthur Judson, whose dream it had been to supply the airwaves with the musicians he managed. Naturally, they were all hired through his bureau. It was clear that what the network planned to pipe its affiliates night after night was music, music, music, of its own making.

At exactly 3 P.M. on that Sunday afternoon, Harry Newman, the network president, stood before the microphone to introduce Harry Browne, who said, "Good evening, ladies and gentlemen. This is the Voice of Columbia." He went on to announce the stations comprising the network, WEAN, Providence, WNAC, Boston, WFBL, Syracuse, WMAK, Buffalo-Lockport, WCAU, Philadelphia, WJAS, Pittsburgh, WADC, Akron, WAIU, Columbia, WKRC, Cincinnati, WGHP, Detroit, WMAW, Chicago, KMOX, St. Louis, WCAO, Baltimore, KOIL, Council Bluffs, and WOWO, Fort Wayne. Each time the network took over WOR and connected with the affiliates, Browne repeated this lengthy salutation.

Then Howard Barlow led his orchestra through a "musical fantasy" entitled "The Vacationist's Return," unsponsored, as the network had failed to complete negotiations with the Kolster Radio Company for the hour. And Berkey and Gay, a furniture company slated to sponsor the next segment, "The Spirit of the Woods," also vanished before signing on the dotted line. Shortly after the dance band got under way, a nasty thunderstorm west of Pittsburgh knocked out those hard-won AT&T lines, and with them the stations to the west. Judson, never dreaming that a concert manager would have to contend with the weather along with all the other variables in a live performance, ran in and out of the control room, where the engineer and an AT&T representative frantically tried to patch the lines. In the name of caution, Judson and White decided to delay by twenty minutes the 9 P.M. scheduled start for the opera, which would then be followed at 10:20 by the first sponsored program, "The Emerson Hour," a musical variety show to which the Emerson Drug Company had given its name. And so the network was launched into the stormy ether.

Three months later, Columbia Phonograph dropped it.

Sterling had departed for Japan and in his place a gentleman by the name of Cox carefully observed the tiny network consume quantities of red ink. When the time came for it to default on its monthly AT&T bill, Cox determined, he would take over completely from Coats, White, and Judson. Throughout the grim fall of 1927, the network managed to attract a few more sponsors, Chrysler, Kolster (at last), and the Cambridge Rubber Company, but it had no equivalent to WEAF's supersalesman McClelland. Losses mounted.

In desperation, Judson sought out his guardian angel, Mrs. Holmes, who happened to be in the mid-Atlantic. From aboard ship she telegraphed her New York office to supply Judson with $45,000, which arrived on the last day of the month, just in time to pay AT&T before they ripped out their precious phone lines. Judson triumphantly confronted Cox, who was ignorant of the last-minute reprieve, and declared, "Well, the chain belongs to us." Judson showed him the telephone company receipt and recalled that Cox called him a "number of violent names." In the end, Cox relinquished Columbia Phonograph's interests in the network in return for $10,000 and thirty sponsored hours. The network was cut free of the Columbia Phonograph Broadcasting System, which left nothing behind but its grand name. At least there would not be another phone bill for thirty days.

Once more into the breach went the enterprising Coats, who this time determined to stay away from New York and the electronic communications field. Thinking, perhaps, that he would have better luck with someone unfamiliar with the problems faced by the network, Coats approached the Philadelphia construction magnate Jerome Louchheim. But Louchheim the builder and Coats the fast-talking promoter proved personally incompatible. Louchheim threw the gentleman from New York out of his office, but his interest in the network had nevertheless been aroused. Next, Judson tried to approach Louchheim, this time through a friend, Dr. Isaac Levy, a retired dentist who with his brother Leon owned Columbia Broadcasting's Philadelphia affiliate, WCAU. This time, Louchheim went in deeply, very deeply, buying a controlling interest in the network. "Now, Mr. Louchheim, you are putting half a million dollars in this thing," Judson remembered Louchheim's lawyer warning. "Next month, you put another half million, a month after that another half million, and it is just a bottomless barrel, I warn you."

"Whose money is it?" the millionaire replied. "Give me the pen." In the process of saving the network, the hapless Coats was dealt out, possibly at Louchheim's insistence.

Under the Louchheim regime, the network underwent two important alterations. First, it acquired a key station it could call its own. The lease on WOR's facilities was about to expire and the station had no interest in renewing. Forced to look for a new home, the network found one in another New York station, WABC, described by Judson as "a little one-horse thing up in Steinway Hall." The call letters stood for the Atlantic Broadcasting Corporation, and the station was one of several owned by the radio manufacturer Alfred Grebe. By mid-1928, the network had arranged to alternate WOR with WABC as its temporary key station, then in September went with WABC full time. In short order, the station, assigned to the 860 wavelength, began doing double duty, providing local programs by day and network programs by night.

Second, the Major, still the member of the network best known to the trade, took to the road to work out more favorable contracts with the affiliates. Those $50 an hour guarantees caused a never ending financial plague. This time around, the network agreed to pay affiliates to carry only those programs that were sponsored. In other words, the affiliates would make money only when the network itself did. Any other shows the affiliates wished to carry would go unpaid. These unsponsored programs came to be known as sustaining, since their costs were sustained by the network rather than a sponsor. Though not as fat a contract as before, it was still a better deal than what the competition offered. NBC's Blue and Red networks actually charged affiliates to carry the sustaining programs, since they were considered a service to the public whose costs must be shared by station and network alike. NBC, torn between two contradictory broadcasting philosophies, tried to force its policy down stations' throats, but the Columbia system had no aspirations to public service at the time. It wanted only to try turning a profit for a change, a goal fully shared by the stations. The terms of the new contract would turn out to be a highly effective weapon in the war with NBC.

Though losing money as rapidly as ever, the new network was now on much firmer footing. Then Louchheim bequeathed his final gift to Columbia in the person of William Paley.

Paley came from a closely knit family of shrewd and successful businessmen, and he shared Columbia's approach to the network as a pure business proposition, dependent solely on advertising. But Paley had more faith in radio's power of advertising than most others in the industry; an experience he had had as an advertiser himself convinced him for life.

Paley's parents, Samuel and Goldie, had immigrated from Minsk. In Chicago, his father, along with other relatives, started up the Congress Cigar Company. The venture soon proved profitable and the family assumed Samuel's son, William, born in 1901, would one day take over. Bill went to the Alton Military School and later the University of Pennsylvania's Wharton School of Business, from which he was graduated in 1922. During summer vacations he worked at the family company, even negotiating a strike settlement one summer when his father was out of town. When Samuel decided to begin manufacturing cigars in Philadelphia, his son assisted. He had learned how to roll and cut tobacco and even visited the Havana plantations where the leaf was grown. Now, upon graduating from Wharton, he became vice-president and advertising manager of the company and by the age of twenty-five was earning a salary of $50,000. Traveling extensively in Europe, Paley played the role of the young heir apparent, pampered, slightly reckless, precocious yet cushioned against the ruder shocks of life and business.

Paley reappears throughout this account, often acting in contradictory, unfathomable ways. As CBS changed over the years, so did he. In fact, an observer can identify at least three stages in his career. Now, in the early phase, he is the smooth-cheeked, fast-moving young blade of the nineteen twenties, his pockets full of his family's money, eager to find himself some amusing playthings. Later, when he has established his business domain, Paley becomes a tougher, more fragmented personality, existing simultaneously in several worlds, yet able to zero in on his first love, broadcasting, and pull off occasional coups of extraordinary resonance which serve to bolster his often fluctuating reputation. The third and current Paley, late in his career, certainly exhibits all the earlier traits, but along with the network they have become somewhat coarser. King of the mountain, he expects to remain in the same crucial role in the foreseeable future, even while a host of new demands clamors all around him.

In 1928, the early Paley, the very early Paley, advertising manager of the Congress Cigar Company, had a problem. Cigarettes had been gaining acceptance, and were now giving the cigar stiff competition. Congress Cigar's best known product was the La Palina, derived from the Paley name (it is said that Goldie served as the inspiration for the figure of the woman on the cigar band), but thanks to the cigarette, sales of that brand dropped in one year from 600,000 a day to 400,000. In the summer of 1928, when Bill was on holiday in Europe, his father arranged for an advertising contract with Columbia's Philadelphia station, WCAU. As it happened, one of the brothers who owned it, Leon Levy, was married to Bill's sister, Blanche. No harm in throwing a little business her way. Paley, Sr., did not suspect that Columbia was losing money as fast as it could borrow it or that his son would leave the family business to own it. The contract between WCAU and Congress Cigar amounted to $6,500 per week to sponsor a locally produced proto-soap opera entitled "Rolla and Dad." The ads took the form of a dramatization, in which wiseacres gather around and banter with La Palina. The campaign scored a striking success. After just six months, cigar sales reached the million-dollar-a-day mark and proved to the twenty-six-year-old Paley, now back from his extended vacation, that radio could be a wickedly effective advertising medium, at least for cigars.

Through his brother-in-law, Leon Levy, owner of WCAU, Paley met Jerome Louchheim, the wealthy owner of Keystone State Construction, and the man who had recently bought a controlling interest in the entire network. Louchheim was old and looking for someone to take the network off his hands. Paley, who had just inherited nearly $1,000,000 from his father, appeared to be a likely candidate, ambitious, well trained, rich, and looking for new worlds to conquer. It was not a deal a cautious businessman would have entertained. No one considered broadcasting a license to print money in those days. Only the manufacture of hardware made much money. The year-old network which Louchheim now dangled in front of Paley's entranced eyes was basically a shambles, little more than a promotion scheme that had never amounted to much. The majestic NBC appeared to have the field to itself. Columbia had drained one investor after another of cash. In all likelihood, Paley would be next in line.

On September 26, 1928, Paley bought the Louchheim interests in the company (2,515 shares, or 51 per cent) for an initial investment estimated at about half a million dollars. He retained 2,085 shares and assigned the others to members of his family. In time, he would invest something like $1,500,000 in the company of which he suddenly, at age twenty-seven, found himself president.

Paley approached the new enterprise in a somewhat less than wholehearted manner. There was still much about broadcasting he did not know, and initially he thought he would devote, say, a few days a week to running the network in New York, then return to home base, and the family business, in Philadelphia. CBS would make a grand part-time endeavor. When Paley came to New York, however, he found both good news and bad. The good was that CBS was capable of unlimited expansion; the bad, that it was still foundering. Paley now occupied the role of chief stockholder, while the Major actually ran the company. Learning of the new infusion of money, stations lined up to close deals with the Major, assisted by Paley, and by the beginning of 1929, CBS could boast to sponsors of a chain comprising forty-seven stations.

Under the new owner's influence, the all-important contract with affiliates underwent further refinements. CBS would provide the sustaining programs free in exchange for five free hours of affiliates' time for the network sponsors to exploit to the hilt. For every hour of sponsored programming in excess of the five, affiliates would receive $50. Several months later, in August 1929, another plan extended the network's edge over NBC. CBS would have priority on affiliates' time for its sponsored broadcasts. The NBC affiliates, in contrast, were a stubborn lot. Clearance along the full stretch of the Red and Blue chains was always a problem, cutting down on premium advertising revenue. NBC could not guarantee a full audience to a nervous sponsor, but CBS could. And the older network was charging affiliates $90 for the first and $50 for subsequent sustaining hours, which CBS supplied free. In 1929, such tiny splashes in the broadcasting ocean spread ripples of goodwill.

Eventually, of course, Paley decided to move to New York and run the network full time, and when he did, the young man drove events forward at an extraordinarily rapid pace. Paley inherited a 1928 deficit of about $380,000 on a gross revenue of over $1,500,000. In swift succession, he merged the Columbia Broadcasting System, the operating company, with the old United Independent, the owning company, eliminating the United Independent name and streamlining the hierarchy. He sold shares to increase capitalization. (At this stage, CBS was still a private company and would not be listed on the New York Stock Exchange until 1935.) Then Paley borrowed $125,000 from the Chemical Bank and Trust Company. With the company on a more secure financial base, Paley decided to move company headquarters, now rapidly outgrowing its quarters in the Paramount Building, to the upper floors of a new, partially completed building at 485 Madison Avenue, in the heart of the advertising community, right where Paley wanted his company to be. Moving into the new home, where CBS was to remain for the next thirty years, proved to be a coup, since the builder did not have full confidence in the fly-by-night network as a reliable tenant; the company's purchase of a lease for $1,500,000 signaled its serious intentions. Later in the year, President Hoover himself dedicated the new studios in a speech originating from his White House study.

Paley found time as well to perfect his persuasive soft-sell approach to potential sponsors. He could be both disarming and direct, a useful talent for a newcomer in the midst of a sea of sharks. To enhance both his own image and that of CBS, he hired the public relations adviser Edward Bernays, a tireless promoter. And he moved into a six-room bachelor flat which had been decorated at the extravagant cost of $10,000 per room. When Paley threw himself a press party at his new digs, he decided to lubricate the Fourth Estate with alcohol. When the word got out that the new owner of the Columbia Broadcasting System was flouting Prohibition, an embarrassing but limited scandal showed Paley the necessity of 1) keeping the press out of his personal life, and 2) cultivating a distinguished and fastidious public image.

In getting CBS on its feet, Paley profited from all the luck anyone could wish for, especially on the eve of the Depression. He brought events to a crescendo by negotiating a risky but vital deal with Paramount's Adolph Zukor. In response to RCA's entry into the motion picture field, Zukor planned to make a move on the radio industry and came to Paley to negotiate an interest in CBS. Paley, always in need of funds at this time, was amenable, selling Zukor half of CBS's not very valuable stock, including his own, in return for a block of Paramount stock worth at the time about $3,800,000. One clause in the agreement specified that Paramount would buy its block back by March 1, 1932, for a flat $5,000,000, provided that CBS earned $2,000,000 during the 1930–31 period. If CBS could not meet this apparently unattainable goal, Paramount would be poised to buy the company out.

The deal, while keeping CBS afloat for the moment and inflating its book value several times over, could ultimately lead to its passing out of Paley's hands into those of yet another investor. The hazards were clear in September 1929, when the deal was negotiated. Then, in October 1929, came the event no one had anticipated, the Crash. On the heels of the market, the Paramount stock, in which CBS and Paley's personal funds were invested, took a plunge.

At this unfortunate juncture, Paley had no alternative but to turn the network around and earn the $2,000,000 in two years. There was no question of the network's operating as a public service or using the public's airwaves in a mutually beneficial manner. The idea was to stay out of hock. This is the atmosphere, then, in which the CBS of today was born—a desperate struggle to earn as much money as possible in a very short time—and the note of desperation was heard loud and clear at NBC, which soon would share the obsession. As Judson declared, the survival of CBS depended on "ideas and hustling ability," for the network had nothing else to sell beyond airtime on affiliates' wavelengths.

How much gold would the network spin from that intangible asset? With the nation reeling under the shock of the Depression, the value of tangible assets diminishing, and people now staying home to listen to radio sets they had purchased when times were better, circumstances conspired to make this intangible asset valuable indeed.

Though Paley preferred to style himself a showman, the key to CBS's survival was salesmanship, the art of convincing potential sponsors to buy time. If they believed broadcast advertising would sell their products, they would, Paley believed, pay handsomely for the privilege of using CBS's vast chain of affiliates to spread their message. From his experience with the La Palina advertising in Philadelphia, Paley knew broadcast advertising was potent, but it was a question of proving the point to others, and for a variety of products. In 1930, the Commerce Department estimated a total of nearly 14,000,000 sets in use, each with slightly over four listeners, adding up to a total radio audience of over 50,000,000. But would listeners buy what they heard? Did they truly constitute a market? It was time for the sales department to go to work.

CBS launched its campaign to lure advertising by temporarily hiring away Professor Robert Elder from the Massachusetts Institute of Technology to conduct an investigation. The fact that he came from an academic rather than a commercial milieu would, CBS hoped, lend credence to his findings. Professor Elder began by contrasting the buying habits of homes with and without a radio. In nearly every case, his survey discovered that products which used broadcast advertising were more popular in homes with than without radios. Pepsodent toothpaste, for example, advertising on a new NBC hit, "Amos 'n' Andy," was twice as popular in radio homes, and Barbasol, assisted by the crooning of Singin' Sam, did nearly as well. The reverse argument was equally compelling. In homes equipped with radio, products which did not make use of broadcast advertising actually gave ground to those that did. This finding implied that companies needed to advertise on radio just to stay even with the competition.

CBS was not alone in its research; both networks began to spew forth statistics confirming the obligatory nature of broadcast advertising. But CBS clearly had the advantage, since the network appeared, to the trade at least, to have taken the lead in this field. Suddenly stodgy NBC found itself upset by its fleet-footed rival. The older network, adhering, more or less, to its service philosophy, lagged in the quest for advertising dollars, until George Washington Hill, the flamboyant president of the American Tobacco Company, persuaded it to try the hard sell. In September 1928, he arranged to sponsor an hour of music performed by the Lucky Strike Orchestra, carried by thirty-nine NBC stations. During four months of the campaign, he claimed a 47 per cent increase in the sale of Lucky Strikes. "We feel that this remarkable increase in sales is largely due to our broadcasting programs," he wrote NBC. Subsequently, Hill became a master of the art of broadcast advertising. He hit upon the technique of endless repetition of slogans, as in L.S.—M.F.T. (Lucky Strike Means Fine Tobacco), and catch phrases ("So round, so firm, so fully packed. So free and easy on the draw").

In pursuit of the lucrative hard sell, both networks wrestled with long-standing inhibitions against specifying prices in the evening hours. The feeling was that such a practice would be too jarring and that it would earn radio the public's ill will, thereby limiting its effectiveness as an advertising medium. For a time, advertisers relied on clever euphemisms. The Robert Burns Panatela, its ads informed listeners, cost only "the smallest silver coin in circulation," and the price of Eno Fruit Salts was but "a little less than two packs of cigarettes." Paley proved to be hungrier than NBC: he allowed CBS to take the lead in shattering the quaint custom. A related inhibition concerned advertising for drugs, toilet articles, or anything that had to do with a bodily function. Though squeamish about offending the audience, the networks yearned for these products, which eventually became a staple of broadcast advertising. An early CBS advertising credo attempted to draw some lines, permitting "no broadcasting for any product which describes graphically or repellently any internal bodily functions." Paley banned laxative advertising, considered the most offensive of the lot, in the summer of 1933, at the same time announcing that he would respect contracts arrived at by an earlier deadline. As laxative manufacturers rushed to grab the last broadcast advertising, CBS enjoyed its best laxative year ever.

The presiding genius of CBS promotion was a true Paley find, Paul Kesten—"the only man," remarked the inventor Peter Goldmark, "who shined the bottom of his shoes." Kesten came to the network as director of sales promotion in 1930 after serving an apprenticeship at Gimbels and the Lennen and Mitchell advertising agency. At CBS he made a specialty of selling radio to the advertiser. With the aid of Professor Elder and others, he broke down the vast unseen radio audience of 50,000,000 according to sex, location, age, and purchasing power. But these statistics only served as raw material to which Kesten would then impart his own brand of poetry. He sold the potential sponsor not just airtime or audiences, but respectability and prestige. This concern dovetailed with Paley's, for the owner knew that CBS could give NBC a run for the money only by appearing to be not the raffish underdog but even more respectable, more elite, and more elegant than its competitor. This image gave the company a psychological edge over its larger rival. In the uncertain, huckstering world of advertising, CBS radiated self-confidence and professionalism. In the depths of the Depression, CBS was betting advertisers would find this pose reassuring.

Kesten promptly began issuing a flood of promotional booklets enhanced by the striking graphic design which became a CBS tradition. The booklets hammered away at a single theme—radio sells goods in a unique fashion, utilizing, in contrast to the print media, the dimension of time rather than space, and thereby monopolizing the listener's attention. Kesten and his crew insisted that the spoken word proved harder to resist than the written. "Nine times out of ten," concluded a typical Kesten promotional piece, "people do what they're told."

This strategy bespoke the networks' obsession with their main rival for advertising. In 1931, magazines and newspapers commanded the lion's share of the advertising market. *The Saturday Evening Post*, for example, had $35,000,000 in advertising as compared to NBC's $25,900,000. CBS had an even smaller share, $11,600,000, as compared to the *Ladies' Home Journal*, which could boast $12,800,000. The gross revenue of all stations reached $78,000,000, but the ten top magazines sold $100,000,000 worth of advertising. It was from print, then, that networks tried to steal customers. Success came in spurts. CBS's major advertisers in the early nineteen thirties included Wrigley's chewing gum, its biggest account, which lavished $22,800 per week on broadcast advertising, Philco, Ford, Chesterfield, and, of course, the La Palina, whose success had started it all. The advertising gravitated toward four related areas: drugs, toilet articles, food, and beverages.

In spite of these impressive figures, most available time went unsold and sponsored programs had the air of an event about them. In 1930, Paley testified before the Senate Committee on Interstate Commerce that only 22 per cent of CBS's programs were sponsored. By 1934, 64 per cent of all programming was still sustaining. There was still plenty of airtime to be sold, and Paley admonished the government to stay out of the networks' way so that they might go about their business in these hard times. "The winning principle of American business is competition," he noted. "This competition has been of almost inestimable benefit not only to network broadcasting but to every listener at American firesides." It was Paley's view—and the industry's—that untrammeled activity would lead to better programming, even though radio was responsible in some measure to the public's elected representatives. Paley would have none of it. Equating program quality with program popularity, he insisted the "best" program would reach the largest audience, benefiting both network and public. "The public will have to accept the fact that it can't have the very best in programming unless advertising pays for it," Paley said. Now, little more than a year after taking control of CBS, he was announcing to the world that advertising was here to stay, on *all* networks. After all, ran the subtext of his argument, there's a depression, and who can afford the luxury of running a network solely as a service? That wild-eyed philosophy, born of nineteen-twenties self-indulgence, was dead.

The apparently harmless device of using advertising rather than a parent company as a network's chief means of support had more profound implications than Paley, advertising's main proponent, would readily admit. The advertising presence created a climate in which programs that sold the best, thereby earning revenue, were the most favored, while less successful sales vehicles came to occupy a special minority class. In short, the demands of advertising selected and shaped programming, rather than just paying for it. Furthermore, thanks to NBC's connection with George Washington Hill, CBS was not alone in its exploration of new commercial frontiers. As we have seen, NBC quickly cast aside its traditional modesty about advertising, and, drawing on WEAF's commercial heritage, made a full-scale effort to introduce new, advertising-oriented formulas. In a 1928 address at the Harvard Business School, NBC's first president, Merlin "Deac" Aylesworth, remarked, "Broadcast advertising is unique in that its advertising and editorial copy are combined in the sponsored program. The two are blended in perfect union." An admitted newcomer to the industry, starting, as he put it, "at the bottom of the top," Aylesworth early on grasped the distinguishing feature of commercial network programming, the integration of advertising and content. Furthermore, he welcomed it. He spoke glowingly of the process as "tacitly and unconsciously coupling the editorial or program features which appeal to us with the advertising message they contain." He went on to define the task of the continuity writer as "weaving the advertising motif into the warp and woof of entertainment."

That was the theory. The reality took the form of live programs built around popular comedians. NBC, as the older, better established network, took the lead in cloaking popular vaudeville comedians—Jack Benny, Bob Hope, Eddie Cantor, and Ed Wynn—in the raiments of advertising. Ed Wynn, for example, in the guise of a fire chief, personified his sponsor's product, Texaco Fire Chief gasoline. Interruptions between entertainment and advertising were carefully blurred. Stars, remaining in character, slipped effortlessly into the role of pitchman. "This is Bob 'Pepsodent' Hope," ran a typical tag line, "saying that if you brush your teeth with Pepsodent you'll have a smile so fair that Crosby will tip his hair!" Another popular comedian opened his show with the greeting, "Jell-O again, this is Jack Benny." The sponsor's products were everywhere: in the show's title, the introduction, worked into jokes, all carefully integrated into the program's content. In the topsy-turvy world of network advertising, commercials strived to entertain while performers strived to sell. Though both NBC and CBS limited commercial time allotments to six minutes per hour, an hour-long variety or serial program with solid sponsor identification amounted to an hour's worth of advertising time. Bob

"Pepsodent" Hope in effect became a walking Pepsodent commercial, as was Jack Benny for Jell-O and later Lucky Strikes. Advertisers had perfected the art of the subliminal sell.

The practice, annoying or corrupt as it seems, gave the networks an edge over their main rival for the advertising dollar, newspapers and magazines, where content and advertising were sharply set off from one another. While mixing editorial opinion and reportage, they did not pepper articles and short stories with the names of advertisers' products, nor did they create advertiser-related personae for contributors. The difference lay in the dimension each medium uses. Print, relying on space, can be rechecked at will. Size and placement makes for impact; endless repetition would seem ludicrous. In contrast, broadcasting uses the dimension of time, from which nothing can be recalled. A word is uttered, then lost. If the listener is to remember a sponsor's message, he needs help, for he cannot go back to refresh his memory on his own. The sponsor must do it for him to keep the product from becoming lost in time and memory. Seizing on this fact, advertisers made repetition—of names, jingles, catchphrases—the keynote of broadcast advertising, often building print campaigns around ideas implanted in the public mind by the airborne commercials.

Though they still had much airtime left to sell, NBC and CBS succeeded in their campaigns to convince the advertising community that broadcasting advertising really worked. As a result, the networks acquired a dual nature, educational and civic-minded in character when it came to network-produced programming fare, yet willing to sell out to the highest bidder. Sponsors, it should be remembered, did more than sponsor; they produced. They leased network facilities and, through an agency, hired performers, writers, musicians, over which the network had no control; nor did they want it. One observer compared the situation to that of an old maid cohabitating with a prostitute. The network had, in effect, taken a new partner into the business, one whose demands had to be met.

The networks counted themselves lucky to find a dependable source of revenue in the depths of the Depression. As a result of the influx of advertising, NBC underwent an abrupt reorientation, causing it more and more to resemble CBS. By 1931, NBC had cast off the last remnants of its not-for-profit philosophy. While the network made its first profit ever, $2,300,000, in that year, the sale of RCA-built and licensed radios fell drastically, reaching deficit levels. If RCA wished to stay in business, it could no longer rely on the sale of hardware to pay its way. Now, advertising from the broadcasting operation was the primary profit center. It was to be encouraged, if only in the name of survival. Dreher notes, "The Depression alone would have driven Sarnoff to unleash the advertisers, but the CBS performance made it imperative for NBC to make the best possible showing on the balance sheet."

Accordingly, NBC assembled ambitious arrangements of its affiliates from which sponsors could pick and choose. In the early nineteen thirties, the Red network consisted of twenty-one stations, reaching west to Kansas City, and the Blue consisted of thirteen, each of which could double on the Red. NBC liked to claim that nearly 10,500,000 sets were tuned to the Red and over 10,000,000 to the Blue, but these figures are probably exaggerations. In contrast, the CBS network consisted of twenty-five stations covering approximately the same territory as NBC's Red and Blue combined, for a total number of sets surpassing the 13,000,000 mark. The estimate was probably at least as inflated as NBC's, but never mind the exact figures, the earning potential of the network was indeed vast. If things could be this good in the teeth of the Depression, imagine how much better they could be when the economy was healthy. Paley and, belatedly, Sarnoff, knew they were only beginning to reap the profits that could be derived from commercial broadcasting.

Once the principle of commercial broadcasting had been established, a rather rigid approach to the business of radio took hold. Of all the various ways a network might affect the public, the commercial bias dictated that an audience should be placated. Second, popularity was of the utmost importance; therefore, shows had to be designed with this factor in mind. And finally, everyone wanted to know how popular a show was. Advertisers needed to know if their product was indeed receiving widespread mention, and networks needed to know how large their audiences were so they could set advertising rates accordingly. Quickly, popularity became the yardstick against which network performance and economic health would be measured, and determining popularity required the invention of a new statistical discipline: ratings.

In 1930, the Association of National Advertisers instituted a survey of program popularity tabulated by Crossley, Inc. (no relation to the Crosley radio-set manufacturing company). Known as the Crossley report, the relatively unsophisticated telephone survey of thousands of homes constituted the first formal ratings service. Callers were asked to keep track of programs to which they listened. Since it depended on memory recall, the survey was rather unscientific. The results, which accorded "Amos 'n' Andy" a 53.4 rating while no CBS offering topped 12.0, brought gloom to 485 Madison Avenue. Nearly all of the ten most popular programs belonged to the NBC roster, and were dominated by the comedians who had been graduated from vaudeville to radio.

AS THE GREAT SHIP WENT DOWN: David Sarnoff on duty at the Wanamaker's wireless station where he first heard of the *Titanic* disaster (1912). *Courtesy RCA.*

WEAF in 1922, when the radio station was owned by AT&T. The announcer is
Helen Hann, who also worked in the Long Lines Department. *Courtesy AT&T.*

WEAF studios at 195 Broadway, AT&T's New York headquarters, in March 1924.
Courtesy AT&T.

LOOK ALIKES: David Sarnoff and Guglielmo Marconi in 1933. *Courtesy RCA.*

Maestro Toscanini and General Sarnoff. *Courtesy RCA.*

FAMILY PORTRAIT: The late Babe Paley, Edward R. Murrow, and William S. Paley at Eisenhower's inauguration in 1953. *Courtesy CBS*.

But CBS fought back. The survey, of course, was not good enough. Kesten hired the accounting firm of Price, Waterhouse to mail thousands of postcards to homes asking them to list the programs they preferred. The results gratifyingly showed a predominance of CBS programs. Never mind the objective accuracy of either survey; it was sufficient that each network have ammunition to support its claims of ratings supremacy. From this time forth, competition for audience as expressed in the ratings came to obsess network thinking. Practically all developments in programming, even technology, were geared to this end. Until this time, network endeavors could be attributed to a variety of motives: to educate, to sell radios, to amuse, to inform, to serve. But at this moment in the evolution of the networks, when the battle is joined, there is a remarkable new unanimity of purpose: to sell. Research, as a corollary, becomes an important tool of network competition. If it cannot prove one network is trouncing another, it can always show how radio as a whole works better than print or how one network reaches a more desirable audience than the other.

While NBC benefited from the proven vaudeville performers, CBS preferred a quieter, less expensive approach to programming, making unknowns into stars, building its own stable at a lower cost. With the assistance of Judson, Paley established the Columbia Artist's Bureau as a CBS subsidiary and vocational school. Under its auspices, Bing Crosby, whom Paley had discovered while listening aboard ship to a recording made by the crooner Morton Downey, and Kate Smith began as hundred-dollar-a-week unknowns and rose to radio stardom. Smith, incidentally, was selected as the entertainer for the all-important "La Palina Hour" with the reasoning that she was not the kind of woman to provoke jealousy in wives.

Paley adopted the same all-embracing approach to serious music. He presided over the merger of several prominent management concerns into a new enterprise called Columbia Artists, which Judson naturally directed while CBS owned a controlling interest. Through Columbia Artists, CBS maintained a much-ballyhooed relationship with the New York Philharmonic, conducted by Arturo Toscanini. The Sunday afternoon broadcasts of Philharmonic concerts were sustaining, but it was just as well, as the presence of the orchestra on the CBS schedule lent an aura of prestige and sophistication to the network and its affiliates. At the same time, it occupied a slot considered to be worth relatively little to advertisers.

Paley gained further initiative over NBC by buttressing his staff with a talented executive corps. In addition to Kesten, the unsung hero of CBS's early success-through-gloss, Paley took on as his second in command a former New York *Times* night city editor, Edward

Klauber. At forty-three, he could be considered elderly in a company in which the employees' average age was merely twenty-six. Klauber's presence allowed Paley to extricate himself from the day-to-day details of running the network and devote himself to more pleasurable pursuits. Here was the beginning of a pattern that was to bring turmoil and tension to CBS as time progressed. Where Paley characteristically avoided direct confrontation, preferring to delegate unpleasant tasks, Klauber seemed to derive a sadistic satisfaction from berating an employee. One of Klauber's young underlings, who would later become network president, Dr. Frank Stanton, recalled that Klauber "had a wicked tongue, wicked in the sense that he could really cut you to ribbons."

Klauber came to CBS at the suggestion of Paley's public relations counsel, Edward Bernays. Once in position, Klauber replaced Bernays, the man to whom he owed his job, with another public relations consultant, Ivy Lee, a well-established socialite thought to be able to introduce Paley to New York's elite WASP enclaves. Here was another Paley trait surfacing rather early in the game, his willingness to drop associates whose services he believed he no longer required. Klauber quickly assumed the role of Paley's strong man, taking care of the unpleasant tasks with which the boy wonder did not wish to deal.

In addition to Kesten, the image-maker, and Klauber, the staff sergeant, Paley took on a former member of the Federal Radio Commission, the regulatory body created by the 1927 Radio Act. This man, Sam Pickard, served as the invaluable liaison with Washington. The FRC offered little resistance to CBS's empire-building. Later, when it was revealed that in return for bringing WOKO (Albany, New York) into the CBS family Pickard became a concealed partner in the station, WOKO lost its license. To complete the executive constellation, Paley brought in as vice-president a socialite acquaintance, Lawrence Lowman, who became known as Paley's constant companion in a taxi or limousine. He supplied the link between Paley's professional and private lives.

The latter, by the way, was becoming more interesting. The confirmed bachelor had become acquainted with Dorothy Hart, a Los Angeles socialite who, at the time, was the wife of newspaper magnate John Randolph Hearst. In 1943, Dorothy divorced Hearst and married Paley in Kingman, Arizona.

Relying to a great extent on his newly acquired executives (Kesten, Klauber, and Pickard in particular), Paley watched his empire prosper. In 1929, CBS managed to sell just $5,000,000 in advertising, earning half a million in profit. In a short time, however, advertising revenue soared: $9,000,000 in 1930, $14,500,000 in 1931, $16,000,000 in

1932. CBS's highest profit in the early nineteen thirties came in the banner year of 1931, when the network earned $2,350,000, a figure that bettered even NBC's profit. To the older network's chagrin, affiliates began to defect to CBS. One desertion stung in particular, that of the powerful WJR in Detroit. In view of this situation, NBC in the mid-nineteen thirties was forced to adopt competitive affiliate contracts based on CBS's formula. CBS's affiliate shoestring lengthened to include seventy-six stations in 1931 and ninety-one by 1933. In terms of numbers of affiliates, it was now larger than either the Red or the Blue (though not both combined). It had a higher profit-to-sales ratio, outsold the Blue, and began to overtake the Red, where most of NBC's popular vaudevillians held sway.

In the process, CBS quietly passed a crucial milestone. The network earned more than the $2,000,000 Paley required to buy back the Paramount stock at the highly favorable pre-Depression price. CBS's success, coming in the depths of the Depression, was a vindication of Paley's judgment and Kesten's salesmanship. At the time of the original agreement between CBS and Paramount, the Paramount shares in Paley's hands were worth $3,800,000. Paramount planned to buy them back in 1932 at $85 a share, or $5,000,000. In the meanwhile, as CBS flourished, the Paramount stock plummeted to $9. Nevertheless, it had to buy back the stock from Paley at more than nine times that amount, something the financially troubled Paramount simply could not afford to do.

Paley could have humiliated Zukor then, but the movie mogul still had something Paley wanted, namely, control over talent. In addition, Zukor was an undisputed power in a related industry. Rather than create ill will, Paley decided on a different denouement. His group elected to ease Zukor's financial situation by purchasing the CBS stock Paramount owned for $5,200,000. Now Paramount could afford to buy back Paley's 48,000 Paramount shares for some $4,000,000. Paley's group had, in effect, paid out $1,200,000 to get Zukor off the hook and to disentangle the two companies. The infusion of Paramount money had served very well back in 1929, but now, with CBS's robust financial health, it was worth that much to Paley to regain unchallenged authority over his network.

In this crucial year of 1932, CBS showed almost exactly the same net profit as its older rival, approximately $2,300,000, and, burdened by a less complex history, achieved its goal with far fewer employees. Though CBS was growing at a faster rate, NBC still enjoyed certain advantages by virtue of having been there first, and not until Paley hired away his rival's highly popular ex-vaudeville stars in the late nineteen forties would CBS actually surpass NBC in the mind of the public, no matter what the research departments' statistics claimed. The success of the newer venture was entirely due to the business acumen of its young owner and his staff, who knew how to play the network game rather better than its originator, Sarnoff.

Though they were head-to-head competitors, the two networks were hardly mirror images of one another; they were as different as William Paley and David Sarnoff. Everything about the careers of the two men stood in sharp contrast. Where Sarnoff came from a poverty-stricken family and rose from messenger boy to chairman of a vast, well-established corporation, Paley, from his well-to-do background, simply bought himself a failing little company to run. If Sarnoff demonstrates the triumph of dogged persistence, then Paley exemplified the advantage of instinct and privilege. Sarnoff grew up with the industry, mastering Morse code, its mother tongue. Experience taught him the value of conscious, laborious effort to solve problems. As his career progressed, the rigidity inherent in this method of operation became increasingly apparent. His mind was profoundly practical, even mechanical. His true family was not his natural one, from which he earned an early independence, but the Company, at first American Marconi and then RCA. Spending most of his waking hours in the corporate environment since the age of sixteen, he was more at home there than anywhere else. He was the quintessential company man. This deliberate, conscious approach meant that every triumph was to be savored, every deed recorded, enshrined in the library at Princeton, every act carefully announced by a vast publicity machine. With David Sarnoff, there is the sense that everything in the man's career came as a result of hard work and merit and therefore is on the record. There is a complete identification between Sarnoff and RCA. The private man does not seem to matter, only the record, the artifacts.

With Paley, however, the momentous events are more difficult to pinpoint. Certainly he does not brag about them; a Paley museum would be entirely uncharacteristic. Sensing that CBS practically fell into his lap, Paley has preferred to remain self-effacing, manipulating from behind the scenes, out of the public eye. One feels the CBS endeavor is merely a facet of a complex existence, sharing attention with other aspects of his life. His career displays what the sociologist Robert Coles identified as a sense of "entitlement" characteristic of the children of the well-to-do. To the manor born, Paley prefers to live well back from the road, keeping the curtains drawn. As a result, his career lacks that inspiring element of surprise, ordeal, and accomplishment that marked Sarnoff's. Paley moved naturally from riches to still more riches. An early description noted, "People who come to

him expecting clever, devious answers are always baffled by his simplicity and the rapidity with which he comes to the point," and "there
is none of the shouting and desk-pounding that is supposed to be
characteristic of dynamic American leaders." That would come with
time. For the moment, the Paley style was deft, shy, adventurous, operating through impulse and suggestion rather than decree. Though
they shared a heritage, Paley and Sarnoff perceived the world in profoundly different ways and acted accordingly.

Thus far, we have seen how their visions shaped the networks, but
within the space of a few short years, the networks themselves became
too successful, too swollen, and too far-flung to yield to the force of a
single personality. For their day-to-day operation, they depended on
crafty cadres of executives, journalists, and, above all, performers. The
reason the networks became as successful as they did while everyone
around them, it seemed, went bust, was that these performers were
purveying a commodity desperately needed by a Depression-ravaged
nation: free entertainment.

Part II

IN THE MONEY

6

Dialogue

ANOTHER BRITISH WRITER AND SOCIAL CRITIC, George Bernard Shaw, found more to admire in broadcasting than did H. G. Wells. "There are three things I'll never forget about America," he remarked, "the Rocky Mountains, Niagara Falls, and 'Amos 'n' Andy.'"

It was not just simple escapism that made the team of Freeman Gosden and Charles Correll the most popular radio comedians of the nineteen thirties, it was their personality, their warmth, their understanding of the everyday foibles and quirks of human nature that endeared them to listeners. The radio stars—Benny, Cantor, and Allen included—remained themselves to a large extent even when playing a role. The characters they created were hardly heroic, instead they were electronic Everymen, the sort of fellows the "average listener" could sympathize or identify with. If they did not live on your block or in your building, they worked in your office, or you were married to one. Radio personalities were near at hand, personable, ordinary people.

As Amos and Andy, Gosden and Correll were the acknowledged masters of portraying the little man. Cheerful in the face of adversity, they obviously struck a chord in a beleaguered nation. Underlying the entire serial lay an analogy between the lot of the black man and the lot of the country in the grip of the Depression. By contemporary standards, of course, those shiftless and lazy characters that Gosden and Correll portrayed so convincingly over the course of four decades are travesties, condescending, cruel, racist stereotypes. But in the blind kingdom of radio, when the entire nation was down on its luck, "Amos 'n' Andy" caught the national mood. "We were all in this together, and Amos Jones and Andrew H. Brown epitomized the men with no money, no jobs, and no future," notes the radio-program connoisseur John Dunning. "Amos 'n' Andy" did not succeed on the basis of mockery and ridicule, but through audience identification.

The program had its origins in a long-standing institution of the Old South, the minstrel show. And the minstrel show itself was just one tributary of the vast mainstream of vaudeville. Before the advent of radio, vaudeville ranked as the most popular entertainment form of its day. Comedians, dialecticians, trained animal acts, singers, dancers, magicians, and everything in between aspired to tour the nationwide circuit of the theaters operated by such vaudeville managers as Keith-Albee, as a prelude to someday playing the Palace in New York. At least that was how things stood before the appearance of the networks. By 1932, this gregarious, pay-as-you-go form of entertainment was largely a memory, and it was the new ambition of vaudeville stars to make the transition from the stage to the radio studio. And so this new medium, free and relatively private, became the home of the most popular comedians, a process which brought about subtle alterations in the nature of their material. First of all, the show was sponsored, naturally, and the sponsor's presence forced performers to make accommodations. Second, with the visual component absent, the quality of writing and characterization became paramount. Without a large audience to respond to gags, the humor evolved into a dialogue with a single, unseen listener, rather than a raucous, sweaty, packed house of paying customers.

Though network radio—especially CBS—served as the incubator of impressive and refreshing experiments in the more serious pursuits of drama and journalism, it was from comedy that the networks gained the popularity they so desperately required to survive the early years of the Depression. And "Amos 'n' Andy" led the way. Without them, it is doubtful that NBC, which first signed them on, would have survived the Depression. The networks had been claiming a potentially huge audience, and they had plighted their troth at the feet of the advertising industry. "Amos 'n' Andy" was the show that proved the networks were as popular as they claimed to be. As such the program came to occupy the role of catalyst between network and advertiser, delivering a vast audience—an estimated half the nation every evening —to a grateful sponsor. Gosden and Correll were more than merely popular; they became a national mania.

Gosden and Correll were, of course, white men playing black characters. The performers' voices were in turn nasal and resonant, wavering and firm, raw and rich as honey. And Southern, of course, for they sounded like nothing so much as a couple of men swapping stories on the front porch. Gosden broke into show business with the Joe Bren Company, an outfit that traveled the country organizing vaudeville and minstrel shows. With Bren, Gosden sharpened his skills as a dialectician and, most important, met Charles Correll, who at the time was playing piano accompaniment for silent movies. As early as 1920, they worked up a blackface act and cut records for the Victor Talking Machine Company. But their careers had yet to take off.

Moving to Chicago, they thought this newfangled thing called radio might hold a future for them, and in short order joined the legion of ex-vaudeville performers trying to adapt their old tricks to the new medium.

At length, they arranged with the Edgewater Beach Hotel to perform a nightly act over the hotel's new station, WEBH, in exchange for free meals. The arrangement was not an uncommon one. Eight months over WEBH gave them a local following, in addition to filling their bellies, and led to an offer in 1925 from WGN, a much bigger station owned by the Chicago *Tribune,* to take paying jobs. The man in charge of the *Tribune's* radio division suggested that the team try a serial patterned after a popular comic strip. In response, Gosden and Correll abandoned their humorous odds and ends in favor of a more dramatic format, in which they portrayed two black men, Sam and Henry. They refined their act over the course of two years, delivering sketches five times a week. When a rival station, WMAQ, offered the team fifty dollars a week more than WGN was paying, they gladly switched, but WGN was hardly about to let them walk off with the names they had popularized. An agreement was reached whereby they would perform at WMAQ under new, untried names. While WGN tried without success to install another Sam and Henry team, the originals, over at WMAQ, experimented with several new sets of names until they settled on Amos and Andy.

The two young comedians were enterprising as well as persistent, and quickly grew wise to the ways of broadcasting. They persuaded WMAQ to distribute transcriptions of their broadcasts to as many as thirty other stations (for a price, of course), thereby creating an informal, but highly popular, network, which they called a "chainless chain." Their operation had only the rudiments of a network and broke with the standard practice of live performances, but it did give them widespread exposure. They were a bona fide Chicago phenomenon, but if they were to go further, they would require more than local exposure and assistance.

This was the era when CBS and NBC were laboring to persuade advertisers to take them seriously. In May 1929, a young Chicago advertising executive, William Benton (later co-founder of Benton and Bowles advertising agency and a Democratic senator from Connecticut), was struck by the omnipresence of "Amos 'n' Andy" in Chicago and hit upon a scheme. At the time, Benton worked for Lord & Thomas, Pepsodent's advertising agency, and he convinced his boss, Albert Lasker, that the program would make the perfect Pepsodent vehicle. Lasker in turn told a receptive NBC that they would have a major new advertiser if they would take on Gosden and Correll. In the meantime, Lasker groomed Pepsodent for stardom, coining the name "irium" for one of its mundane ingredients. NBC, now feeling pressure from the highly commercial CBS, rapidly agreed to Lasker's proposition and that summer offered the "Amos 'n' Andy"–Pepsodent contingent a fat contract, $50,000 a year for both Gosden and Correll, a considerable improvement over their $150-a-week salaries.

The young men hastened to New York, where they made their debut over NBC's Blue network, the one emanating from WJZ, on August 19, 1929. After an initial six-times-a-week schedule at 11 P.M., NBC received complaints from listeners that the show was on too late. The network responded by moving the team to a five-times-a-week schedule at 7 P.M., an hour of the day they soon came to control across the country. Or, rather, in the East. The West now complained that the show was on too early, and to oblige, Gosden and Correll undertook repeat performances for the West Coast three hours later. At the same time they switched to NBC's more commercial Red network.

The show rapidly attracted an audience of 40,000,000 each night, a seller's paradise for Pepsodent. Movie theaters, finding they were deserted at 7 P.M., announced on their marquees that they would pipe the show to their audiences. Department stores, encountering the same problem, followed suit. Calvin Coolidge and then Herbert Hoover were confirmed "Amos 'n' Andy" addicts while they were in the White House.

For the first seven golden years, Gosden and Correll wrote the 1,500-to-2,000-word scripts themselves every afternoon before the broadcast, then read them off before the microphones. They performed all roles themselves, creating a total of 550 characters through voice intonations alone. While the serial was built around developing characterizations, "Amos 'n' Andy" also relied on the traditional comedy device of the malapropism, the intentional substitution of one word for another with a similar sound but a different, often nonsensical, meaning. Gosden's and Correll's malapropisms worked their way into the national consciousness and were endlessly repeated. "I'se regusted," Amos would complain. "Is you mulsifyin' or is you rividin'?" Andy would ask.

The nucleus of the original serial consisted of Amos Jones, played by Gosden, and Andrew H. Brown, played by Correll. Together, they ran the Fresh-Air Taxicab Company of America, Incorpulated. In the early days, Amos played the straight man, a churchgoer, the one who did all the work his partner took credit for. In a popular ritual at Christmastime, it was Amos who explained the Lord's Prayer to his daughter.

Over the years an interesting development took place in the serial. Gosden eased out the recessive Amos in favor of a character able to match wits with or even dominate Andy. This new Gosden creation was George Stevens, known as the Kingfish, an appealing double-dealer who held court at the lodge hall of the Mystic Knights of the Sea. Among other things, then, the series charted the intricacies and pitfalls of an evolving relationship between two buddies. Gosden and Correll, doubtlessly pouring a lot of themselves into their daily program, expressed elements of their own highly charged relationship.

Among other regular characters there were the straitlaced Henry Van Porter (Correll) and the slow-witted, slow-moving Lightnin'. Women were present, too, playing crucial roles. Initially, Gosden and Correll did not attempt to imitate women's voices. They simply referred to them as off-microphone characters whose presences were so real that listeners often thought they had actually heard them. By the late nineteen thirties, when "Amos 'n' Andy" switched to CBS, Gosden and Correll relinquished bit parts to others, and actresses entered directly into the action. By that time, the comedians had taken the two-character serial about as far as it could go; they had succeeded in creating a miniature universe which 40,000,000 Americans visited for a quarter of an hour five times a week.

Gosden and Correll won their audience's loyalty with a dramatic formula in which humor and sentimentality were intertwined. They introduced endless postponing of climaxes in plot development, a technique that would serve as the basis of most soap operas. "Amos 'n' Andy" could very well be considered the granddaddy of situation comedies, and in certain ways it remains the best. As with most representatives of the genre, characters met with dire circumstances, but somehow the show's premise never altered. Andy's skirt-chasing provided excellent opportunities to build excitement in the serial's early days. The best known incident involved a breach-of-promise suit brought against Andy by the Widow Parker. The prolonged denouement stirred listeners into frenzy. Later, in 1939, Andy appeared on the verge of making the commitment; he went to the altar with his bride, but there, in mid-ceremony, he was cut down by gunfire as the episode came to a raucous conclusion. The press raised a fuss over whether Andy had been married or not. Prior to writing the episode, Gosden and Correll heard that a minister must actually say, "I now pronounce you man and wife" for a marriage to be binding. Andy remained a bachelor, of course.

In the midst of the merriment, there remained the specter of racism. Gosden and Correll denied that they were portraying a picture of black life that had nothing to do with the reality of black existence and black aspirations. Gosden, for one, believed his characterizations were valid, based on his childhood experiences in the South and a boyhood friendship with a certain "Snowball." He said he was qualified to impersonate a black man because he possessed a "thorough understanding of the colored race." When social realities caught up with the entertainment industry's distorted and condescending attitude toward minorities, Gosden and Correll, identified with an earlier, almost willfully blind era, retreated into obscurity. Much later, in the nineteen fifties, a CBS television version of the serial (in which black actors starred) drew fire from black groups. The addition of a visual dimension revealed the racism which had been latent in the original serial. Even in the America of the nineteen fifties, and in the lily-white world of network television, "Amos 'n' Andy" was an anachronism, an embarrassment.

In the early nineteen thirties, however, a little laughter covered a multitude of sins. "Amos 'n' Andy" not only enhanced the status of commercial network radio on the American scene but also gave rise to a wave of serials. The industry discovered that the serial, with its ability to attract an audience and keep it coming back for more of the same, and commercial sponsorship were made for each other. In the best efforts, writing remained of primary importance, as evidenced by two much-admired early serials, "Easy Aces," which was launched on CBS in 1931 (it later switched to the Blue network), and "Vic and Sade," which appeared on all three networks, the Red, the Blue, and CBS, at one time or another.

A pleasure to listen to, "Vic and Sade" defies adequate description. Its creator, Paul Rhymer, wrote of the day-to-day events in the life of a family named the Gooks, who lived in Crooper, Illinois. He imparted to the episodes a highly peculiar rural charm and fantasy. Audiences delighted in such characters as Rishigan Fishigan of Sishigan, Michigan, who was married to (wouldn't you know it) Jane Bane of

Pane, Maine, and places like the Little Tiny Petite Pheasant Feather Tearoom. The fifteen-minute-long episodes, broadcast five times a week, dealt with the minutiae of everyday existence. High drama had no place in "Vic and Sade." A typical episode showed Vic breaking in his new pipe under his son Rush's watchful eyes:

"Picture of a lady *kissin'* a fella on the front," Rush notes, examining the tobacco pouch.

"She's supposed to be Nicotine, the Goddess of the Tobacco Harvest," his father blithely explains. "The picture is somewhat allegorical. Represents a pipe-smoker tasting the joys of tobacco."

Goodman Ace not only wrote "Easy Aces" but performed in it with his wife, Jane Ace. He often wound up playing the straight man to Jane's dizzy whirl of malapropisms, the device "Amos 'n' Andy" had popularized in radio and which the Aces raised to the status of a parlor game. During their fifteen-minute-long sketches, Jane related how she had been "working her head to the bone," puzzled over "the fly in the oatmeal," and proclaimed that "Congress is still in season." She talked of the "ragged individualist," those who were "insufferable friends," complained of having risen "at the crank of dawn." Unlike Gosden and Correll's malapropisms, which were nonsensical, Jane's peculiar vocabulary often made a quirky psychological sense. Her malapropisms were akin to Freudian slips.

In contrast to other comedians, particularly those coming out of vaudeville, who bent over backward to accommodate sponsors, Goodman Ace, with his background in journalism, demanded stringent separation between sponsor and performer. He refused to meet with representatives of Anacin, his sponsor in later years, when he moved to NBC. And when, in 1945, an Anacin official ventured to criticize the program's music, Ace took Anacin to task for packaging aspirin in cheap cardboard rather than sturdy tin boxes. Whereupon Anacin immediately canceled its sponsorship, and the Aces left the air for three years.

Similarly, the performer who was to become radio's most popular comedian and master salesman took several years to make his peace with sponsors, carving out a delicate, revealing, and influential truce with the forces that ruled the air. He first appeared on radio in 1932, in a weekly program broadcast over CBS moderated by a New York *Daily News* columnist named Ed Sullivan. As millions listened, Sullivan yielded the microphone to a monologuist. "Ladies and gentlemen," he said in a youthful, distinctively nasal voice, "this is Jack Benny talking. There will be a slight pause while you say, 'Who cares?'" With this slightly snide note of self-deprecation which was to run through all of Benny's humor, the man who would eventually become radio's single most successful comedian—and salesman—introduced himself. His appearance on Sullivan's show amounted to an audition not so much for audiences as for potential sponsors for his own program.

As it happened, Benny went over well with the N. W. Ayer Agency, representing Canada Dry ginger ale, and they signed him up to appear on CBS as "The Canada Dry Humorist," pun intended. Benny alarmed his sponsors, however, by deprecating not just himself but them as well. The audience might have appreciated Benny's quips about Canada Dry, but the sponsor did not. After seventy-eight programs, the Canada Dry Humorist found himself sponsorless. At the time, the company, indeed, the industry, did not realize that Benny had hit upon a potent way of selling products. As "Amos 'n' Andy" established the conventions and popularity of the serial format, so Benny shaped the format of the popular variety program. Fred Allen, perhaps the most admired of the radio comedians, concluded, "Practically all comedy shows on radio owe their structure to Benny's conceptions. He was the first to realize that the listener is not in a theater with a thousand other people, but is in a small circle at home."

It is worth looking for the origin of some of "Benny's conceptions." He was born Benjamin Kubelsky in Waukegan, Illinois, in 1894. As a teen-ager, his stage appearances consisted solely of violin performances. Not until the First World War, when trying to hold the attention of a restless audience of sailors, did he crack a joke onstage, to the delight of the crowd. After the war, he returned to the stage as the monologuist Ben K. Benny. The violin was now purely incidental. After a fling in films, Benny returned to New York to appear on Broadway, and it was at this point in his career that he received his invitation from Ed Sullivan. He had at last found his medium, but it took a while for the medium to adjust to his ways. After the Canada Dry debacle, Benny found a new backer, Chevrolet. Though he now rose to the very top of the ratings, Chevrolet did not care for his style either and soon canceled. Later, when the company reconsidered, it was too late, for General Tire and subsequently Jell-O and Lucky Strikes reaped the rewards of Benny's barbs on the Red network. Furthermore, his style of salesmanship bent slightly under pressure. Rather than denigrating the product itself, he made a practice of mocking the commercial format. That was the nature of his uneasy truce.

This evolution paralleled a growing sophistication among radio performers, audiences, and sponsors. A comedian like Benny, playing virtually the same character throughout his broadcasting career, established an unusually close rapport with his audience, almost a pact.

To turn around and become pitchman would have violated this pact, ruined the credibility of the performer, and reflected poorly on the product. By kidding the product, the performer salvaged his rapport and managed to continue with his integrity apparently intact. Broadcasting's most successful salesman-personality in the post-World War II era, Arthur Godfrey, relied on the same principle. This peculiar strategy sprang from the fact that radio performers, unlike their vaudeville predecessors, were beholden not to the audience but to the sponsor. The sponsor maintained a booth at the studios where broadcasts originated and decided then and there what script material would be acceptable and what would not. With every gag a comedian delivered, the sponsor's reputation was on the line. Nervous about deviations from prearranged formulas, they eventually realized that this novel method of advertising did not hurt sales, only pride. The context of the product mention was not nearly so important as the mention itself.

Other comedians adopted the repertoire of conventions Benny established, such as the affable, overweight, middle-aged announcer, and the conception of the cast as a kind of extended family consisting of wife, servant, neighbors, and friends. But Benny displayed a unique knack for generating listener interest with his artificial on-air feud with Fred Allen, carried on solely in the name of publicity.

Also a vaudeville veteran, Allen shared many of Benny's qualities, the crispness of timing and the slightly crotchety or exasperated manner, but he relied less on characterization and more on writing. In this realm, Allen was the acknowledged master, the comedian's comedian. In his book, *The Funny Men*, Steve Allen wrote that he possessed a "poet's regard for peculiarities of sound and expression and he never seemed so happy as when he could roll off his tongue some glittering allegory, metaphor, or simile." Allen broke into radio months after Benny, in October 1932. Like Benny's show, Allen's featured his wife, Portland Hoffa, and a collection of fanciful characters including Mrs. Pansy Nussbaum, played by Minerva Pious, and Senator Beauregard Claghorn, who quickly had the country repeating his tag line, "That's a joke, son."

In 1937, Allen and Benny, on their separate programs, embarked on the ten-week-long feud, hurling barbs between studios. Allen took Benny to task for his violin playing, remarking that the instrument's strings would have been better off left in the cat. Benny, known to rely heavily on gagmen, replied to such insults, "You wouldn't dare talk that way if my writers were here."

As Benny established audience rapport by kidding his sponsors, Allen went after the network, contriving sketches which mocked the petty preoccupations of NBC vice-presidents, whom he described as "a bit of executive fungus that forms on a desk that has been exposed to a conference." Occasionally NBC would retaliate by momentarily cutting him off the air. At times Allen was forced to rewrite his scripts at the last minute to suit the network's pleasure. But the last word was his, since he reserved the excised comments for the studio audience.*

For the comedians working inside the network system, lightning struck again and again. Comedy provided an endlessly renewable source of national diversion and network profits. It was remarkable how, in the depths of the Depression, network broadcasting, that most commercial of enterprises, flourished, feeding the national hunger for diversion. The industry succeeded because it offered entertainment for free and through its wide reach succeeded in creating a desire for products—cigarettes, toilet articles, and food items mostly—where there had been little or none before. By 1932, CBS was able to offer sponsors a "basic network" consisting of twenty-two stations for over $2,000 for a quarter hour, night rate. This guaranteed at least $32,000 in gross revenue a night every night, and in fact the figure was substantially higher. Furthermore, overhead was low. The affiliate stations, cornerstone of the network, were for the most part independently owned, though both NBC and CBS realized they would fortify their position by owning more outlets in addition to the key station in New York. Affiliates, then, bore the burden of costs. All the network had to do was pay AT&T line charges for the linkup and maintenance of the New York studios. These were fixed costs, not rising in proportion to revenue, but remaining the same for a sponsored or sustaining program.

The networks jealously guarded their monopoly on New York entertainment, the kind the public and sponsors clamored for, by broadcasting solely on a live basis. At first a condition for receiving a relatively uncrowded frequency assignment, live broadcasting now served to consolidate the networks' power over programming. By making a strict policy of forbidding transcriptions of comedians, singers, correspondents, bands, or announcers, the networks kept the

---

* The audience, incidentally, was originally separated from the performers by a glass partition designed to screen out all laughter and other unscripted reactions. But in April 1932, Ed Wynn, Texaco's "Fire Chief," decided to remove the glass, setting a precedent that other comedians soon followed. The following year, Wynn, riding the crest of his popularity, left NBC to form his own network, called the Amalgamated Broadcasting System, consisting of six stations fed by WNEW in New York. By this time, however, it was too late. NBC and CBS had the field to themselves, since virtually all worthwhile stations belonged to one camp or the other. The poorly organized venture succumbed within a few months.

talent to themselves, and they did not even pay for the talent; sponsors did. The network broadcasting system quickly became a highly efficient moneymaking mechanism, for the main commodity networks offered their sponsors, time on the schedules of affiliates across the country, was as free as the air. The network did not pay affiliates money until it made money from a sponsored program, and for sustaining programs costs were held to a minimum until that fine day when they, too, found a sponsor and joined the cavalcade of cash.

During a typical day in March 1932, CBS began wringing substantial amounts of money out of the air early in the evening. Advertising rates doubled at 6 P.M., when an estimated one fifth of the nation's radio stations would be operating. For forty-five minutes the network broadcast sustaining music programs, including Bing Crosby's. The pecuniary procession kicked off at six forty-five with the evening's first sponsored program, "Frank Strels Orchestra," which went out twice weekly to thirteen stations. The sponsors, Seek and Kade, makers of Pertussin, paid CBS over $3,000 a week in "time costs" (plus another $1,000 a week to the orchestra). The evening's first big serial program was "Myrt and Marge," one of those backstage dramas about a naïve young performer and the veteran who looks out for her. Popular in the West, "Myrt and Marge" had a much wider reach—thirty stations five times a week, for which Wrigley Chewing Gum, CBS's largest early sponsor, paid a handsome $73,250 a week to the network in time charges (and just $2,000 for talent). It was at this point, after the saga of Myrt and Marge, that the efforts of Paley and Kesten and staff really began to pay off. An estimated two fifths of the nation's radios were in operation, and most of these were tuned in to the sophisticated byplay of the Aces, sponsored by the mouthwash Lavoris, which paid $15,615 a week to present the program on sixteen stations, plus $1,000 for the talent.

And so it continued throughout the evening. At seven forty-five Morton Downey reached a grand total of seventy-four stations. R. J. Reynolds Tobacco Company, makers of Camels, paid $204,084 each week to present the six-times-a-week orchestral program. Talent costs were high, too: $3,500 for Morton Downey plus $9,000 for Tony Wons and orchestra. At eight-thirty Kate Smith sang for Congress Cigar's La Palina over twenty-three stations. (And there was no favoritism here; Paley charged his family business $34,576 for the four-times-a-week program. Since several family members, including Paley's father, Samuel, sat on the CBS board, the family was, in a sense, paying itself.) By now, 8:45 P.M., the radio audience was thought to be nearing its peak, with three fifths of sets operating. Once a week Ed Sullivan held forth on behalf of La Gerardine hair lotion. He received $1,000 (less agency commission), and CBS received $1,884 in time charges. And so on into the night with bands of every description. Here was capitalism indeed, unfettered as yet by any notions of accountability or public service: a very particular kind of dream come true.

And it was all largely due to the vaudeville performers who supplanted the earlier broadcasting staple of band music. The Red network, the premiere comedy chain, had Eddie Cantor, Ed Wynn, Al Jolson, Rudy Vallee, and, of course, "Amos 'n' Andy." CBS had Jack Benny, Burns and Allen, and Fred Allen. Later, when Benny switched to the Red, he further intensified the concentration of comedy at NBC and became the perennially highest rated program of them all. Despite the bigger attractions on the NBC marquee, however, CBS remained the more nimble operation, capable of wringing more profit out of the air than either the Red or the Blue. In this matter the fine managerial hand of Paley is evident. Concentrating solely on broadcasting, he became a master at deploying programs for maximum commercial advantage. Yet, while CBS in 1932 looked better on paper than NBC, having come a long way since its frantic debut just five years before, the network still toiled in enormous Blue and Red shadows.

7

Exhibit A

IN THE END, CBS countered with prestige programming—minority-oriented, high-quality, and sustaining. While Sarnoff, with his "pipeline" approach to the function of a network, took relatively little interest in programming and devoted his greatest attention instead to the development of new technological innovations, especially television, Paley, limited to broadcasting alone, did what he could to enhance the prestige of CBS, to make it seem in the public mind the more advanced, dignified, and socially aware network. The sustaining programming, the music of the New York Philharmonic and the drama of Norman Corwin and Orson Welles, was meant as a dividend derived from the network's undeniable commercial success. While Sarnoff assumed the role of technocrat, Paley played that of programmer.

Or rather hired a thoughtful man who would. Alerted by an article in the June 1935 issue of *Fortune* magazine about CBS's sudden rise and the clever young man who made it happen, William B. Lewis approached Paley for a job after his own advertising agency had foundered. As it happened, the network was running an impressive ad in a trade journal for a head of programming, someone to develop network- rather than sponsor-controlled efforts. The position was a particularly sensitive one, for sustaining programs could be construed as conveying the beliefs, political or otherwise, of the management. Though the network awarded this category of programming skimpy budgets and lame-duck time slots, they bore a disproportionate amount of editorial importance.

The CBS ad declared the company wanted "a big man" with a "brilliant flair for entertainment." Lewis received the coveted position quite by accident when his application was misfiled and his name came up for review. Beginning in 1936, he proceeded to gather around him not ex-vaudeville stars or other show business luminaries, but directors such as Irving Reis, William Robson, and Orson Welles, then making his name in New York with striking adaptations of classic plays, composers such as Bernard Herrmann, and writers such as Archibald MacLeish and Norman Corwin, a journalist who wrote verse in his spare time. Together, these individuals proposed to overturn the tenets of commercial broadcasting. Where the Red network, for example, offered listeners the anaesthetic of laughter in the face of the Depression, they would devote their creative energies to sharpening public awareness of the great social issues of the day, especially the coming turmoil in Europe. For the rise of serious drama on radio quickly became inextricably linked to the rise of fascism in Europe. Today, we recall the comedians of the era more clearly than the dramatists; memoryless broadcasting has usually favored personality and the spoken word over issues and the written word, but the Lewis crowd was undeniably in touch with the issues of the era and tapped vast public anxiety about them.

CBS commenced its weekly dramatic anthology series, "The Columbia Workshop," in July 1936. For a time, the series struggled to define itself, serving as a laboratory for experiments with sound effects, filters, microphones, and echo chambers. Salaries were at the subsistence level. Writers received about $100 for a produced script and actors only $18.50 for a half-hour performance, including rehearsal time. As a result, the series attracted men and women who were young, untried, exposed to the raw edge of the Depression, and hungry. Furthermore, they were laboring in thankless time slots. "The Columbia Workshop" competed against Jack Benny, who came on the air Sunday evenings at 7 P.M. over the Red network. CBS time salesmen's rate cards marked "The Columbia Workshop" "withheld from sale," but it is doubtful the network could have lured substantial sponsorship for any program running opposite Benny. On the brighter side, ratings, now firmly in control of all sponsored programming, did not enter into consideration. CBS made no attempt to determine the workshop's popularity.

These were the terms, then. Archibald MacLeish, for one, accepted them. The Pulitzer Prize-winning poet and playwright perceived a natural kinship between poetry and radio stemming from a reliance on

the ear. "My theory of radio as a medium of verse is that the imagination works better through the ear than through the eye," he wrote.
MacLeish set himself the task of employing the workshop's technical
daring in the service of a powerful statement about the spread of fascism. The result, a 1937 verse drama entitled *The Fall of the City*, syn-
thesized recent political events in Europe: the Civil War in Spain, the
rise of Mussolini and Hitler, and the chilling prospect of totali-
tarianism. In MacLeish's parable, the inhabitants of a city rush to
prostrate themselves before an approaching conqueror. They prefer
enslavement to the burden of responsibility implicit in a free, democratic society. Through this heavily ironic replaying of recent history,
MacLeish wished to illustrate for the radio audience the perils of iso-
lationism and apathy. In so doing, MacLeish sounded themes many of
the workshop's subsequent productions were to echo. Furthermore, he
introduced often imitated dramatic techniques. To tell his story, Mac-
Leish's script relied on a device borrowed from Greek drama, the in-
teraction between a speaker and a chorus. In *The Fall of the City* this
device was transformed into a dialogue between announcer and
crowd. "For the radio play the announcer has become a great dramatic symbol," MacLeish wrote. "He has become a dramatic device
far beyond expectations as revealed by the European crisis, and
chiefly by those announcers who went on the air at Prague. The announcer as a narrator becomes a most colorful and useful tool for the
dramatist." MacLeish did not waste time on a detailed plot. "Bold
outlines and simplicity" were what he thought radio drama called for.
The net result, in the words of the New York *Times* radio critic of the
day, Orrin Dunlap, amounted to a "dramatic recitation with sound
effects."

MacLeish set the tone for the entire workshop. His themes were
further developed by a younger writer, an unknown named Norman
Corwin, who championed the "little guy" in his struggle against ty-
rants everywhere. Like MacLeish, Corwin wrote in a verse based on
the vernacular and relied on those "bold outlines" and dramatic sound
effects espoused by MacLeish. This was, in essence, didactic drama.
Its aim: to raise the nation's political consciousness.

In the wake of MacLeish's drama, which was hailed as a milestone
in the development of radio writing, the workshop found itself flooded
with dramatic scripts by the likes of W. H. Auden, William Saroyan,
Stephen Vincent Benét, and Maxwell Anderson. The enterprise began
to shed glory on all of CBS, bringing just the luster and prestige Paley
wanted. And, for the moment, the risk of controversy was minimal, for
the workshop caught the spirit of the times. Hoover, after all, was
long gone, and this was the era of the New Deal, with its antibig-

business, antimonopoly stance. Furthermore, Congress had buttressed the Radio Act of 1927 with a new Communications Act of 1934, which created a Federal Communications Commission endowed with sweeping powers. As a cornerstone of its charter, the FCC sought to determine whether the industry, among other things, took care to "serve the public interest, convenience, and necessity." By 1935, Paley was known to be the highest paid executive in radio, earning $169,097. As such, both he and his network were sitting ducks, inviting government scrutiny. Through the workshop and other prestigious programming, Paley wished to make a good showing not only to ease his conscience but also to enable his executives, when questioned by this or that congressional subcommittee, to point with pride to the workshop or the Sunday afternoon New York Philharmonic concerts. Such concerns were not entirely misplaced, moreover, because as the nineteen thirties drew to a close, the FCC would move to disband the NBC dual network structure. In the process, the networks did a dramatic about-face. NBC, the originator of the service concept, abandoned such notions in the face of the Depression and competition from CBS. And CBS, in the meanwhile, which had begun as a thoroughly commercial proposition, could now afford to take the lead in service-oriented programming, if only as a matter of self-protection.

A year after his first effort, MacLeish wrote another play for the workshop, *Air Raid,* which turned out to be a rehearsal for events in the very near future. He wrote the play in June. By September, the events foreseen in the play tragically came to pass as German troops crossed the border into Czechoslovakia. And just two years later, a young CBS News reporter, Edward R. Murrow, would narrate London's efforts to survive air raids akin to the nightmare MacLeish imagined.

The man of the moment, Lewis, now turned to a workshop regular, Orson Welles, to start another dramatic anthology series. To Lewis, the proficient and multitalented Welles must have seemed like a natural candidate to produce a dramatic series. He had appeared in workshop productions, including *The Fall of the City,* in which he played the pivotal role of the announcer, and another MacLeish script, *Panic,* about the Wall Street crash. He had also created the role of Lamont Cranston in the popular radio series "The Shadow," not to mention participating in a summertime Shakespeare series the network had produced. His directing credentials matched his acting career. With the Federal Theatre in New York, he had staged a *Macbeth* with a black cast and a Marc Blitzstein opera, *The Cradle Will Rock.* When the Federal Theatre interfered with the radical opera, Welles and an actor-producer named John Houseman formed a splinter group, the

Mercury Theatre. Their first production—an interpretation of Shake-speare's *Julius Caesar* as a fascist drama—reflected the workshop's po-litical preoccupation. When Lewis offered Welles, Houseman, and the Mercury Theatre the opportunity to perform a series of hour-long ad-aptations of literary classics, they were taking on board not only a prodigiously talented actor-director, but a theatrical group with strong leftist leanings. In 1937, such political beliefs were not considered es-pecially threatening, only noncommercial. Later, the networks, shift-ing with the nation's political climate, would interpret such beliefs as a threat to national security.

"The Mercury Theatre on the Air" made its debut in July 1938 with an adaptation of Bram Stoker's *Dracula*. Regular cast members in-cluded Agnes Moorehead, Martin Gabel, and Joseph Cotten. Bernard Herrmann, the CBS in-house composer, was responsible for the music. In the fall, CBS moved the series opposite another of radio's exceed-ingly popular comedians, Edgar Bergen, whose show, the so-called "Chase and Sanborn Hour," was broadcast over the Red network on Sunday evenings. As with the workshop, "The Mercury Theatre on the Air" was sustaining, occupying a time slot considered unsellable. Seven weeks into the season, it managed to reach just 3.6 per cent of the radio audience, as compared with Bergen's 34.7 per cent, a disap-pointing showing even for a "prestigious" program.

As its offering for October 30, 1938, the series scheduled an adapta-tion of H. G. Wells's science fiction tale "The War of the Worlds." Howard Koch, the series writer, disliking the musty Victorian at-mosphere of the story, requested an alternate choice, possibly *Lorna Doone*. Welles preferred to stick with Wells as the Mercury Theatre's Halloween offering, and Koch and Houseman set to work updating the story. They moved the locale from London to Grover's Mill, New Jer-sey, and employed MacLeish's dramatic device of the announcer. In this case, the announcer would repeatedly interrupt a supposed pro-gram in progress with news bulletins about strange happenings in Grover's Mill. CBS, thinking the script, loaded as it was with refer-ences to President Roosevelt and the Biltmore Hotel, too real, re-quested thirty-eight changes.

The broadcast, live, as always, began at 8 P.M., when much of the networks' audience tuned in Edgar Bergen and Charlie McCarthy. As a result, few people heard an announcer on CBS explaining that the Mercury Theatre would be offering their version of the H. G. Wells story. They also missed Orson Welles setting the scene: "In the thirty-ninth year of the twentieth century came the great disillusionment. It was near the end of October. Business was better. The war scare was over. More men were back at work. Sales were picking up. On this particular evening, the Crossley service estimated that thirty-two million people were listening in on radios." The program, then, was not taking the audience to some strange world for its horror story, but stayed resolutely in the present. It was a seductive and brilliant ploy. The broadcast then revealed what the audience was supposedly listening to, one "Ramon Raquello and his Orchestra" from the "Meridian Room of the Park Plaza in downtown New York," in short, a perfectly acceptable counterfeit of a humdrum radio program.

At the same moment, in one of those coincidences that have the feel of fate about them, Edgar Bergen yielded the microphone to a singer. Dials across the country went spinning in search of another program, and many of them tuned in CBS. None of the newcomers had heard the multiple, unambiguous introductions to the drama in progress. What they did hear was an announcer breaking into an innocuous program of dance music with alarming accounts of an object's having landed in Grover's Mill. They heard that a creature had emerged from the object and sent out destructive rays. All the while, the Mercury Theatre crew was doing a devilishly good imitation of remote broadcasts of the day. Some listeners, made uneasy by Hitler's aggressive actions against Czechoslovakia, began to take the accounts at face value. They reacted with terror to the following description delivered by a hysterical actor: "Ladies and gentlemen, this is the most terrifying thing I have ever witnessed. . . . Wait a minute! Someone's crawling out of the hollow top. . . . It's indescribable. I can hardly force myself to keep looking at it." The announcer was clearly modeling his performance on Herbert Morrison's well-known account of the crash of the *Hindenburg* zeppelin at Lakehurst, New Jersey, in 1937. By the time another announcer described how the monster was taking control of central New Jersey, cutting off rail lines and creating a state of martial law, havoc struck. Meanwhile, safe in the cocoon of the studio, the broadcast continued and a real announcer pointed out that "you are listening . . . to an original dramatization of 'The War of the Worlds.'" Though the invaders did die in the end, victims of bacteria, it was too late. In defiance of all logic, hysteria mounted, releasing a remarkable amount of accumulated apprehension. Welles, with that rich, impudent voice, concluded the program with the thought that it had merely been "the Mercury Theatre's own radio version of dressing up in a sheet and jumping out of a bush and saying 'Boo!'"

The press seized the opportunity to chastise its upstart rival for irresponsibility. Newspaper accounts actually fed the hysteria and labeled it as a certified public calamity. The New York *Times*, for example, gave the story front-page play, describing a night of horrors during which the fraudulent broadcast drove decent citizens out of their homes in panic.

Shortly after the broadcast, when Welles realized what he had wrought, he figured he was finished at CBS. Unlike MacLeish, his goal had been simply to entertain, rather than to make a political statement, but his entertainment had backfired. Yet Welles was not disgraced. As a result of the notoriety surrounding the broadcast, the series acquired a sponsor, Campbell Soup, and began its 1939 season as "The Campbell Soup Playhouse," of all things. It seemed that sensationalism had accomplished what no amount of earnest intentions had managed to: attract a sponsor for this sustaining dramatic series. In radio, as in advertising, there could be no such thing as bad publicity.

While Welles's reputation continues to thrive, that of another writer-director Lewis launched, Norman Corwin, has languished, no doubt because he was so closely allied with the brief flourishing of serious radio drama. In the later nineteen thirties and forties, Corwin came to be known as the dramatic poet of radio *par excellence*. Unlike MacLeish and Welles, who drifted in and out of radio, Corwin developed his craft primarily within the confines of CBS. Lewis encouraged him; Paley entertained him at home. "In the early days," Corwin recalls, "there was a family feeling about the network. It sounds a little bit sentimental to say, but that was really the case."

Born in Boston in 1910, Corwin began his career as a newspaperman, with the Springfield *Daily Republican*. Eventually becoming the paper's radio editor, he doubled as newscaster for WBZ. In 1936, he went to New York, where he found himself delivering a fifteen-minute poetry program over a local station, WQXR, which liked to bill itself as "the station for people who hate radio." But Corwin aimed his sights still higher, at the prestigious "Columbia Workshop," which he considered "the peak for writers and directors." In the spring of 1938 he signed on as a director. Later that year, Corwin approached Lewis. "I had a suggestion for a series of broadcasts and asked him if I could have $200, which was then the budget to make [the equivalent of] a pilot," Corwin remembers. "Lewis liked it very much, and the meeting in his office changed my life."

The idea consisted of adapting an assortment of nursery rhymes to radio. On the strength of the pilot, Lewis offered Corwin his own program immediately following the Sunday afternoon New York Philharmonic concerts, when a culturally inclined audience was thought to be tuning in to CBS; furthermore, Lewis gave the new series the title "Norman Corwin's Words Without Music." "This stroke at once went far beyond anything an agent could have asked for me, because I hadn't got any credits, and offering me billing at the head of a show was an extraordinary act of generosity, if not faith."

By Christmas 1938, just two months after Welles's *succès de scandale*, Corwin ventured to produce the first program he himself had written, rather than adapted from other sources. The holiday offering was entitled "The Plot to Overthrow Christmas," and the lighthearted fantasy about satanic efforts to subvert the Christmas holidays established the young poet of the airwaves. "That was, of all the programs I've written, one of the easiest," says Corwin. "The search for a rhyming pattern sometimes forces you into insouciant and wry and funny combinations, and that's what happened all the way through this for me." In the process of spinning out his light verse, Corwin managed to parody the conventions of radio and mock the powers of fascism. The concoction went down well, and the program became a Christmas perennial. Part of the success of this and subsequent Corwin efforts stemmed from their buoyant, optimistic, slightly naughty, tongue-in-cheek tone. There was none of MacLeish's admonitory nihilism here.

Corwin now expanded his range. Just a few weeks later he presented another startling verse drama which drew a large public response, "They Fly Through the Air with the Greatest of Ease," a vigorous attack on fascism. Corwin was on the offensive and the public responded to his let's-roll-up-our-sleeves-and-get-down-to-work attitude. That response, incidentally, came in the form not of stellar ratings, but of mail, one of the principal methods by which Corwin and his colleagues gauged the impact of their programs.

While the programs continued on a sustaining basis and salaries remained low, Corwin's reputation and, by extension, that of CBS, blossomed. "I suddenly went from being a new recruit on the eighteenth floor of 485 Madison Avenue to having my picture in *Time*," Corwin recalls of his sudden accession to celebrity. Next, Lewis turned over "The Columbia Workshop" to Corwin for a series of programs, the first time the series had become the domain of one man. Now called "Twenty-six by Corwin," the series taxed his abilities to the utmost. "I didn't know what I was getting into," he says. "I had to turn it out each week: not only conceive it, write it, and direct it, and produce it, but get scripts out far enough in advance for an original score to be written." Corwin returned to lighthearted efforts from time to time: "The Undecided Molecule," for instance, featured Vincent Price, Groucho Marx, and Robert Benchley. But as the nation pitched toward war his radio plays took on patriotic themes. Corwin's influence soared even higher with a pro-Roosevelt program which all the networks carried in 1944. He was now working on a vast aural canvas, employing a seemingly limitless number of actors and effects.

Radio finally found its poet laureate in Norman Corwin. His plays were printed as popular books. CBS spared no expense to design handsome promotional material featuring Corwin. As he continued with one successful series after another, "Columbia Presents Corwin" (1945), for example, and individual programs like "The Lonesome Train," about the train bearing Lincoln's body, it seemed he could do no wrong. Paley was solidly behind CBS's poet in residence. "I never got a negative stroke from him," Corwin recalls. "CBS told me they never bothered to take ratings on my programs. 'We don't care,' they said, 'how many people are listening or not listening to your program. We believe in it.'"

In producing the work of Corwin and others, CBS gained self-confidence. The network was no longer merely a linking of coast-to-coast affiliates, a commercial proposition with a cluster of studios for hire; it was a program source itself, endowed with a sense of identity. More than any commercial effort, no matter how popular, the network drew on the sustaining "Columbia Workshop" and related series for its self-definition. In this respect, the prestigious programming defied good business practice, yet became, as much as anything could, the heart and soul of the network, simply because it was not for hire by advertisers.

The development held widespread implications. If a network was to be not merely a highly profitable program carrier but a program source, it was now venturing into a legal *terra incognita*. Was the network, for example, entitled to protection under the First Amendment, as newspapers and magazines most certainly were? The question applied even more acutely to the networks' rapidly growing news divisions. For the moment the networks straddled approaches to broadcasting. On the one hand, they had developed undeniably lucrative and apparently inexhaustible sources of commercial programming over which they had little influence, merely supplying the pipeline for sponsors' messages. On the other hand, CBS had pioneered a new, network-originated type of programming, editorial in nature and unsponsored. Geography aggravated the dichotomy, for by 1937 nearly all the top-rated comedians had moved from New York to new network studios in Hollywood. No longer did sustaining and sponsored programs habitually originate from the same studios in New York. Increasingly, commercial entertainment emanated from the West and prestigious programming—drama, news, classical music—from the East. And the networks, as a result, were at odds with themselves.

For a brief interval, the CBS sustaining dramatic anthology series appeared to exist within the commercial network desert as oases of higher cultural aspirations. They were apparently innocent of the competitive motives behind all other aspects of broadcasting life. Yet the prestige programs soon became exceptions proving the competitive rule, for in no time NBC began to foster its own prestigious programming, created quite obviously in the CBS image. Not only that, but NBC took to scheduling it at the same hours as its rival's cultural offerings. Very quickly the networks became as combative on the prestige front as on the commercial, although their motives for engaging in such a struggle were not as clear-cut. This new, murkier form of competition had as its point of origin a fit of pique in the NBC executive suite, specifically that of John F. Royal, the network's cagey vice-president for programming.

Appropriately, Royal came from a background in vaudeville theater management with the Keith-Albee chain. He drifted into radio, and when the Red network acquired the station employing him, he entered the network hierarchy, where he was conditioned to perceive the networks in terms of two competing vaudeville chains rather than becoming attuned to the nuances of network broadcasting. In short, he was a student of the big draw, the star system aimed at packing an invisible house. Furthermore, Royal had an invaluable asset, ready access to David Sarnoff, who proved quite willing to act on his schemes.

By the summer of 1937, when "The Columbia Workshop" had become a recognized success and source of CBS pride, its godfather, William Lewis, decided to follow up with a warm-weather dramatic series consisting of more popular fare. In June, the network announced a summer Shakespeare series scheduled for Monday evenings from 9 to 10. The cost for the series would be a modest $60,000. As series director, Lewis engaged Brewster Morgan, who, as a Rhodes scholar, had made a name for himself as the first American to direct Shakespeare at the Oxford University Theatre. Unknowingly, Lewis had just fired the first shot in what became known as the Shakespeare War.

For several weeks, no more news from CBS about the series was forthcoming. Nonetheless, the network had wounded NBC's pride once too often, and the great Red and Blue beast was stirred to action. Suddenly, at the end of June, NBC announced with great fanfare that it would present its own summer Shakespeare series, which it called "Streamlined Shakespeare," giving the impression that the plays would be cool as a summer breeze, and fast. Furthermore, and this was the doing of Royal, the series would have a glamorous star, John Barrymore, the brilliant but unstable brother of Lionel and Ethel Barrymore. Barrymore's six-play "Streamlined Shakespeare" would be carried over the less commercial Blue network. The unkindest cut concerned the time at which the series had been scheduled, Monday evenings from 9:30 to 10:15, or almost head-to-head with CBS's Shakespeare. Giving the sword a last twist, NBC planned to begin the series almost immediately, on June 21, weeks ahead of the competition. CBS had been outmaneuvered.

NBC had not tried to steal CBS's thunder for reasons of financial gain; both series were sustaining. In all likelihood it was not out of respect for the Immortal Bard of Avon, either. Said Royal, "We didn't put it on because we were great enthusiasts for Shakespeare. To be strictly honest, we put it on for Exhibit A, to show educators, etc., that we were adding something to culture. It didn't add anything to our rating."

Royal's troubles with the crash series began in earnest when an aide, dispatched to track down Barrymore in California, found him "drunk in the gutter."

"Drunk in the gutter he is a better Shakespearean actor than some of these people we have on Broadway," Royal insisted, referring to the likes of John Gielgud.

"He can't stand," replied the aide.

"Go in the gutter and tell him," Royal ordered, "tell him to direct it, produce it, cast it, do everything."

Barrymore responded favorably to the proposition of appearing on radio. "Nothing like it to carry those flowery vowels," he remarked. On June 21 he presented his streamlined version of *Hamlet*, and, according to Royal, "the war was over in two minutes." When the CBS series finally got under way with its *Hamlet*, it would merely appear to be imitating NBC, even though CBS had first proposed the idea.

To recapture the initiative, Paley retaliated with a publicity barrage. CBS announced an impressive array of motion picture stars to appear in its series: Burgess Meredith as Hamlet, Edward G. Robinson as Petruchio in *Much Ado about Nothing*, Walter Huston as Henry IV, Tallulah Bankhead as Viola and Orson Welles as the Duke in *Twelfth Night*. CBS even tried to hire Barrymore away from NBC. Earning $1,500 per Shakespeare play at NBC, he refused to be tempted by a higher offer. Since it started several weeks later than the short NBC series, CBS's "Summer Shakespeare" hoped to gain a larger audience when its rival left the air, but Royal continued to harass the series. He scheduled a four-play Eugene O'Neill series in the same time slot as its "Streamlined Shakespeare" to vex CBS throughout the summer. As a result, series designed explicitly as noncommercial offerings fell victim to the same competitive mania afflicting sponsored programming. Certainly the public was not well served when its Shakespeare series were broadcast simultaneously.

Royal extended NBC's battle for pre-eminence in prestige programming to several fronts. In the field of drama, where CBS had its Corwin, Royal cultivated Arch Oboler, whose thrillers, tinged with an element of the fantastic, relied on virtuoso production techniques rather than language for their full effect. Another NBC answer to Corwin came in the person of Alfred Kreymbourg, who went so far as to write "Fables in Verse." The inspiration for such efforts was clear; NBC was paying its rival the ultimate compliment even while trying to overwhelm it.

Royal's most intricate maneuvering in the name of prestige took place in the classical music field. Since 1930 CBS had pointed with pride to its broadcasts of Sunday afternoon concerts by the New York Philharmonic. The series cost CBS a mere $40,000 a year, and the network even had offers for sponsorship. Nonetheless, they were not to be taken up, because it was more important to keep the series a prestigious CBS effort—Exhibit A, to borrow Royal's terminology. In 1937, Royal encouraged Sarnoff to go CBS one better with an NBC Symphony Orchestra. As a lover of classical music, Sarnoff reacted with enthusiasm. The time seemed ripe because the year before, the Philharmonic's conductor, Arturo Toscanini, had left the United States in the midst of a heated controversy. Furious at the treatment the New York Philharmonic accorded him, he vowed never to return. If NBC could lure the ex-CBS star to its orchestra, the move would legitimize the entire project, declare its high musical purpose, and, hopefully, siphon away the radio audience Toscanini had cultivated during his seasons on CBS.

However, bringing Toscanini back to the United States promised to be a formidable task. In 1931, when the conductor had refused to conduct a fascist anthem, Mussolini had had him beaten by thugs. The dictator would not gladly permit this conductor to travel abroad and spread the cause of freedom. Sarnoff decided to engage the New York *Post* music critic, Samuel Chotzinoff, to undertake a bit of informal diplomacy. Dispatched to Italy, Chotzinoff caught up with Toscanini in seclusion at his villa. There the two began gingerly to discuss the terms for the conductor's proposed tenure with the NBC Symphony Orchestra. Toscanini finally agreed to accept the post in return for an unusually high fee, equivalent to $40,000 after taxes, for conducting ten concerts. All would be well, if Toscanini could find a way to leave the country.

The effort to liberate Toscanini from his homeland involved the intercession of diplomats from several nations. At one point, the conductor planned to flee by seaplane. In the end, negotiations were successful, and Il Duce was persuaded to let Toscanini go. He took up his post with the NBC Orchestra the day after he arrived in New York aboard the *Normandie*, and on December 25, 1937, conducted his first concert with the orchestra. Sarnoff succeeded in scoring just the impressive coup he had wanted. Toscanini received an ecstatic welcome and continued to conduct the NBC Symphony Orchestra until his retirement in 1954. He even had an opportunity to gain a musical revenge on Mussolini. In 1943, while leading the orchestra through a performance of Verdi's *Hymn of the Nations*, the Maestro took care to change the words of Boito's text from *Italia, mia patria* (Italy, my fatherland) to *Italia tradita* (Italy betrayed).

That Sarnoff was able to leapfrog ahead of CBS in the field of serious music testified to his passion for opera and orchestral music, rather than his sensitivity to the full spectrum of network programming. Both networks could, in the uncertain year of 1937, afford to indulge in this battle since both were in strong financial positions. NBC's two networks showed gross time sales of $38,000,000: $27,000,000 for the Red, and $11,000,000 for the Blue. NBC further enhanced its position by owning or operating 15 radio stations, in addition to its 135 affiliates. Though smaller, CBS was in even rosier financial health. Owning nine stations claiming 106 affiliates, the network tallied nearly $37,000,000 in sales. Together, CBS and NBC accounted for over half the time sales in all domestic broadcasting.

Though both networks were able to afford prestige or public service programming, CBS manifested the stronger social commitment. Soon that social commitment became obsessed by one central issue, the inevitability of war. The dramatists—Corwin, MacLeish, and others—were the first to sense it, and their concern spread to the news division. In fact, both the news division and "The Columbia Workshop" had much in common. They were both sustaining, and they were both in New York. It was inevitable that their concerns would overlap. Out of this supercharged milieu emerged one of the very few heroes in the history of the networks, a commentator with an imagination so poetic and a personality so forceful that he left his mark on CBS long after he had departed—Edward R. Murrow.

On the strength of Murrow's new kind of broadcast journalism and the organization he built to maintain it, CBS won an unassailable lead in news coverage, a lead the network managed to keep throughout the late nineteen thirties, the Second World War, and the McCarthy era. By the mid-nineteen fifties Murrow was revered as a patron saint of broadcast journalism. Yet by that time, he had outlived his usefulness to the network. When he resigned from CBS in 1961, he was inflamed by what he perceived as the networks' betrayal of their mission, their public trust. By then, sustaining programming was all but extinct, but

Murrow persisted in his belief in the service ideal and lived long enough to lay the groundwork for a new network, the Public Broadcasting System. Had he lived beyond 1965, the year he died of lung cancer, he would have been the logical choice to become the first head of PBS when Congress legislated it into existence in 1967. The rise and fall of Murrow at CBS, then, is more than a biography of a single reporter, but the embattled history of a special philosophy of broadcasting.

This urbane, well-tailored world traveler was born in 1908 in a North Carolina hamlet called Pole Cat Creek. Upon graduation from Washington State College in 1930, he became head of the National Student Federation. With a tiny office in New York and a salary of twenty-five dollars a week, he spent much of his time organizing debates on foreign affairs. Soon he moved on to the Institute for International Education, under whose auspices he traveled in Europe. As yet, there was little journalism in Murrow's experience, but a great deal of concern with foreign affairs, as well as a taste for travel.

Network journalism, as it stood at the time, hardly seemed appropriate for the ambitious young man. In fact, it suffered from a positively scandalous reputation. In 1935, both press and radio disgraced themselves with imflammatory coverage of the Lindbergh kidnapping trial in Flemington, New Jersey. In the wake of the carnival atmosphere the news media created at the trial, the American Bar Association decided to banish the microphone and camera from the courtroom. This ban still stands today in most states.

Yet the record was not entirely bleak. In 1930, CBS stumbled across the inherent immediacy of broadcast journalism during a riot and conflagration at the Ohio State Penitentiary. From within, a prisoner called the Deacon described the ghastly events taking place around him for a remote hookup to the network. CBS had scored a shocking journalistic coup.

Sensing the possibilities of full-scale network journalism, Paley, assisted by former New York *Times* editor Klauber, encouraged the development of an independent-minded news operation. During the nineteen thirties, the CBS news department, through its various formulations, developed a split personality. On the domestic front there was the hard-nosed *Front Page*-style journalism of former United Press editor Paul White, a Klauber recruit. Foreign news, especially the European beat, was another matter, however. The type of story and personality covered seemed to lend themselves to a different breed of correspondent, one who was more self-reliant and editorially inclined. Foreign news quite naturally invited comment and interpretation, placing a new and complex responsibility on the news-

gatherers. For the moment, there were precious few. One was a former reporter for the New York *Post*, César Searchinger, who, as CBS's
director of talks, tirelessly tracked down Pope Pius XI, Trotsky,
Gandhi, and George Bernard Shaw, persuading all to speak to
America via the conduit of CBS. Shaw, incidentally, took the opportunity to address his American cousins as "dear old boobs" for condemn-
ing the Russian experiment with socialism. In presenting controversial points of view, CBS adopted an educational approach,
allowing the influential or powerful to present their views, even if re-
pugnant, as a means of informing the American public.

Domestic news, hard news, however, faced serious problems, thanks
to the presence of an established rival, the newspapers. To the publishers' way of thinking, it was bad enough that the networks were luring their advertisers away; worse was the thought of being scooped by
a new and relatively untried form of journalism. Under Paul White,
CBS did not hesitate to develop its own news service, and even managed to enlist the support of a sponsor. In 1933, General Mills proposed to the network to split the cost of a news service, provided that
its share did not exceed $3,000 per week. In short order, the Columbia
News Service went on the air, supported by bureaus in New York,
Washington, and Los Angeles; stringers, or part-time correspondents,
in smaller cities; and news agency reports from abroad. This far-flung
operation contributed just two five-minute broadcasts each day and a
fifteen-minute wrap-up at 11 P.M. Commentary at this stage occupied
but a tiny niche, with former WEAF commentator H. V. Kaltenborn
delivering a news analysis once a week.

In setting up an expanded news department, Paul White oversaw
the development of a more listenable style of news writing featuring
shorter, easier-to-pronounce sentences, and accounts that relied less on
a recitation of facts than on conclusions. Of this era, White records
that "our biggest triumph, which caused us to go around back-slap-
ping for days," was an interview with Doris Duke, then regarded as
the wealthiest woman in the world.

As both networks realized, however, any expansion of news coverage would inevitably be interpreted by the press as a direct provoca-
tion. In retaliation, newspapers began to eliminate from their listings
the formal, sponsor-given names of programs in favor of short, rather
unappetizing descriptions. Listeners would have to know that what
the network called the "Linit Bath Club Review," and what the newspapers listed simply as "comedy," was actually Fred Allen. Similarly,
"The Chase and Sanborn Hour," also listed as "comedy," featured
Eddie Cantor. Then there was the suspicion that newspapers limited

their coverage of companies that sponsored radio shows. Under the weight of these pressures, both CBS and NBC were ready to deal.

In December 1933, NBC vice-president Frank Mason set up meetings at the Biltmore Hotel that included the networks, the wire services, and the American Newspaper Publishers Association. "You could tell from the start that these were peace conferences because of the warlike attitude of all the participants," Paul White wrote. Out of these meetings came a series of compromises. CBS would give up its fledgling news service. Together, the networks would finance a Press-Radio Bureau, which would get its news, in bulletins of thirty words or less, from the wire services. The networks, then, would not be gathering news in their own right, but would become adjuncts of the wire services. Furthermore, their broadcasts would have to be unsponsored, which of course guaranteed that news broadcasts would receive a low priority. This unwieldy arrangement went into effect in March 1934, only to die a short time later. When Esso proposed a series of sponsored news broadcasts the wire services quickly broke rank and began selling their bulletins. But in the meantime, the networks' ability to relay fast-breaking news, which the press viewed as the greatest threat, had been seriously hobbled.

Commentary, on the other hand, began to flourish. Less controversial, at least as far as the newspapers were concerned, it was an area in which Paley sensed CBS could make an original contribution. After Searchinger's departure in 1935, the network began looking for a new director of talks. The individual who held this job would have to be practiced in public speaking, knowledgeable in world affairs, and well connected. Searchinger initially offered it to the respected commentator Raymond Swing, who declined. He preferred to remain in front of the microphone, not behind it, lining up interviews. As a result, the young man from the Institute for International Education, Edward R. Murrow, got the job. He probably added a few years to his age to seem more qualified, but he did bring the necessary expertise.

Lacking a background in broadcasting, Murrow very quickly learned the tricks of the broadcaster's trade from announcer Robert Trout, the man considered the voice of CBS News. Trout encouraged Murrow to treat the intimidating microphone not as an inanimate audience, but simply as a means of communication, a telephone which happened to be hooked up to millions of listeners. After a Christmas Eve party, Murrow, who had himself imbibed heavily, persuaded Trout to let him deliver the evening news. Trout waited for mike fright to seize the cocky youngster, but, according to Murrow biographer Alexander Kendrick, "he marched through the news clearly and precisely, as if it had been made for him and he for it."

Not so coincidentally, a rivalry quickly sprang up between the suave, young director of talks and Paul White, master of backroom bravado. White counted on becoming a network vice-president, an ambition he did not want any rival to thwart, even unintentionally. And Murrow's eventual supplanting of White would indeed be unintentional since his primary interest lay in the field of news commentary, not administration.

Quincy Howe, himself a commentator, described this new breed as "the journalist who had learned to talk, the lecturer who had learned to write, the broadcaster who had learned to read—something more, that is, than the script before him." H. V. Kaltenborn, a founding father of broadcast commentary and among the most important of Murrow's precursors, could be classed as the journalist who had learned to talk and talk and talk.

Hans von Kaltenborn was born in the United States of German parents. After being graduated from Harvard and touring the world as tutor to the young Vincent Astor, he embarked on a twenty-year career as a widely respected journalist for the late Brooklyn *Eagle*. In the mid-nineteen twenties, Kaltenborn became a commentator for AT&T's WEAF, where he assumed he would enjoy the same freedom of expression he had at the newspaper. Unfortunately this was not to be. When he undertook to criticize a judge before whom the phone company had a case, he discovered, in his words, that the "Vice-President-in-Charge-of-Litigation suggested to the Vice-President-in-Charge-of-Radiobroadcasting that it was suicidal for the telephone company to lend its facilities to a radio commentator to criticize an important judge whose ill will might prove very expensive to the company." Kaltenborn was admonished to toe the company line, but when he repeatedly refused to do so, AT&T dropped him.

He promptly resurfaced as the CBS news analyst. Where Murrow would later hammer away at two or three related themes in the course of a broadcast, Kaltenborn ranged freely over the full spectrum of world events, a professor at large in a global classroom. Endowed with great mental stamina and never at a loss for words (though nowhere near as incisive as Murrow), Kaltenborn could extemporize with ease. He continued to be quite strict and stubborn about sponsor noninterference with news, as might be expected after his WEAF experience. When Eddie Cantor invited the commentator to appear on his popular show on the Red network, Kaltenborn refused to participate in a skit that led into a commercial.

At CBS, Kaltenborn's outspokenness created so much turmoil that Paley delegated Klauber to keep the man in line. In 1937, Paley appeared to state a company policy when he said, "We must never have

an editorial page. We must never try to further either side of any debatable question." The idea was to keep from scaring off sponsors who
would not wish to be associated with a controversial commentator,
program, or network. CBS devised a euphemism for the term commentator, the analyst. An analyst discussed issues but did not persuade audiences. While CBS policy uttered one position, its sustaining
program took quite another. "The Columbia Workshop" productions—
and later Murrow's reports from London—were animated by a strong
political point of view. The sustaining and sponsored sides of CBS's
personality existed in a state of delicate balance. Kesten worked his
beat, polishing the CBS image for advertisers; Klauber, White, and
Searchinger (and later Murrow) worked theirs, and William Lewis
his, "The Columbia Workshop." Somehow Paley managed to embrace
all these blossoming divisions and philosophies. His network could be
rich *and* cultivated *and* well informed.

But Kaltenborn continually threatened to disrupt this balance. To
CBS's relief, NBC hired him away in 1940, and there he ran into similar problems, which hounded him until his retirement in 1953 at the
age of seventy-five. The former WEAF commentator, incidentally, remained on the air long enough to declare Dewey the victor over
Truman on election night in 1952, and for a triumphant Truman to
mock his high-pitched voice before the newsreel cameras.

In 1937, CBS, wishing to solidify its pre-eminence in the field of foreign affairs, began looking for a new European director. By this time,
Murrow had become acquainted with the staff of "The Columbia
Workshop," particularly William Lewis, its director. Lewis, recognizing talent when he saw it, now proposed Murrow for the job. The
recommendation was accepted, and Murrow, not yet thirty, found
himself in a position which, with the coming of the war, would be crucial. Where Kaltenborn, Howe, Elmer Davis, and Swing advanced the
art of commentary, Murrow would remake it in the light of the momentous story now developing in London.

Murrow was no doubt relieved to leave the hothouse atmosphere of
the New York office behind him. But upon his arrival in London, he
was hardly plunged into a maelstrom. Still under the influence of
CBS's slightly musty "educational" approach to public-service programming, he passed the time arranging hookups for concerts. He did
devote attention to building his staff, which would form the nucleus of
the CBS News division in the postwar era. Under Murrow's influence,
the CBS news-gathering operation evolved during the course of the
war from a simple headline service to a worldwide ring of sophisticated, often headstrong correspondents. For Murrow had chosen reporters in his own image, sartorially impeccable, literate, often liberal,

and prima donnas all. These were not self-effacing company men but journalists with an independent turn of mind. By the war's end, the CBS cadre of foreign correspondents included William L. Shirer, Eric Sevareid, Charles Collingwood, Howard K. Smith, Richard C. Hottelet, Winston Burdett, and Larry LeSueur. In 1950, Murrow succeeded in hiring a young former UPI correspondent named Walter Cronkite to cover the Korean situation.

At first, the shop, as New York headquarters was known, was taken aback by the profusion of new untutored voices, no matter how informed or expert their reports might be. Murrow was told his staff sounded "terrible" on the air; he retorted, "I'm hiring reporters, not announcers." Shirer was a particular case in point. His thin, reedy voice contrasted sharply with the golden-throated announcers in New York, especially Robert Trout.

In March 1938, Hitler marched on Vienna, and the newly assembled correspondents were put to their first major test. Prompted by a desire to demonstrate the accomplishments of their correspondents and the swift reactions of the network's news department, Paley and Klauber decided to present an unprecedented news roundup, a series of brief, live reports by correspondents positioned around the Continent. The moment came with Murrow in Warsaw, arranging one of the concert hookups. There he was contacted by Shirer, his man in Vienna, who told him, "The opposing team has just crossed the goal line." Shirer departed for London as Murrow contrived to reach a city on the verge of occupation. In the heat of the moment, he chartered a Lufthansa aircraft for $1,000 to take him to Vienna, where he arrived ahead of Hitler. Immediately he sensed the chilling air of expectation in the city. The scene eerily recalled MacLeish's *The Fall of the City*. The first roundup took place on March 13 when, at 8 P.M. Robert Trout in New York introduced Shirer in London. His analysis was followed by those of correspondents in Berlin and Paris, and Murrow's from Vienna.

The Murrow-Shirer broadcasts continued as Hitler prepared to move against Czechoslovakia. During the eighteen days of that crisis, which finally took place in September 1939, Kaltenborn, still with CBS at that time, undertook the superhuman task of rendering the complex, swiftly moving events intelligible for American listeners. The network had prepared for the challenge. "The mechanical setup to tie and untie the entire network in a matter of seconds or to bring together New York and five European capitals for a round-robin discussion involved the most ingenious devices, some of them developed on the spot by inventive radio engineers," Kaltenborn recalled. Mussolini, Hitler, Chamberlain—they were all heard over CBS. By his own reckoning, Kaltenborn delivered 102 spontaneous connecting discussions. Here were events that did not lend themselves to condensation into a simple headline or bulletin. "News bulletins were handed to me as I talked," Kaltenborn wrote. "Speeches of foreign leaders had to be analyzed and sometimes translated while they were being delivered." Kaltenborn, furthermore, had to make substantial allowances for the exigencies of scheduling. "I had to keep a constant eye on the control room for signs telling me when I was on or off the air. Sometimes when I had just launched into an analysis of some foreign leader's speech I was given a signal to wind up my talk in exactly one minute." The entire operation was a triumph. Kaltenborn even acquired a sponsor, but for White these broadcasts were also something of a last hurrah, as he soon found himself overshadowed by his young rival, now stationed in the eye of the storm known as the Battle of Britain.

"This is London at three-thirty in the morning." Thus began Murrow's broadcast of September 13, 1940. He usually climbed to the roof of the British Broadcasting Corporation or another large, solid building at such an ungodly hour so that his reports, crackling with the immediacy of live testimony, would reach American shores at a more reasonable hour. "This has been what might be called a 'routine night,'" Murrow continued: "air raid alarm about nine o'clock and intermittent bombing ever since. I had the impression that more high explosives and fewer incendiaries have been used tonight. Only two small fires can be seen on the horizon. . . ." Apparently spontaneous, Murrow's on-the-spot reporting of the Blitz was in fact carefully rehearsed improvisation. In preparation for broadcasts Murrow practiced ad-libbing. He rehearsed details. And he excelled at the task of rendering an abstract menace as a palpable and frightening presence. "One becomes accustomed to rattling windows and the distant sound of bombs, and then comes a silence that can be felt. You know the sound will return. You wait, and then it starts again. That waiting is bad. It gives you a chance to imagine things. I have been walking tonight—there is a full moon, and the dirty-gray buildings appear somehow ill timed and out of place."

His resonant, insistent voice communicated the high tension of the hour, the sense of impending disaster. The CBS London bureau, where he was based, was bombed out several times, finally relocating to 49 Halloran Street, near Murrow's flat at number 89. Though never wounded, he was sorely taxed. During one particularly harrowing broadcast, his voice broke into sobs of tension-induced despair. "The British aren't all heroes," he told Americans, "they know the feeling of fear; I've shared it with them. . . . They will cheer Winston Churchill when he walks through block after block of smashed houses and offices as though he'd brought them a great victory. During a blinding raid when the streets are full of smoke and the sound of the roaring guns, they'll say to you 'Do you think we're really brave, or just lacking in imagination?'

"Well, they've come through the winter; they've been warned that the testing days are ahead. Of the past months, they may well say, 'We've lived a life, not an apology,' and of the future, I think most of them would say, 'We shall live hard, but we shall live.' "

By containing and mastering the panic and danger he sensed, Murrow communicated it all the more effectively to American radio audiences. He was not a reporter in the sense of being a fact-gatherer, but rather a mind at large, a commentator, a voice of conscience. He did not report news so much as interpret it, and his conclusions were so clear-cut that they did not need to be stated. He had the knack of combining simplicity of expression with subtlety of nuance. Of his formula for reporting, Murrow said, "You are supposed to describe things in terms that make sense to the truck driver without insulting the intelligence of the professor." Even in print, without the benefit of his manly, tormented voice, Murrow's accounts painted a picture of London during the Blitz with many telling details.*

But Murrow had more on his mind than transmitting a sense of grotesque local color. Through his broadcasts he subtly but forcefully advocated an American commitment to the British fight for freedom, a commitment he perceived as inevitable. "If the people who rule Britain are made of the stuff of which the people who work with their hands are made, and if they trust them, then the defense of Britain will be something of which men will speak with awe and admiration so long as the English language survives," he commented on August 18, 1940. The following March he proclaimed the same theme with even greater urgency:

> The course of Anglo-American relations will be smooth on the surface, but many people over here express regret because they believe America is making the same mistakes that Britain made. For you must understand that the idea of America being of more help as a non-belligerent than as a fighting ally has been discarded, even by those who advanced it originally.

As the war took place before his eyes and ears, Murrow put it into instantly identifiable terms for Americans. The fate of Britain not only could but will be yours, he was telling them, and what will you do

* The now defunct New York paper *PM* printed transcriptions of his broadcasts as news dispatches.

about it? How you feel about their fate, ran the subtext, reflects how
you feel about your own. His reports took on the character of a bibli-
cal lamentation, a jeremiad aimed at a complacent people. In this role,
Murrow functioned as the eyes and ears of a nation. He could see further than most of the nation, and could instantly transmit his findings.

Though filled with bits of intimate, even novelistic detail, Murrow's
broadcasts from London eventually reached such a pitch that they
could not be construed as anything but a call to arms:

> The number of planes engaged tonight seems to be about the same as
> last night. Searchlight activity has been constant, but there has been
> little gunfire at the center of London. The bombs have been coming
> down at about the same rate as last night. It is impossible to get any es-
> timate of the damage. Darkness prevents observation of details. The
> streets have been deserted, save for a few clanging fire engines, during
> the last four or five hours. The planes have been high again tonight, so
> high that the search-lights can't reach them. The bombing sounds as
> though it was separated pretty evenly over the metropolitan district. In
> certain areas there are no electric lights.
>
> Once I saw *The Damnation of Faust* presented in the open at Salz-
> burg. London reminds me of that tonight, only the stage is so much
> larger. Once tonight an antiaircraft battery opened fire just as I drove
> past. It lifted me from the seat and a hot wind swept over the car. It
> was impossible to see. When I drove on, the streets of London re-
> minded me of a ghost town in Nevada—not a soul to be seen. . . .
>
> And so London is waiting for dawn. We ought to get the all clear in
> about another two hours. Then those big German bombers that have
> been lumbering and mumbling overhead all night will have to go
> home.

A man can stand only so much. After three years of broadcasting
from London and other European hot spots, Murrow returned to the
United States for a visit in November 1941. On his arrival, Paley arranged an extraordinarily elaborate reception for the young CBS correspondent at the Waldorf-Astoria. The remarks were recorded,
menus became souvenir items, as did table seating charts. During the
three years of his broadcasts, Murrow had acquired the status of a
prophet with honor in his own land, a status Paley now encouraged,
as it shed glory on the network. Through its newly established news
division, CBS had found a unique, sophisticated, and responsible identity that greatly appealed to Paley. At the banquet a thousand guests
heard Murrow declare what he had implied in his transatlantic broadcasts from the rooftops of London in the wee hours. "Unless the
United States enters this war," he said, "Britain may perish or at best

secure a stalemate peace—a delayed-action defeat." MacLeish, the poet who had imagined the events Murrow reported, spoke for those in attendance: "Over the period of your months in London you destroyed in the minds of men and women in this country the superstition that what is done beyond three thousand miles of water is not really done at all."

Paley had skillfully seized upon the occasion not only to honor the outstanding CBS correspondent but to call attention to the network's attitude toward the war. Suddenly the network was transformed into more than a facility for hire, more than a dramatic workshop. It was at last in the news business in its own right, not cribbing stories from the wire services or newspapers. It was from this activity that the network as a whole took its identity, more so even than from its successful (and sponsored) entertainment programming. This was not to say that news would receive more attention or greater budgets than sponsored programming, but it would at least stand above the fray.

Curiously, the man credited with being the patron saint of network journalism was not really a journalist in the usual sense. In a profession that considers an apprenticeship with a wire service or print journalism highly desirable, Murrow never worked for a newspaper, never rushed through his copy to meet a deadline, bridled under an editor's idiosyncrasies, or received a thorough grounding in the fundamentals of journalism. He did not come to broadcasting while trying to adapt old methods; he made up new ones as he went along. In the end, he devoted himself to the development of commentary. In this enterprise he had few predecessors and few descendants. Over the years, and especially in the postwar era, commentary became an anachronism as broadcast journalism, following a national trend toward disengagement from great public issues, relied instead on so-called objective presentation of news. As Murrow the committed journalist knew, there could be no such animal; he would have considered a pretense of objectivity in itself an admission of confusion and occasionally collusion.

As Murrow discovered, the function of the commentator proved to be a natural and effective response to the limitations of broadcast journalism. Murrow assumed the listener had read the morning newspaper. He pondered the question of what the informed listener would wish to know and tried to supply the insight and understanding. He was interested in discussing issues rather than informing. He aimed to provoke a moral commitment, an active response to issues of the day. In this role he went beyond Kaltenborn's musings. If Kaltenborn resembled a rather stuffy editorial page, Murrow was a clarion call in the night. The man did not waste words. He generated tension, concern, clarity. He dealt with essences. As a commentator he complemented rather than competed with the papers. Where they remained, as Murrow well knew, the ideal medium for the record, for all the news that was fit to print, broadcast journalism, with its short memory span, emphasis on the correspondent's voice, and inevitably, personality, found itself admirably suited to the role of commentary, the task of sharpening the listener's perceptions of events.

Through Murrow and the team he had assembled, CBS gained not only identity but authority. The prestige and credibility for which Paley had longed since the late nineteen twenties now finally clung to CBS. Yet with them came new perplexity, new contradictions, and redefinitions of the network's role, ones which the success of the network's sustaining dramatic programming had already provoked. One of Murrow's protégés, Eric Sevareid, put the approaching dilemma of the networks this way: "They thought, originally, that they were just in the advertising business and found, often to their discomfort, that they had become co-trustees of the First Amendment." Were networks or stations entitled to the extent of protection that print media enjoyed? Should the law of the land—that Congress shall make no law respecting or abridging the freedom of speech—apply to broadcasting? At the time Murrow returned to the United States, the question remained unanswered. A no-man's-land existed between the networks and the government as each tried to formulate answers to engulf the other side.

The brilliant gathering in honor of Murrow took place on a Tuesday evening. The following Sunday, December 7, the Japanese bombed Pearl Harbor and the nation went to war.

As the networks geared for the conflict, most of the commercial struggles in which they had been engaged were suspended. The questions about freedom of speech raised by CBS's adventurous sustaining program were also shelved for the duration. Murrow would have his way, at least until peacetime.

Also placed in the deepfreeze was a master plan of David Sarnoff's, one which he calculated would knock CBS and its advanced programming into a cocked hat. Overseeing the development of an RCA-designed and -manufactured television system, he envisioned a recurrence of the boom created by the introduction of radio in the nineteen twenties. Then, the field had been wide open. Inventors labored in the public eye. Now, they were largely sequestered in laboratories, especially RCA's. This time around, Sarnoff would not allow events to pass him by as they had with the radio music box. He was no longer a young executive fighting to be heard, but at the peak of the broadcasting industry, backed not only by NBC's two networks but also by

RCA's vast manufacturing capabilities. His position could be compared to that of a general who had spent years building an army for some vast campaign. Sarnoff's campaign would be to develop and introduce television to the American public.

However, Sarnoff omitted to consider several variables in this grand equation. The complexity of the technology involved, for one. A world war, for another. And, most surprising of all, the introduction of an astonishing CBS color system which threatened to render RCA television obsolete.

My Way

As EARLY AS 1923, even before radio had gained widespread acceptance, Sarnoff was advocating the commercial introduction of television. He summarized the advances of widely scattered inventors and
tried to persuade his superiors to mass-produce a relatively inexpensive version of television for home use. In this he repeated his radio
music box strategy, and he chose a propitious moment to launch his
campaign, for in 1923 RCA was just beginning to reap the rewards of
selling the radio music box Sarnoff had for so long advocated. In a
memo to the RCA directors he predicted, "I believe that television,
which is the technical name for seeing instead of hearing by radio,
will come to pass in due course. Therefore, it may be that every
broadcast receiver for home use in the future will also be equipped
with a television adjunct by which the instrument will make it possible for those at home to see as well as hear what is going on at the
broadcast station." Though Sarnoff was coming to be known as a recognized technical prophet, the question he had yet to answer was,
What kind of television? At the moment, there were two rival systems,
one electronic, still untried and primitive, the other mechanical,
simpler and close to completion.

The mechanical approach to television dominated early efforts. This
system had one foot in twentieth-century electronics and the other in
nineteenth-century scientific thought. In 1884, the German inventor

Paul Nipkow received a patent for a television system relying on a mechanical means of converting visual images into transmittable electronic impulses, then back again into a visual image. Nipkow's device contained a perforated disc that revolved thirty times a second. This was placed between the subject and a photocell that converted the dots of light seen through the disc into electronic impulses. At the receiving end, the impulses varied a light source. The viewer looked at this source through another disc spinning in exact synchronization with the first and saw a picture composed of lines of varying brightness.

It was not a particularly clear or bright image; nonetheless, the mechanical system appeared to be the coming thing. Ernst Alexanderson, the inventor of the alternator that had spurred the creation of RCA, conducted television tests in 1928 over an experimental station operated by General Electric. Similarly, RCA had its experimental television station, W2XBS, in operation using the mechanical system. In England, mechanical receivers were on sale. By this late date, when NBC was all of two years old, Sarnoff could safely predict that television would be as prevalent as radio. It was only a matter of time.

It had been seven years from the time Sarnoff wrote his radio music box memo to the commercial introduction of RCA's radio. Television, it seemed, might come to pass even more quickly, but that would be to underestimate one factor that would extend its incubation period to a full twenty years. It so happened that Sarnoff, under the influence of the great man himself, Marconi, now concluded that the mechanical system would never form the basis of the satisfactory home television receiver of the future. Already in 1928, the device, with its whirling discs, was an antique. Sarnoff determined that an all-electronic system was needed, one rooted firmly in the twentieth century and one, not so incidentally, to which RCA could own all the patents. The disc-system patents were too widely dispersed for the company ever to have the complete control it wished to have. Sarnoff required his own, in-house device, but where would he find one or the inventor willing to create under the RCA aegis?

It so happened that the man who would develop such a system for RCA was, like Sarnoff, a Russian immigrant, born in Murom, Russia just two years before Sarnoff, in 1889. After a long international odyssey, Vladimir Zworykin finally met up with Sarnoff in 1929, but only after years of tribulation, for Zworykin had been cursed with living in interesting times. Initially planning to become a physicist, Zworykin attended what was then called the St. Petersburg Institute of Technology, where he studied under the physicist Boris Rosing. Eventually Rosing hired the young student to help in his laboratory, where he was seeking new ways to extend man's sight. By 1907 Rosing had developed a television system which employed a disc at the transmitting end but relied on a blown-glass tube to re-create the image at the receiving end. To convert the electronic impulses into visual ones, Rosing employed a cathode ray tube with a fluorescent surface. The system was more electronic than mechanical, but still quite primitive. When the Revolution came, Rosing went into exile and died shortly thereafter, but his young assistant carried on.

Upon graduation, Zworykin was not sure in which direction he should turn: "I had three difficulties," he recalls. "First of all, my father wanted me to work in his business. Second, the institute wanted me to go to England. And Rosing wanted me to go to France." Following Rosing's advice, Zworykin went to France, studied under Paul Langevin, and returned to Russia to begin his career. Unfortunately, the First World War intervened and Zworykin found himself drafted into the Tsar's army. Realizing that Russia at the time was no place for an inventor concerned with the development of all-electronic television, Zworykin decided to leave the country when the Revolution broke out in earnest. It took him months to extricate himself, but eventually Zworykin wound up in the United States, a country he considered to be hospitable to an inventor. It was here that one of his idols, Edison, was flourishing. Fortunately, perhaps, for inventors such as Zworykin, Edison did not foresee a great future for the broadcasting industry. In 1922, at the beginning of the radio craze, he remarked, "It will die out in time so far as music is concerned. But it may continue for business purposes."

Zworykin's theories were, by American standards, highly speculative. His most useful skill turned out to be the ability to fashion glass tubes. On the strength of it he found a job with Westinghouse in Pittsburgh, about the time Conrad was attracting attention with his KDKA experiments. Zworykin "hated" the task of dipping vacuum tubes into chemical baths, "so I started to think about ways to avoid this manual work." He befriended a glassblower, and working overtime together they developed an automatic tube-manufacturing system. The company recognized a significant innovation and declared the laboratory a restricted area. Then Zworykin happened to come down with the flu. In his absence, an explosive gas was accidentally employed in the manufacturing process, and when Zworykin, ignorant of the substitution, returned to work, he found "everything working like a charm. Then I pulled the switch and everything blew up!" Rather than exploding Zworykin's career in the process, the incident brought the young Russian immigrant to the attention of Westinghouse officials, who, recognizing his initiative and capabilities, transferred him to

Edgar Bergen and Charlie McCarthy on "The Chase and Sanborn Hour," a Sunday evening staple throughout the late nineteen thirties. *Courtesy The Museum of Modern Art/ Film Stills Archives.*

THE HIGH PRICE OF TALENT: Jack Benny, Mary Livingston, Dennis Day, and Eddie Anderson in 1939, before being lured to CBS. *Courtesy The Museum of Modern Art/ Film Stills Archives.*

Bob Hope and Bing Crosby at the NBC microphones. *Courtesy The Museum of Modern Art/Film Stills Archives.*

Orson Welles cuts loose on "The Mercury Theatre," 1938. *Courtesy CBS*.

The Columbia Workshop's production of Archibald MacLeish's *The Fall of the City* took place in New York's Seventh Regiment Armory, 1937. *Courtesy CBS*.

A formidable array of talent gathered to perform Norman Corwin's "Bill of Rights," produced in CBS's Hollywood studios and broadcast on all networks. Left to right: (standing) Orson Welles, Rudy Vallee, Sterling Tracy, Bernard Herrman, Edward G. Robinson, Bob Burns, Jimmy Stewart, Norman Corwin, Walter Brennan, Edward Arnold; (seated) Lionel Barrymore, Marjorie Main, Walter Huston. *Courtesy The Museum of Modern Art/Film Stills Archives.*

The young Edward R. Murrow in 1939, four years after joining CBS. *Courtesy CBS.*

more advanced work. "Every time they asked me what I wanted, I said 'television,'" recalls Zworykin, but Westinghouse considered his notions commercially impractical.

On his own, then, Zworykin saw no reason why Conrad's pioneering experiments with KDKA in radio could not be extended to television. Perhaps the new motion picture industry would be responsive. Warner Brothers tried to hire Zworykin away, but the inventor ended the flirtation by deciding to remain with Westinghouse. Working nights, fashioning his own tubes, he continued to refine an all-electronic television system. By 1923, the year Sarnoff advocated television before the RCA directors, Zworykin was able to demonstrate a crude system for Westinghouse officials and applied for a patent. Though Zworykin could transmit only high-definition shapes, his system served as the basis for all television's future developments.

The problem all inventors—Zworykin was by no means alone in the field—in search of all-electronic television faced was to find a way to transmit differing levels of light, i.e., to find a visual equivalent for the radio microphone, which changed audible waves into electrical impulses. Nipkow's disc only partially solved the problem because the resultant image was quite dim. Zworykin went to work developing a more light-sensitive camera, one that broke the image down into electronic points which could be stored and amplified. In the Zworykin system a camera lens focused the visual image onto a flat surface, called a mosaic, because it was covered with thousands of dots of light-sensitive metal. When the light struck a dot, it gave off electrons, the amount varying with the light's intensity. (This phenomenon, known as the photoelectric effect, had first been noticed by Albert Einstein in 1905.) Next, those renegade electrons gathered onto a metal plate located behind the mosaic. At the same time an electron gun shot a rapidly moving beam of electrons at the mosaic. Hitting each light-sensitive dot thirty times a second, the scanning beam replaced the lost electrons the dots had shed when exposed to light. This in turn caused the renegade electrons on the plate to flow out of the tube and into a wire for transmission. Zworykin called his camera an iconoscope. For the receiver he initially relied on a cathode tube based on Rosing's model, and he employed De Forest's audion to amplify the signal as required.

The 1923 demonstration, which Zworykin has described as "scarcely impressive," used this technology to transmit a cross "with low contrast and rather poor definition." But it was all electronic, if nothing else. Still, Westinghouse officials were not about to undertake television broadcasting on such a flimsy basis. They suggested that the inveterate tinkerer devote his time to more practical endeavors.

Undeterred, Zworykin continued to labor after hours. The laboratory guard was instructed to send the inventor home by 2 A.M. if he found the lights on in the laboratory. "Zworykin rhymes with workin'," the inventor today insists in his Russian-accented English. Under these conditions he developed a more sophisticated receiver to take the place of the cathode tube. The kinescope, as he called it, again used an electron gun working in synchronization with the gun in the iconoscope or camera. The kinescope's gun swept the television screen, which had been coated with a chemical that would glow when bombarded by electrons. Both guns operated in synchrony, hitting the dots, line by line, thirty times a second. The kinescope in essence reversed the process taking place in the iconoscope, converting electronic impulses into light. As with the disc, the system relied on the "persistence of vision" phenomenon to blur the scanning gun's rapid pulses of light into a moving picture. Zworykin's kinescope serves as the basis for television picture tubes in use today.

In November 1929, Zworykin was at last able to demonstrate both iconoscope and kinescope before an appreciative audience, the Institute of Radio Engineers. Here was just the all-electronic device Sarnoff was looking for. Even better, it was developed at Westinghouse, which had a cross-licensing agreement with RCA covering patents. Sarnoff immediately summoned the inventor. Technology would, at last, meet with commercial enterprise, and another broadcasting revolution was in the making. "I went to see Sarnoff," Zworykin recalls, "told him the story, and he was very interested. 'Well,' he asked, 'how much do you think it will cost you to take it into production?'

"Oh, about two hundred thousand a year," Zworykin replied, naming a figure off the top of his head.

"'Is that so?'" Zworykin recalls Sarnoff saying. "'I'll think it over.'" Soon thereafter, the inventor was transferred to the RCA laboratories, where he has spent the remainder of his professional life, eventually becoming director of the Electronic Research Laboratory in Camden, New Jersey. In later years, Sarnoff was fond of calling Zworykin the best salesman he had ever met, for the total RCA investment in television reached $50,000,000 before earning some financial return for the company. The speed with which Sarnoff took up Zworykin's invention did not attest to the inventor's powers of persuasion so much as to Sarnoff's desperate need to find an all-electronic television that RCA could call its very own. Zworykin came along at precisely the right time. Had he not, it is quite possible that RCA would have continued to develop and introduce the mechanical system, whirling discs and all. Finally, Sarnoff was shrewd enough to realize that with his invention Zworykin was too important a man to fall into the hands of an RCA rival. RCA considered itself in the business of owning patents and licensing others to manufacture equipment using them, if it wished. Sarnoff was counting on Zworykin to deliver the patents that would give the company an unassailable commercial advantage.

Under Sarnoff's watchful eye, Zworykin pressed on. In 1930 NBC commenced experimental television broadcasts from a transmitter atop the Empire State Building. This system employed Zworykin's kinescope, but relied on a mechanical camera. By 1933, however, all vestiges of the mechanical system were supplanted by Zworykin's electronics. Along with a team of RCA engineers, he turned his attention to improving picture resolution. The challenge here was to make the electron gun slice the image into as many lines as possible; the more lines, the greater the detail. When Zworykin first met Sarnoff, the system yielded just fifty lines. Throughout the nineteen thirties RCA steadily refined the system, increasing the number of lines and consequently the resolution. Experimental systems boasted 120 lines by 1931, 240 lines by 1933. In 1935 Sarnoff made RCA's commitment to television public, announcing what was considered to be a lavish million-dollar development plan. Despite all the signs of progress, television went into limbo.

Factors both within and outside Sarnoff's control converged to slow its commercial introduction. First, there was the inescapable fact of the Depression. The nineteen thirties were hardly the time to introduce a costly television receiver onto the market. Ten years before, perhaps, an indulgent society would have accepted the novelty, but not now. Second, the success of radio lessened the need for such a system. Both NBC and CBS were getting rich from their broadcasting endeavors, not from the sale of hardware. Switching to a new medium appeared to be a wasteful extravagance. Besides, the stars who had labored to make radio a success were hardly inclined to try their luck in an even more demanding medium. Radio was just too new and too successful to be supplanted.

Then there were factors operating within RCA, primarily its monopolistic tendencies, which were attracting increasing government attention. Rescuing RCA from the government maw and restructuring it to better suit his own ends siphoned off the greater part of Sarnoff's energies for several years.

On the night of May 30, 1930, David Sarnoff, the new president of RCA, attended a lavish dinner party in his honor. He had spent the last three years climbing to the uppermost rungs of the RCA corporate ladder, outmaneuvering and outlasting those who had stood in his way. After the triumphs of cajoling RCA into manufacturing highly profitable radios and inaugurating two broadcasting networks, now also moving into profitability, Sarnoff went even further out on a limb by announcing the purchase of the Victor Talking Machine Company for the sum of $154,000,000. Sarnoff wanted the company badly, both to keep it out of CBS's hands and to increase RCA's manufacturing capability. He threatened to resign if the deal did not go through, but by now David Sarnoff was the indispensable man around RCA, and he got his way.

Luckily for Sarnoff, he eased into the power position just in time, for months later RCA began to reel under the first blows of the Depression. Profits from the manufacture and sale of radio equipment dropped precipitously, reaching deficit levels in 1932. In the simplest terms, people could no longer afford to purchase the radio sets RCA sold or licensed others to manufacture and sell. RCA employees took salary cuts. The industry was in a state of siege.

Then came news that rocked the already weakened industry. On the way to the dinner party, Sarnoff, anticipating an evening of genial toasts and praise, was met by a federal marshal who served him with a copy of a major suit the Justice Department intended to bring the following day: *The United States* v. *RCA et al.* Beneath that jovial evening, then, lurked a profound anxiety. The government was planning to drain the patent pool in which RCA, GE, Westinghouse, and AT&T had been swimming. Since its inception in 1919 to permit the manufacture of radios, the pool had swollen until it numbered about four thousand inventions. Now the companies would be left high and dry. The patents had served as the bedrock of RCA's existence. Without them, it was no more than, well, CBS.

At first glance, the Justice Department action appeared to be highly inconsistent with the government attitude toward RCA. Had not the Navy helped to create RCA? Had not the government permitted the patent pool to exist over the last eleven years? However, the RCA the government had midwifed and the RCA of 1930—in other words, Young's RCA and Sarnoff's RCA—were vastly different enterprises. The earlier version, Young's, had served as a selling agent for the products of other manufacturers. The latter, under Sarnoff's direction, not only became a manufacturer in its own right but also the owner of two highly profitable broadcasting networks.

In the end, however, the adversity would be sweet for David Sarnoff. He transformed the government's intention to dismantle RCA into an opportunity to extend his power within the company until, by the time the suit was withdrawn, he was able to run it virtually as his own fiefdom. "The Department of Justice handed me a lemon and I made lemonade out of it," Sarnoff boasted. The government set a trial deadline for November 1932. AT&T quickly made a separate peace with the Justice Department. The other parties negotiated for two harrowing years. During this time, Sarnoff served as the company's liaison, apparently fighting for its best interests. RCA argued that it was not, in fact, a monopoly, merely a government-sanctioned patent pool which licensed hundreds of competing manufacturers. However, RCA had no hope of winning with this argument. Times and administrations had changed vastly since the post-World War I era when the patent pool had come into existence. Rather than struggling to save the status quo, Sarnoff in fact participated in a complex maneuver to cut RCA, his RCA, loose from the alliance with the other electronics giants. The fruits of his labors were contained in a consent decree of November 22, 1932, announced just before the trial deadline.

All the chips fell Sarnoff's way. Under the terms of the agreement, RCA retained the right to manufacture equipment. So did GE and Westinghouse, but at a great disadvantage. They had to wait a full two and a half years before competing directly with RCA, and when they did begin manufacturing equipment, they would have to pay RCA royalties on its patents. In return for this remarkable concession, RCA turned over property and debentures to its future rivals, who now withdrew their representatives from the RCA board of directors and promised to sell at least half their RCA stock within three years. Finally, RCA chairman Owen D. Young, closely identified with the old patent-pool arrangement, would step down. Here was an important, concealed victory for Sarnoff, because Young was his last superior, and now even he would be gone. During the exhausting negotiations, Young had often fallen asleep while Sarnoff tirelessly fought over details. Through sheer force of will Sarnoff managed to supplant his one-time boss. In sum, then, it looked as if the Justice Department suit amounted to one of the best things that had ever happened to David Sarnoff. "RCA had been praised, damned, investigated, stipulated," ran the assessment of Robert Landry, *Variety*'s veteran correspondent. "It had been multiplied, augmented, expanded, revised, reorganized, refinanced, reoriented, and reformed." And now it was in Sarnoff's pocket. He had picked up the corporate pieces and reshuffled them one last time to suit his pleasure.

In this he echoed Paley's maneuvers at CBS, for at the same time the younger rival had been disengaging his company from its financial involvement with Paramount, and in the process brought it firmly under his control. Nineteen thirty-two turned out to be the year both Sarnoff and Paley crowned themselves emperors of their empires. But the consent decree would hardly be the last time RCA had to submit to government scrutiny. It had indeed disbanded one monopoly, the patent pool linking several major companies, but in its place it created a new one. RCA's new, improved monopoly extended from the manufacturing of radio equipment to the operating of not one but two networks, and, finally, the owning of major radio stations. For the rest of the decade at least, Sarnoff and RCA would have the industry coming and going.

As if to set off the old RCA from the new in as dramatic a way as possible, the company moved in 1933 from its old headquarters at 711 Fifth Avenue to the palatial setting of the newly opened Rockefeller Center, then the focal point of mid-Manhattan's surge in business activity. Sarnoff assumed his command post on the fifty-third floor of a Sixth Avenue skyscraper assigned the address of 30 Rockefeller Plaza. The surrounding buildings came to be called Radio City. NBC now had thirty-four studios at its disposal, including one of the largest in the world, Studio 8H, whence the Toscanini broadcasts originated. Despite the handsome surroundings, Sarnoff did not succeed in bringing better management to the company. In the eyes of many observers, he became increasingly remote, authoritarian, and arbitrary. Behind the rigid exterior, NBC shuffled along in a state of confusion. Hoping to ameliorate the company's image, Sarnoff retained Edward Bernays, the public relations expert Klauber had dismissed at CBS, and there at NBC Bernays encountered "infighting" and a "waste of manpower, time, and energy" that shocked him. But Sarnoff hardly bothered to raise his eyes from the drafting board. The exploitation of new broadcasting technology was his forte, not organizational niceties. Free for the time being of government interference, Sarnoff could now focus his full attention on television once again. But what he found was not to his liking. Disturbing news of inventions taking place beyond his control began reaching Sarnoff. As the self-appointed arbiter of television, he would deal with the mavericks in his own fashion.

One of them, anyway, looked like an easy mark. His name was Philo Farnsworth, and, if reports could be believed, he had succeeded in developing an all-electronic television system to rival Zworykin's. Because his approach closely paralleled RCA's, Farnsworth represented a potential threat. The last thing Sarnoff wanted was other companies introducing systems in advance of RCA, systems employing incompatible components. It was of the utmost importance to the Sarnoff approach that RCA television come first, with others conforming to its patents and electronic design. Therefore, he would have to do what he could to hold back random developments until RCA could, like an immense wave, sweep across the field, overwhelming all obstacles.

Farnsworth himself was an unlikely candidate to send shivers up Sarnoff's spine. Born in Utah of Mormon parents, Farnsworth was a self-taught inventor who in his early twenties developed another all-electronic substitute for Nipkow's whirling disc. The Farnsworth system relied on an "image dissector," for which he received a patent in 1930. Instead of the photo-emissive mosaic employed by Zworykin, the image dissector depended on a plate for collection. Lacking the recharging dots, the system did not have storage capacity, and therefore required a great deal more light than the Zworykin design.

However, in certain ways the Farnsworth image dissector outperformed Zworykin's iconoscope, and there was just enough of a difference to present potential entrepreneurs with an alternative to RCA's system. That threat came nearer to reality as Farnsworth went about lining up private investors in Los Angeles and San Francisco, all the while trying to maintain enough secrecy to avoid attracting undue attention. Police even raided his laboratory, in which he kept the blinds drawn, expecting to find a distillery. When the time came for Farnsworth to apply for his patent, RCA attorneys carefully questioned the young man, hoping to prove he was impinging on RCA patents, but they did not succeed. Armed with his patent, Farnsworth moved quickly. At a radio conference in Washington, D.C., in December 1930, he formally announced his invention and asked for government authority to operate an experimental television station in New York. Rubbing salt into the wound, he boasted that his system already had a greater resolution than RCA's, achieving a picture comprised of three hundred lines.

Deeply concerned, Sarnoff dispatched Zworykin himself to California in 1931 to examine Farnsworth's image dissector. Upon his return, Zworykin assured his boss that the RCA system did not require Farnsworth's technology to succeed. Sarnoff was still worried. The young inventor, sensing the possibility of becoming the Marconi of television, continued to improve his system, acquiring more patents in the process. He stung RCA badly when he hired away one of its executives, E. A. Nichols, to become the president of his company. In short order, Farnsworth found a manufacturer willing to back him, Philco. It is important to note that the Farnsworth and Zworykin systems were complementary, not mutually exclusive. Though they employed different techniques of image conversion in the camera, the receivers for both were the same. The two systems could have coexisted, but RCA would not settle for less than the entire market. After years of the clumsy patent-pool arrangement, Sarnoff was not about to share and share alike. At stake of course was not only prestige but money. Patent owners could earn a 3.5 per cent royalty on the wholesale price of licensed sets built by other manufacturers. By this time Farnsworth had invested a million in development and RCA far more. Both wanted their investment back.

Eventually Sarnoff made the pilgrimage to Farnsworth's laboratory, and what he saw caused him to conclude he would be better off to co-operate with Farnsworth as a way of limiting the potentially damaging competition. Locked into a cross-licensing agreement with RCA, Farnsworth would pose less of a threat. This rare example of compromise controverted every business principle in which David Sarnoff believed. He wanted RCA to own all patents, and thereby be in a position to license others, not the other way around. For an instant, David appeared to have slain Goliath. At the signing of the agreement, Farnsworth biographer and financial backer George Everson thought he saw tears come into the eyes of the RCA patent attorney. Nonetheless, Farnsworth had consigned his invention to oblivion, for RCA naturally had no intention of promoting it at the expense of Zworykin's. Having been thus co-opted, the Farnsworth campaign gradually lost momentum.

The next challenger to appear on the horizon was Allen DuMont, head of a small cathode ray tube business. The DuMont threat never became as serious as the Farnsworth, because patents were not involved, only a cheaper way to mass-produce television sets. DuMont liked to claim that, in contrast to the prodigious amounts of money RCA was spending in development, he had invested only eight thousand dollars in his set. He managed to attract substantial backing from Paramount in return for a half interest in his company. DuMont went so far as to bring out television sets in the fall of 1938. At the time the primary television station in operation happened to be RCA's W2XBS. By the strangest of coincidences, RCA ceased its experimental broadcasts when the DuMont sets came out, and as a result, the DuMont sets sold poorly. After World War II, sales of high-quality DuMont sets picked up, but the company eventually went out of business, never having succeeded in cornering a sufficient share of the market to survive.

Edwin Howard Armstrong posed a threat to Sarnoff's relentless campaign to monopolize the technology of television that was far more complex and personal in nature than the competition offered by such remote figures as Farnsworth, DuMont, and even Paley. Though Armstrong was the man's friend, his ability to devise the inventions Sarnoff never could stirred the darker passions within Sarnoff's breast. Their relationship was charged with ambivalence: admiration and envy, support and betrayal. It can be read as a cautionary tale about the position of the inventor in the age of the giant corporation, for Sarnoff, using RCA's might, did not simply ignore, compete with, or co-opt Armstrong; he destroyed him. It has been noted how Sarnoff, through an arduous process of conscious exertion, gradually mastered the complexities of the corporate existence. In time this trait hardened into rigidity, an inability to tolerate unpredictable external influences. It was Armstrong's fate to have been such a wayward influence in Sarnoff's ever more highly ordered universe.

The two first met as far back as 1913, a year after Sarnoff had come to prominence with American Marconi as one of the telegraph operators who had reported the sinking of the *Titanic*. At that time, Armstrong had recently developed a radio circuit which greatly improved reception. He even succeeded in bringing in signals from a British Marconi transmitter in Ireland. After receiving a degree from Columbia University, he took a position as a $50-a-month assistant in the Engineering School, and there, in its laboratories, he carried on his radio experiments. After taking the precaution of filing for a patent, the ambitious young inventor took the logical step of inviting American Marconi representatives to examine his device. One of them turned out to be David Sarnoff, 22 at the time, slightly younger than Armstrong. The inventor, incidentally, hid his circuitry in a black box to prevent unauthorized borrowing of his ideas. Already the combination of admiration and mistrust that was to mark their relationship was present. Armstrong was hoping that American Marconi would pay handsomely for his invention. "I was hard up in those days," he recalled in later years. "If somebody had said, 'Here's $10,000 and a job at $75 a month,' I'd have sold out so fast!" But Sarnoff's company was not buying, yet.

The technical wizardry Armstrong had attempted to promote came to be known as the regenerative circuit, a concept based on an earlier invention, De Forest's audion, which itself stemmed from the work of Edison and Maxwell. De Forest had noticed that when tuned to a specific frequency, his modified vacuum tube emitted a faint whistle. Armstrong realized the whistling was actually the tube amplifying. If he fed the tube's signal back to itself, it reinforced the signal several thousand times, thus making a previously undetectable radio signal loud and clear. During World War I, Armstrong developed another circuit, this one called the superheterodyne, which mixed, or heterodyned, radio signals to bring about greatly improved reception. After the war, Armstrong, still in Europe, received this unnerving telegram: "De Forest pressing action. Your presence urgently required."

Armstrong returned to the United States to become embroiled in a bewildering array of lawsuits and countersuits, the net result of which was a $40,000 debt for Armstrong. Then Westinghouse arrived on the scene, a corporate *deus ex machina* offering Armstrong an irresistible

$335,000 for his patents on the regenerative and superheterodyne circuits. Armstrong hastened to accept and received further confirmation of the originality of his inventions when, in 1922, De Forest finally lost his case. Yet by now the pattern of the inventor's career was set: invention followed by promotion, highly expensive lawsuits, and last-minute rescue by means of a sale at a whopping price.

By the time Armstrong received the Westinghouse offer, he had already succeeded in developing still another important circuit, the superregenerative, again based on the audion. The new circuit promised to eliminate aerials for many radios and reduce the number of tubes, and, consequently, the size of the set. RCA, then in its first and profitable year of radio production (1922) perceived immediate commercial potential in the superregenerative circuit and decided to buy. But in order to obtain the most favorable terms possible, the company first attempted to weaken Armstrong's position by negotiating for another, similar patent held by one John Bolitho, an Englishman. The enterprising inventor caught on to the RCA strategy, however, and managed to catch up with Bolitho first, in Egyptian Sudan, as it happened. Armstrong bought the patent, thus blocking the RCA tactic. Now in a position of strength, he called the shots, selling the superregenerative circuit to RCA for $200,000 and 60,000 shares of stock, making him the company's single largest stockholder, larger even than David Sarnoff. As the RCA stock soared throughout the nineteen twenties, reaching a 1929 high of 549, Armstrong enjoyed the status of a multimillionaire inventor. Here was living proof that the lone inventor could still, even in the twentieth century, achieve fame and 'fortune. Never again would an Armstrong victory taste as sweet.

There is considerable doubt that RCA ever received full value for its enormous investment in the circuit. "The trouble with it was that it didn't have selectivity," the inventor said, "and the art was developing in such a way that the ability to tune in a number of closely spaced stations became all-important." All was not lost, though, for another Armstrong circuit, the superheterodyne, did have the needed selectivity, and it too wound up in RCA's patent pool.

In that same heady year of 1922, Armstrong forged a personal as well as a professional alliance with Sarnoff and RCA by wooing none other than Sarnoff's secretary. During the negotiations with RCA, Armstrong made a practice of dropping by the office of his old friend, and while waiting to see him became acquainted with Marian Mac-Innis, the secretary. Like Sarnoff, Armstrong knew the value of a stunt. "I'm leaving for France on a vacation," he boasted to Miss Mac-Innis, "and I intend to buy the biggest and most expensive car I can find." True to his promise, when Armstrong returned from the Continent, he took the attractive young lady for a whirl in a brand-new Hispano-Suiza. In another stunt with far more disturbing implications, Armstrong climbed to the top of the transmitter of WJZ, key station of the Blue network, and while perched about four hundred feet above the ground posed for photographs, which he sent to his ladylove.

In the end, inevitably, they wed, but though wealthy, renowned, and married to the woman he loved, Armstrong did not live happily ever after. Both the force of circumstances and his own litigiousness would see to that.

De Forest was at it again, no doubt provoked by the attention surrounding the huge remuneration Armstrong received for developing circuits based on the audion. In 1924 a Washington, D.C., court decided that the relationship between the audion and Armstrong's circuits was so close that De Forest should have been credited with all the inventions. In 1928 the Supreme Court upheld the decision without reviewing the evidence. In 1934, the issue again came before the Supreme Court, this time in the form of a patent-infringement suit against RCA. But Armstrong, not the company, footed the lawyers' bills, so intent was he on seeking vindication in the courts. The Supreme Court again found for De Forest, declaring he had invented the regenerative circuit because he had noticed the whistling effect. The engineering community quickly pointed out that simply noticing the whistling effect meant no such thing. It was Armstrong who had realized what it was and then applied his discovery.

But Justice Benjamin Cardozo, who had written the Court's opinion, held his ground. Over the next several years the scientific and engineering professions rallied on Armstrong's behalf, stating for once and for all that it was De Forest who invented the audion and Armstrong who was responsible for the regenerative circuit.

This scientific, economic, and legal tangle was only partly due to the inventors' covetousness. Both men had come along rather late in the invention game, when the primary inventions of a Morse or a Marconi were already part of history. What was left to Armstrong and De Forest was to refine pre-existing technology in an era of the corporate impresario. The age of the inventor was fast yielding to the age of the salesman. The corporate atmosphere lent itself not to revolutionary inventions or breakthroughs so much as to minute, commercially valuable refinements.

During the protracted court battle with De Forest, Armstrong received a tantalizing challenge, one that would ultimately lead to his undoing. The man from RCA, David Sarnoff, was looking for a way to eliminate static from radio reception. Armstrong no doubt expected that lightning would strike twice. RCA would again pay handsomely for another magic circuit.

At the time, static was officially considered an insoluble problem. "Static, like the poor, will always be with us," said an AT&T executive. Armstrong worked on the problem intermittently for ten long years, finally filing for a patent in 1932. At last he had a solution to the problem, but what he had invented was not the simple improvement Sarnoff may have had in mind, but a revolutionary approach to transmission. Between lawsuits, Armstrong tried broadcasting with a different kind of radio wave. The one in use depended on varying the amplitude, or strength, of the waves carrying the sound. This system is known as amplitude modulation, or AM. Armstrong now decided to vary the frequency of the waves (rather than their amplitude) as a way of transmitting sound without static. He was not the first to try frequency modulation, or FM. AT&T had once looked into the system, but again, Armstrong was the first to apply successfully a previously known but overlooked method.

In 1933 he demonstrated his FM system for Sarnoff and RCA engineers, who had the privilege of hearing a remarkably clear and lifelike sound along with the total absence of static. Soon after, the company invited Armstrong to begin experimental tests from the RCA installation in the Empire State Building. As the system proved eminently successful in further testing, NBC engineers took the opportunity to swarm around the equipment, completely familiarizing themselves with it from June 1934 to October 1935. Armstrong, it turned out, had succeeded only too well.

The industry had undergone profound changes in the decade between Sarnoff's challenging of Armstrong to solve the static problem and the inventor's refinement of FM. In 1922, when Armstrong began work, lucrative network broadcasting was still five years in the future. Technology was changing rapidly and at small expense. But now, in the early nineteen thirties, the industry was mature, the vast networks in operation and already set in their ways. For both the consumer and the network the expense of converting to an entirely new transmission system, even in the name of high fidelity, seemed out of the question. The network system was just too profitable to tinker with in the midst of the Depression. Sarnoff had made lists of priorities for the future, and at the top came television, to which FM posed a direct threat. Both would use the same high frequencies, of which only a limited number were available. Sarnoff naturally wanted as much of the spectrum assigned to television as possible. And both would drain company resources to implement. Sarnoff perceived a greater future and a greater return in RCA-controlled television rather than a maverick's

FM system. Finally, he knew that if the company should ever want to implement FM broadcasting, RCA had by now mastered enough of the technology involved to do so on its own, without Armstrong's direct assistance or even his patents. Those engineers examining the Armstrong installation in the Empire State Building had done their homework. Now the company would not have to be in the thrall of this lone inventor, but could continue to collect rather than pay royalties. It was for all these reasons, then, that Sarnoff made his 1935 announcement of the million-dollar commitment to television and proceeded to boot Armstrong out of the Empire State Building.

By now, reversals in Armstrong's career were becoming as predictable as the seasons, but this one, entailing a direct confrontation with Sarnoff, promised to be particularly threatening. The unsuccessful circuit Armstrong had sold to RCA and the costly De Forest lawsuits had created a well of bitterness waiting to be tapped. Armstrong and Sarnoff circled each other uneasily. At RCA's 1935 annual meeting, Armstrong spoke up for Sarnoff's role in the company, then added, "I have a row on with him now. I am going to fight it through to the last ditch." Though Sarnoff sent a note of appreciation, pertaining to the favorable part of the speech, it was too late for a reconciliation. Armstrong, true to his word, applied in his own right to the newly formed Federal Communications Commission for permission to operate an experimental FM station. He had decided to go the De Forest route, inventing technology, then operating a station to demonstrate it to the public. Chief rival for a frequency allocation was, of course, RCA, which sought the same part of the spectrum for television alone. After an initial refusal, the FCC granted Armstrong a tiny frequency allocation, and the inventor put his plan into action. First he sold off a block of his RCA stock to finance the venture, and by 1938 was operating his own 50,000-watt FM station, W2XMN, located in Alpine, New Jersey, overlooking the Hudson River. W2XMN's 400-foot-high transmitting tower again brought out Armstrong's daredevil climbing instinct. He often scaled the structure, ostensibly to chip ice away.

Just a year later, RCA performed a most curious about-face by applying for its own FM station license. Sarnoff offered Armstrong a flat $1 million for his patents. Though apparently generous, the offer did not include the principle of royalty payments on patents, an arrangement which would have enhanced rather than diminished Armstrong's prestige. This move amounted to an offer to buy him out, and he refused.

Armstrong had, in a sense, succeeded in his campaign to convince the industry to adopt FM. In a short time, the FCC received no fewer than 150 applications for FM station licenses, all demanding that part of the spectrum coveted by Sarnoff for his television master plan. The commission went so far as to remove a tentatively assigned television frequency, Channel 1, and give it over to FM. Seeing this, radio-set manufacturers now approached Armstrong, not RCA, for a royalty arrangement to manufacture sets. In 1940, the FCC gave its final approval to commercial FM operation. Here indeed was a second chance for radio, an opportunity to correct past mistakes, to learn the lessons of history. FM even became a component of television, for the FCC ruled that television sound would require FM circuitry. Armstrong appeared to have won his riskiest battle of all.

Then history intruded. Again, the specter of war halted the rapid pace of broadcasting developments. Armstrong assigned the FM patents to the military for purposes of war communications. The vindication he was on the verge of savoring suddenly was snatched away. If the war had not come, however, Armstrong's FM would have gone a long way toward supplanting the accepted network structure. As it happened, the five-year period of limbo provided Sarnoff with crucial time to perfect and adapt television for the consumer market, and in time its appearance relegated radio's potential second chance to a less important role. In the postwar era, the appearance of television swamped every other development. Furthermore, the FCC gradually permitted FM stations to duplicate AM programming, thus strangling the incentive to purchase FM sets and the desire to create new programming especially for the FM spectrum. Armstrong had, in short, been thwarted by world history. He would never again be able to regain the initiative.

Yet this was by no means the end of the Armstrong saga. In 1948, the ever-litigious inventor sued RCA, NBC, and, subsequently, other radio- and television-set manufacturers, claiming that they were attempting to co-opt his invention and scuttle FM altogether, a charge Sarnoff vigorously denied in his later testimony.

As the trial progressed, RCA lawyers subjected the inventor to rigorous, occasionally humiliating questions in their offices. Armstrong succeeded in preventing them from besmirching his reputation, but he did not succeed in proving that RCA had, indeed, swiped FM. The complexity of the technology involved made the task well nigh impossible. His inventions were not clear-cut creations, but carefully and intricately conceived refinements of existing, often misunderstood, technology. The lengthy suit drained Armstrong of his funds and diverted his energies from scientific applications. Obsessed with vindication, he slowly gave way under the strain. In 1954, the tragic underside of his old daredevil stunts emerged. He leaped to his death from the thirteenth-story window of his comfortable apartment on Sutton Place. He was sixty-four. Shortly after his death, Sarnoff, hands on his chest, protested to an associate, "I did not kill Armstrong." Though his statement was literally true, Sarnoff and his corporate juggernaut had helped create a climate that aggravated his friend's mental instability. RCA made a $1,000,000 settlement with Armstrong's estate, while settlements from other manufacturers brought the figure to approximately $10,000,000. Armstrong had won his battle, in a sense, for he is today considered the inventor of FM, even though he did not succeed in proving RCA had infringed on his patents. And Sarnoff won *his* battle, for the most visible technological challenger to RCA's control over broadcasting technology was gone.

The reason Sarnoff carried on as if Armstrong never existed was, of course, television and his desire to be there first with it. He had made his first announcement in 1935. The FCC, trying to balance RCA on the one hand and Armstrong's FM on the other, never gave him unequivocal permission to proceed. Not that Sarnoff believed it was required. He decided, four years later, to try again, to *re*-introduce the marvel of the twentieth century to the public as if for the first time. The occasion would be a perfect example of the Sarnoff *fiat* at work. The site, the 1939 New York World's Fair.

On April 20, 1939, he stepped before a television camera at the fair to proclaim:

> On April 30th, the National Broadcasting Company will begin the first regular public television-program service in the history of our country; and television receiving sets will be in the hands of merchants in the New York area for public purchase. A new art and a new industry, which eventually will provide entertainment and information for millions and new employment for large numbers of men and women, are here.
>
> . . . And now we add radio sight to sound. It is with a feeling of humbleness that I come to this moment of announcing the birth in this country of a new art so important in its implications that it is bound to affect all society. It is an art which shines like a torch of hope in a troubled world. . . .

And so on. Sarnoff, it seemed, was speaking on behalf of the sole network in existence. It had now in its wisdom decided television was ready for a public which should be prostrate with thanks. Never mind the stalling, negotiations, and chicanery which had combined to stifle nearly as many developments as they had fostered, never mind the impending world war, never mind the impending FCC investigation of the networks' antitrust violations—all of these facts of life were temporarily suspended in the face of Sarnoff's desire to be the one and only to bring television to the American public. Following his speech, President Roosevelt addressed the television camera, and his presence further enhanced the official aura of the announcement. CBS might as well not have existed.

The introduction of television, then, was quite different from that of radio, which had begun at the grass roots, as an amateur hobby, and only later would come under the control of the networks. Television began life as an exclusively network preserve, and woe unto any adventurous tinkerer who tried to develop a system outside RCA's auspices.

There was, of course, much less to Sarnoff's elaborate introduction of television than met the eye. Primarily, it was premature. The system Sarnoff used employed 441 lines, but the FCC eventually adopted 525 as the U.S. standard. Television sets had hardly begun to appear in stores, and when they did, they cost a whopping $625. Available programs were extremely limited: demonstrations, some performers, a few documentary films, together totaling fifteen hours a week, most of which was sustaining since sponsors could pay only token amounts for commercials. But what really took the wind out of Sarnoff's pronunciamiento was the fact that not until February 1940 did the FCC allocate eighteen channels for limited commercial television broadcasting. (The FCC had assigned channels before, but these had been experimental.) Of the new channels, eleven were set aside for military use, and none of the remaining were in the frequency RCA had been using for its television broadcasting. Here was a provocative move indeed. By forcing RCA to revamp its transmitters in accordance with the new spectrum allocations, the FCC appeared to be sending a message that it, not RCA, would have the final word in organizing the nation's television service. Sarnoff reacted to the provocation by placing a limited number of television sets on sale (twenty-five thousand in all) in the New York area in conjunction with an impressive full-page advertisement in the New York newspapers announcing the inauguration of a regular television service. Never mind the 1939 announcement; the FCC's maneuver had rendered that plan obsolete. Through this aggressive strategy, Sarnoff planned to wrest the initiative away from the FCC. The advertisement, carrying his signature, strongly echoed the renowned 1927 newspaper notice of the creation of the National Broadcasting Company:

It is now possible for the RCA to announce the extension of its plans to provide, first, a regular television program service in the New York area; second, the offering to the public of receiving sets at moderate prices within the reach of the average American family; and third, the initial step in the construction of a television radio relay system as a means of interconnecting television transmitters for simultaneous service to and from other communities.

In other words, RCA promised a lot of pie in the sky to those who purchased enough sets to block the introduction of rival systems. NBC at the time had but a single television studio operating in a single city —New York—and no television network. With this meager support Sarnoff was still hoping to legislate RCA television into existence in the forum he knew mattered most, the marketplace. Others aspiring to enter the television market had little to do with the terms set forth in the announcement. CBS and DuMont seemed to be invisible, exactly as Sarnoff wished. He now could claim to be sole owner and proprietor of the nation's television system.

He did not, of course, expect to launch such a bold move without generating some controversy. He had taken the precaution of showing the advertisement to the FCC chairman, James L. Fly, before publication. But Fly was no ordinary FCC chairman. A Roosevelt appointee, the new chairman was determined to reverse the tradition of FCC acquiescence to industry demands. In an era of the New Deal and antitrust legislation, the networks' monopolistic tendencies bothered the chairman, who, when he eventually showed his mettle, proved to be as cagey as Sarnoff. Fly let RCA run the ad, then attacked it for all it was worth, calling the plan a monopoly, a positive menace to the public. This chairman was indeed different in that he confronted rather than maneuvered, challenged rather than persuaded. Sarnoff abhorred the confrontation, preferring to work behind the scenes, trying to persuade the FCC to allow him to introduce television to the public, but Fly took his case to the people. The loosely linked chain of stations known as the Mutual Network gave Fly an hour of time to take RCA and big business to task. And to make certain that RCA realized his complaints were not just so much hot air, in May 1940 he reversed the FCC's decision to allow television broadcasting by withdrawing the limited frequency allocations. Suddenly, the RCA–FCC conflict became more than an anonymous clash between two bureaucracies; it was now a contest between two personalities.

Before congressional hearings Sarnoff bewailed the FCC reversal. He countered Fly's broadcast by giving a sympathetic senator airtime on NBC to rebut the chairman. Fly, of course, was opposed not to the introduction of television, but to RCA's attempting to introduce the system singlehandedly. But Sarnoff would not be satisfied. From his point of view, the FCC existed primarily to assign frequencies, to function as an aerial traffic cop, not to shape business conditions in accordance with the prevailing political winds. This had been the function of the FCC's predecessor, the Federal Radio Commission, in the nineteen twenties, and before that the Commerce Department. The government agency did not provoke disputes, but rather mediated after they had begun. Sarnoff remained implacable. Interestingly, the man caught in the middle of the dispute was Roosevelt himself. He had appointed Fly while maintaining a long-standing relationship with Sarnoff going back to the days when he had helped the man from RCA acquire a transmitter to broadcast the Dempsey-Carpentier fight. "David," the President told his friend, "I'll pay for the meal if you and Fly take lunch together and settle this argument."

To this jaunty suggestion Sarnoff replied, "No useful purpose would be served by a goodwill luncheon."

Despite the lack of a summit meeting, the contest of wills temporarily relaxed. On April 30, 1941, the FCC reassigned eighteen television channels for unrestricted use. But Fly's gesture meant very little, in fact. During the delay, RCA had lost valuable time and its unchallenged initiative. And in May, immediately following the reassignment, Roosevelt declared a national emergency, meaning that RCA materials and production capacity would be devoted not to television but to war, now only six months away. Nonetheless, RCA maintained the facade. On July 1, 1941, its experimental TV station, W2XBS, which had been in occasional operation ever since 1928, finally traded its experimental denomination for the regular letters WNBT and broadcast its first commercial, a ten-second pitch for Bulova watches. The sponsor paid a token nine dollars for the message.

Fly's crusade would have a more profound effect on the future of RCA and its Red and Blue networks even than the war. The surge of patriotic feeling that the war aroused, in fact, fitted into Fly's plans perfectly. RCA was now in effect nationalized, its resources devoted toward achieving national rather than corporate aims. Government influence over the company was at its highest point since the first few years of its life. Any serious RCA resistance to government policy would look positively dastardly with a world war in progress. If there ever was to be an historical moment for the FCC to seriously affect the course of the company, it was now, before the war's end and the gradual disengagement of the company and its military customers.

Undertaken in the name of enlightened liberal principles, the Fly crusade carried some of the marks of a grudge. He set off a chain reaction over which he gradually lost control. Fly would win his fight to dismantle what he perceived as RCA's industrywide monopoly, one which would only intensify with the introduction of television. But he could not have taken much delight in the victory. The third national network he helped to create merely added to problems he was trying to eliminate. But how was he to anticipate this turn of events from the vantage point of 1941, with the nation on the brink of war?

9

Monopoly

As WAR SWEPT ACROSS EUROPE in the dark year of 1941, most of the massive conflicts in which RCA had been engaged were suspended. With Armstrong's patents assigned to the government for military use, the introduction of FM was inevitably postponed. Television, too, went into limbo; production facilities once intended for the manufacturing of sets were now given over to the war effort. Television sets disappeared from the stores. Even Zworykin turned his attention to military research. For the second time in three years, Sarnoff had miscalculated the proper moment for the commercial introduction of television.

On one front, however, RCA's battles still blazed. James L. Fly, Roosevelt's appointee to the chairmanship of the Federal Communications Commission, spurred an investigation of network monopolies. War or no war, he continued to stalk Sarnoff, and with the close government-business relationship brought on by war climate, he had more power than Sarnoff supposed. The investigation had begun—slowly—back in 1938, even before Fly became FCC chairman. Now the President wanted his appointee to bring the desultory investigation to a quick conclusion.

The main reason Sarnoff—or anyone else in the industry—did not fear the FCC's powers at the time was that the commission was responsible for licensing stations, not regulating networks. This remarkable state of affairs had come about through an accident in timing. When the first comprehensive government regulation of broadcasting was under debate, as early as 1923, the idea of a network was but a twinkle in David Sarnoff's eye. By the time the Radio Act of 1927 finally came into existence, the industry that it was designed to regulate had developed so fast that the act was already obsolete. However, the networks' sudden appearance caused Congress to tack on a last-minute provision. The newly created Federal Radio Commission could make regulations about "stations engaged in chain broadcasting." As is clear from the wording, these regulations could affect only stations, not the chains themselves. Effects, but not causes.

Here was a remarkable fluke. The single most influential event in the development of broadcasting—namely, the creation of networks with their centralized programming and sales forces—remained beyond the control of the nation's elected representatives. The omission left a glaring loophole, and the networks barreled through.

Subsequent refinements in the laws did not make much difference until 1933, when President Roosevelt requested a study of the nation's electronic communications, ranging from broadcasting to telephones. As a result of the study, Congress passed the Communications Act of 1934, which superseded the Radio Act of seven years before and established the FCC as the FRC's successor. For all its comprehensiveness and complexity, the new body still regulated only stations, not networks. It was a licensing and regulatory agency modeled on the Interstate Commerce Commission, which had been devised back in 1887.

It was with this rather clumsy bureaucratic ammunition, then, that Fly attempted to take on lofty NBC. The role of the FCC was riddled with inconsistencies. On the one hand, Section 303 of the 1934 Communications Act charged the body to exercise its powers as "public convenience, interest, or necessity requires," but on the other, the FCC had but a single tool for accomplishing the task, the authority to license stations. Fly made the most of it.

After three long years of investigation, the FCC finally issued its Report on Chain Broadcasting on May 2, 1941. The date would prove to be Sarnoff's day of reckoning, the day he learned NBC would have to part with one of its networks. No wonder Fly permitted television to go commercial just before the report came out. He was convinced he had taken the necessary steps to safeguard the future of network television against the RCA–NBC monopoly.

Most of this brilliant but doomed document was devoted to tracing the economic histories of the networks then in operation, NBC's Red and Blue, CBS, and the seven-year-old newcomer, the Mutual

Broadcasting System, but the crux of the report was set forth at its
very beginning: RCA was, in effect, born with a mission to monopolize. The company "could not fail to assume a dominant position in
the field of network broadcasting as a result of its purchase of WEAF
and the Telephone Co. network." The assault continued, "following
the purchase, the only two networks in the country were under the
control of RCA," which amounted to a "practical monopoly of network broadcasting." Before going further with the unraveling of the
report's charges, it is worth considering how outlandish its point of
view was. RCA was well beyond the limits of the FCC regulatory
powers, which were confined to individual stations. Much more likely
candidates to investigate possible antitrust violations were the Justice
Department, the Federal Trade Commission, or even the Interstate
Commerce Commission. Of all the possible trust-breakers, the FCC
was among the least qualified. Its home truths were being uttered in a
void, but what truths they were.

The RCA monopoly, according to the report, began with "its control of thousands of patents and its experience with an ownership of
pre-broadcasting wireless transmitters, as well as its support from
General Electric and Westinghouse." All these factors combined to
"give it a running start in the radio-broadcasting industry." Then the
report zeroed in on the company's transformation from foreign communications to domestic manufacturing and broadcasting. This was of
course the work of David Sarnoff during the period from 1922 to 1932,
and Fly's presence is almost palpable as the report condemned
Sarnoff's purchase of the Victor Talking Machine Company, calling it
a "step-by-step invasion of the phonograph business," which "gave
RCA entering wedges into the transcription and talent supply business." As a result, RCA and its subsidiaries, including NBC, enjoyed a
"marked competitive advantage over other broadcasting companies,
other radio manufacturers, and other phonograph-record companies."
Along the same lines, the report viewed with alarm RCA's entry into
the motion picture field through its association with RKO and its entry
into FM broadcasting. Here were two more Sarnoff specialties. Never
naming him, the report obviously considered his policies to be the primary cause of the monopoly. It disapproved of practically everything
he had ever done for the company since the day the *Titanic* sank.
Curiously, it omitted mention of the quintessential Sarnoff monopolistic enterprise, the introduction of television. The report stuck to
demonstrable facts, not the potential for future abuses. After the FCC
finished with RCA, Fly knew, the RCA television monopoly would be
no more.

The report, in short, conveyed the impression that RCA and later

NBC, having systematically eliminated most competitive conditions in the broadcasting marketplace, had cleared quite a field for itself. "RCA was originally founded to utilize wireless techniques for the transmission of messages; today it bestrides whole new industries, dwarfing its competitors in each," the report eloquently noted. "Every new step had not only increased RCA's power in fields already occupied, but had enhanced its competitive advantage in occupying fields more and more remote from its beginnings."

In the context of the report's analysis, however, the recitation of RCA's monopoly served mainly as a preamble, setting the tone for its primary concern, NBC. Though the FCC could do little besides bemoaning RCA's monopoly, it was on much firmer ground when it dealt with individual stations. In 1927, it noted, just under 7 per cent of all radio stations were NBC affiliates. But over the course of the next decade, the percentage more than doubled, reaching the level of 25 per cent at the time of the report and still climbing. This concentration of power served to strangle new networks hoping to enter the field. The report noted the overwhelming obstacles the Mutual Broadcasting System faced in trying to make headway against NBC, a company which operated two of the three networks in existence at the time of Mutual's debut in 1934.

Of greatest significance among all of its observations—both those it was entitled to make and those it was not—was an account of how NBC manipulated its two networks to stifle competition. "The Red and Blue networks are not separate business enterprises," it decided. "Nor are they even two distinct operating divisions of departments within NBC." The Red and Blue did not compete against each other, but acted in unison to compete against others. As anyone with a radio could attest, NBC used its Blue network as a "buffer" for the Red, allocating its high-rated, high-priced entertainment to the Red while loading the Blue's schedule with public-service programs, where they would do the least damage to company profits. They did not compete, and that, in the report's eyes, amounted to a cardinal sin. NBC was in the enviable position of being able to counterprogram against itself to achieve an overall competitive advantage against non-NBC networks. As the report saw the situation, "available radio facilities are limited. By tying up two of the best facilities in lucrative markets—through ownership of stations, or through long-term contracts . . . NBC has utilized the Blue to forestall competition with the Red."

Well, the FCC had a point, but it wound up destroying a crucial facet of network broadcasting in the process of trying to save the industry from itself. The logical remedy for the situation was to force

NBC to divest itself of one of its two networks. Naturally, it would choose the less profitable Blue over the Red. Once in the marketplace, for sale to the highest bidder, the Blue could bid farewell to any pretense of public service. Without the profitable Red network to support it, market forces would cause the Blue to become commercial just to survive. Fly's reformist zeal blinded him to this fact of network life.

Furthermore, the impending shake-up at NBC promised to affect CBS programming. Once NBC lost its public-service network, CBS, reacting, as always, to its older rival, would feel less pressure to emphasize that kind of programming. And the addition of a third competitor in the network race for shares of the advertising market would make such programming seem more than ever like wasteful indulgence. Fly, then, upset the delicate competitive balance between NBC and CBS which had permitted a certain amount of sincere, sustaining, minority-oriented programming to exist. Where networks had once maintained a halfhearted commitment to the prestige program, there would, in the future, be virtually none. Fly's dilemma pointed up a classic problem with government regulation of industry. With only limited powers, an agency, in trying to rectify the abuses of a current situation, can, unintentionally, instigate an even worse situation.

Fly, incidentally, also found things at 485 Madison Avenue to wave his finger at. Clearly, CBS was not as vulnerable as RCA–NBC to charges of monopoly. Concentrating primarily on broadcasting, it did not have the patents, manufacturing capacity, or twin networks that the report took its rival to task for. But it did have William Paley, and in the report's opinion, he exerted an undue amount of influence within CBS itself. At the time of the investigation, the report found that Paley and family held "a total of about 33 percent of all the stock of CBS" and "the power to elect a majority of the entire board of directors." The report also criticized the practice of both CBS and NBC of maintaining management agencies. Through its association with Arthur Judson, for example, CBS controlled Columbia Concerts as well as an artist bureau. NBC also maintained an artist bureau. Since the bureaus' owners also happened to be their best customers, they were not in a position to get the best fees for their clients. "NBC's dual role necessarily prevents arm's length bargaining and constitutes a serious conflict of interest," the report concluded.

So much for the report's bad news, which is to say so much for the report. It failed to mention or commend a single *pro bono* network activity, series, or program. In the heat of the moment, the FCC neglected to take into account any of the services the networks provided, in employment, entertainment, advertising, or news, an area in which CBS especially had been making tremendous strides. Fly ignored these factors at his—and ultimately the industry's—peril. The report justified its extreme position in part because the networks had grown very rich at a time of a national depression. "Both have reaped, and reaped richly, almost since the time of their foundation," the report said, noting the "tremendous returns on investment which each has received, amounting in 1938 alone to 80 percent of the investment in tangible property in the case of NBC and 71 percent in the case of CBS." For their part, the networks had made a practice of justifying their enormous rate of return on the basis of the risks they took, a correlation Fly chose to ignore. Without the profits, even the minute trickle of service programming would have been cut off long ago.

The report promised a dire remedy indeed, one that would be effective at the network level. In the hope of stimulating better public service and more freedom of expression, Fly decided to legislate more competition into the business. "Where competition has not been effective in protecting the public interest," the report noted, "Congress has substituted detailed governmental control of rates, prices, finances, or other matters for the principle of free competition. But in regulating radio, 'Congress intended to leave competition in the business of broadcasting where it found it,'" because "it has long been a basic hypothesis of the American system that competition in a free market best protects the public interest."

In short, Fly wanted more networks. Testifying in June 1941, before a Senate investigation committee, he expressed the opinion that the country could do with perhaps six competing networks, not just two. However, the history of the networks until this point has shown that full-scale commercial competition leads only to full-scale commercial programming. It does not necessarily lead to the best service, only the most profitable. Furthermore, Fly's competitive utopia was, for the time being, technologically impossible. There might be radio stations aplenty, with their limited range, but a network was almost by definition a monopolizing influence. There was hardly room on the broadcast spectrum—there were hardly enough stations—to accommodate six full-blown competing networks, another factor Fly chose to ignore.

To get at the networks' monopoly, Fly employed an indirect approach, via the stations, a tactic that proved awkward indeed. Fly may have wished to chop NBC into tiny subdivisions à la Standard Oil, but he did not have the power to do so. Since he could only license stations, Fly decreed: "No license shall be issued to a standard broadcast station affiliated with a network organization which maintains more than one network." In other words, if NBC wished the affiliates of one of its networks to retain their licenses, it had to divest itself of the other. Fly had; after all, accomplished the feat of wagging the net-work dog through its tail.

Needless to say, Fly's impressive feat of bureaucratic maneuvering caused a howl of protest. The man was attempting to rewrite broadcasting history. NBC's president at the time, Niles Trammell, insisted that the order to divest would "destroy freedom of the air." NBC, he said, would be forced to bite off its nose to spite its face. He threatened that given the new set of circumstances the network would have to forgo such indulgences as the glorious NBC Symphony Or-chestra conducted by Toscanini (which, incidentally, did not happen until the Maestro's retirement in 1954).

Interestingly, Paley went along with the NBC line. CBS did not re-ally stand to gain from having its greater rival maimed. It had, over the years, managed to carve out a very cozy niche for itself. Its success had been built on the foundations—both technological and conceptual —laid down by RCA and NBC. And when that foundation was shaken, CBS trembled. It too would be facing stiffer competition. Said Paley, "The first paralyzing blow will have been struck at the freedom of the air, because a commission which can exercise such drastic powers without even going to Congress for authority to exercise them will have reduced the networks and stations to impotent vassals."

The networks' impassioned arguments did not bear close scrutiny. Where NBC claimed it could not survive without operating two net-works, CBS had demonstrated beyond a doubt that a single network could flourish. NBC, the more threatened of the two companies, took the matter to court, but since the Supreme Court at the time con-tained a number of Roosevelt appointees, the network could count on little support from this quarter. In 1943, Justice Felix Frankfurter confirmed the FCC's right to force NBC to divest itself of one of its two networks. In the meantime, the industry as a whole, not just the networks, mounted a campaign to discredit Fly. Invited to attend a meeting of the National Association of Broadcasters, a body represent-ing station owners, Fly was attacked, then refused permission to reply. After the meeting, Fly told the press that the NAB reminded him of "dead mackerel in the moonlight—it both shines and stinks." Fly's *mot* generated further ill will.

Rhetoric aside, NBC had no choice but to divest itself of a net-work. Despite the distraction of wartime activities, Sarnoff made sure that NBC would, in the process, be giving up as little as possible. Ob-viously, he would not part with the popular, profitable Red network, home of the top-drawer comedians, but rather with the low-profit, public-service Blue. Furthermore, he would not sell off the Blue en-tirely. He stripped it of important assets even while calling attention to its profitability. In 1940, the Blue yielded little more than $10,000,000 against the Red's nearly $40,000,000. By 1943, the year of its sale, the Blue was claiming $25,000,000 worth of advertising time sold. But when the Blue went on the market, it was missing several important affiliates: KDKA in Pittsburgh, WBAL in Baltimore, and WHAM in Rochester—all of which joined the Red's roster. What was up for sale, then, was little more than airtime on the remaining affiliates (approximately 100), three company-owned radio stations (WJZ in New York, WENR in Chicago, and KGO in San Francisco), and the services of network employees. RCA's massive technical support and established talent were not part of the bargain. CBS had begun in circumstances nearly as humble, but that was the point. In order to survive, that network had had to adopt a thoroughly commercial posture, and so would the new Blue. Sarnoff's service philosophy of network broadcasting, then, became a casualty of Fly's strategy. More competitive, the three separate networks would now be more commercial than ever before.

Sarnoff appointed Mark Woods, a self-effacing veteran NBC vice-president, as the head of the cast-off network, which was called, for the time being, simply the Blue. The asking price was $8,000,000, an astonishingly low figure considering the network's potential earning power. The Blue, however, attracted no buyer endowed with the entrepreneurial daring, social commitment, or long-standing involvement with the broadcasting industry characteristic of Sarnoff or Paley. Instead, the eventual buyer would be a skillful businessman and advertiser who had made a fortune promoting Lifesavers candy, Edward J. Noble.

The "Lifesaver King," as Noble came to be called, had plenty of cash (his sale in 1928 of the Lifesaver Company had netted $22,000,000) and limited broadcasting experience derived from his ownership of WMCA in New York, a station he eventually sold as a condition of buying the Blue.

The major obstacle to Noble's acquisition of the network was getting Fly's confidence that the sale would indeed serve the ends of the report. At a hearing to determine the orientation of the network's new management, Mark Woods, the Blue's president, said, "We are in the advertising business, gentlemen, and that is the business of selling goods to the American people." In his hands, then, the Blue would, inevitably, make the transition from a service to a full-scale commercial network. To assuage the commission's misgivings, Noble submitted a less than wholehearted statement to the effect that his network would accept sponsorship from groups of all political persuasions. To the commission's way of thinking, this amounted to a guarantee of diversity of opinion. But sponsorship was sponsorship, and once a network became indebted to its sponsors, its programming would invariably be affected. There was no way the FCC could enforce its conditions once the network was in Noble's hands, just as there was no way the FCC could prevent Noble from selling his network to someone with even less interest in diversity or service than he.

Nevertheless, Fly gave his consent to the deal with Noble. The new owner promptly renamed the Blue the American Broadcasting Company.*

Noble started off ABC just as Fly would have wished. He said he hoped to make the network into the New York *Times* of the business. He soon, in his words, "discovered that if we intended to remain in this business—we had to get shows that a great many million people want to hear." In 1944, the first full year of Noble's ownership, ABC's time sales climbed past $44,000,000, and the competitive spiral continued to whirl upward. History was repeating itself. Back in 1927, the appearance of CBS and the Depression two years after that forced NBC to adopt a more commercial course than Sarnoff had anticipated. Now, at the end of the Second World War, the appearance of ABC and the expense of introducing television increased the competitive frenzy. The FCC could only watch and wait as the networks went about their primary business, making money. Now that he had played his hand, there was little left for Fly to do. In 1944, he stepped down.

The surprising turn of events at ABC had not been entirely his fault. He had tried to make the best of a bad situation. The root of the problem was that the FCC just did not have the power to carry out his good intentions. For all of Roosevelt's New Dealing and Fly's crafty maneuvering, the 1927 loophole mattered more than the ensuing welter of legislation about stations. The networks would continue to flourish just beyond the wiggling fingers of the long arm of the law. Eventually, Congress would create its own network to satisfy the need for public-service programming on a grand scale, but that plan still lay twenty years in the future.

* ABC naturally wanted its flagship station, WJZ, to bear the call letters of the new network, hence the emergence of WABC. Since WABC happened to be the call letters of CBS's flagship station, it in turn acquired a new appellation, WCBS.

10

Color War

As SARNOFF STRUGGLED with an increasingly belligerent FCC, still another challenge to the RCA television monopoly sprang up from a predictable quarter. Goaded by the ever-present urge to beat Sarnoff at his own game, William Paley allowed himself to be lured onto unfamiliar territory: the development and manufacture of hardware. Paley, who was about as uncomfortable with technology as Sarnoff was with show business, at first met with astounding beginner's luck. But eventually his attempt to emulate his rival would degenerate into CBS's major postwar fiasco.

The CBS challenge began in March 1940, when a thirty-three-year-old inventor working at CBS named Peter Goldmark went to see his first color movie, *Gone With the Wind.* For the previous four years, the Hungarian émigré had labored to mount some kind of CBS challenge to RCA's formidable television campaign. Under Paley's and later Kesten's direction, CBS had conducted experimental television broadcasts from the Chrysler Building and even built a television studio at Grand Central Station. "The urge to beat RCA and its ruler, David Sarnoff, was such an overriding force that it eventually began to shape my own career," Goldmark wrote. Despite the brave show, the CBS experiments amounted to a token effort in the face of RCA's multimillion-dollar campaign. Paley would have been content to see radio as it existed continue indefinitely. Profits and prestige were good and getting better all the time. But, as always, if RCA pioneered a development, CBS would try to go the behemoth one better.

At first Goldmark saw no choice but to select either the Farnsworth or the RCA (Zworykin) system as his point of departure. Having decided on RCA's, Goldmark discovered that the arch rival was only too glad to help. By selling its system to CBS, RCA would eliminate a competitor while gaining a prestigious customer. "Such benevolent marketing rattled us a bit," he recalled.

Then, while watching *Gone With the Wind*, Goldmark had a brainstorm. "All through the long, four-hour movie I was obsessed with the thought of applying color to television," he wrote. The inventor shared his obsession with Kesten, who gave Goldmark a go-ahead. By the end of August 1940—record time, indeed—Goldmark demonstrated a full-color television system to FCC chairman Fly. Again, CBS was shot with luck, because Fly, as an avowed enemy of RCA's monopolistic tendencies, was only too glad to give rival CBS a boost. According to Goldmark, Fly "right then and there announced he was a champion of color." CBS began carefully cultivating publicity for its color system, and the press seized on it. Here was a new marvel of science, grist for the Sunday-supplement mill. In September, the St. Louis *Post-Dispatch* ran brilliant, sharp full-color photographs of images transmitted on the CBS color system. The company appeared to enjoy a sudden advantage over RCA, which had also demonstrated its version of color television, but with poor results.

The secret ingredient—and, ultimately, the downfall—of the CBS–Goldmark color system was its reliance on a spinning disc to scan the image. Goldmark had resurrected the old mechanical system, the one Sarnoff and Zworykin had labored to render obsolete, then modified it to produce color. It produced sparkling color, too, but had one other important characteristic—incompatibility with the RCA system. That meant the signal put out by the camera of one system could not be decoded by the set of the other. It also meant war.

The development of color television turned into a contest because the FCC, acting as referee, would eventually have to approve one system or the other. The loser would fall by the wayside, along with the development costs. In fact, the contest held implications beyond color, for whoever controlled it controlled the future of the industry. In the CBS scenario, the industry would switch directly from radio to color television, skipping the intermediate black-and-white phase. Once the consumer saw those glowing electronic colors, and the advertiser saw the consumer's reaction, RCA's black-and-white television would be about as up to date as the steam-powered automobile.

As expected, the FCC initially came out in favor of CBS color. In

1941 the agency approved the introduction of experimental broadcasts. At this moment, commercial introduction seemed inevitable. It looked as though Paley really had accomplished the astonishing feat of leapfrogging over the vast RCA empire. But that would be to underestimate the wily Sarnoff. Despite its obvious qualities, the CBS system never gained even the most tentative acceptance in the marketplace.

Goldmark called his color system field-sequential. That is, it scanned the image, or field, to be transmitted through a sequence of colored filters, red, blue, and green. The filters were built into a disc that rotated between camera and subject. The system scanned an image three separate times, once through each filter. Though photographed through a colored filter, each image was transmitted as black and white. The color was added at the receiving end, where another disc, spinning in synchronization with the camera's, added the red, blue, and green to those separate black-and-white images. The resulting images, though separately colored, passed so fast across the screen that through the "persistence of vision" phenomenon they merged within the eye into a full-color image. When harried by RCA criticism of the awkwardness of employing rotating discs in sensitive electronic equipment, Goldmark maintained that the essence of his system was not mechanical at all. He said he could, in time, replace the filter-bearing discs with electronic equivalents. Rather, the essential feature of the system was that it was *sequential*, that is, it transmitted images in three separate color-coded versions, one after the other. The color system RCA eventually proffered transmitted all colors *simultaneously*. The notorious disc, then, did not turn out to be the barrier to compatibility between the CBS and RCA color, but the method of transmission most definitely did.

Goldmark continued to refine his system. His original tests, sparkling though they were, did not include transmission of live, moving images, which were beyond the grasp of Goldmark's mechanical camera. Deciding to modify Zworykin's all-electronic camera tube to the sequential system, he called upon the services of RCA technicians, who hastened to comply with the request, delivering the camera tube in two weeks' time. The technicians were hardly attempting to subvert the RCA system, merely to co-opt the competitor. In the process, they endowed him with live-transmission capability. So, by June 1941, when the FCC gave CBS permission to conduct experimental color broadcasts, the company was in a position to launch a major offensive. But so were the Japanese and Hitler. It would be a full ten years before color would again be on the verge of going public, a full ten years for Sarnoff to orchestrate its eventual introduction.

In the meantime, CBS's inexperience in matters electronic became embarrassingly evident. The company naïvely believed that even after Fly's departure the FCC would continue to back its system. Furthermore, it assumed that when the final approval came and those fateful spectrum allocations were handed down from on high, they would assign CBS color to ultra high frequency wavelengths, where the experimental broadcasting was now going on. RCA had staked out a different part of the spectrum, very high frequency, and was only slightly disgruntled to find it would have to make space for the intrusion of FM radio.

CBS color marked time during the war. Kesten, who had first believed in it, departed. In 1944, when Fly stepped down from the FCC to return to private law practice, his successor turned out to be Charles Denny, who ultimately proved how wrong CBS's assumptions about continuing FCC support could be.

As a prelude to full-scale television broadcasting, the FCC now decided on commercial frequency allocations which, with only minor alterations, are still in use today. It reserved space for thirteen very high frequency television channels falling at intervals between 44 and 216 megahertz. FM found a home in the midst of the television bands, just above Channel 6, in an allocation stretching from 88 to 108 megahertz. (To those who could read a cryptic code, the peculiar arrangement concealed a victory for RCA and a defeat for FM proponents, especially Armstrong, for the displacement of FM rendered all FM sets in use obsolete. RCA and others would have to manufacture new sets, and people would have to buy them, if FM was to get off the ground.)

Finally, the allocation reserved a plentiful number of ultra high frequency television channels, numbered 14 to 83, between 470 and 890 megahertz.* It was in this region that CBS petitioned for and expected to receive FCC permission to transmit its brilliant color signals.

To demonstrate its goodwill and sincerity about going ahead with color transmission, CBS actually withdrew four major applications for television stations in the black-and-white, VHF part of the spectrum. Now the network retained but a single VHF license, for New York City. It applied instead for UHF licenses for color transmitting. For a brief moment, it appeared that the two networks might be broadcasting on entirely different parts of the spectrum, RCA in black and white on VHF, and CBS in color on UHF, and never the twain shall meet. But would RCA manufacture or license others to

* In 1970, the FCC removed channels 70 to 83 from television broadcasting.

manufacture sets capable of receiving CBS signals? Of course not, especially if they were incompatible with the RCA system. Whoever began transmitting television signals, then, needed to make arrangements for sets to receive them. RCA had the manufacturing capacity; CBS did not. Probably no one had understood the full extent of the problem when Kesten first gave Goldmark the go-ahead. The requirements of the situation, then, practically guaranteed a monopoly, for whoever ran a television broadcasting operation also had to make the receiving equipment to go along with it. And RCA was the natural candidate for maintaining the dual functions, even if its black-and-white television system—never mind color—was the inferior of the two systems available.

Then came the bombshell. In March 1947, Denny refused to approve the CBS color system, or any other color system for that matter. Now the CBS UHF licenses were practically worthless, and along with them the entire CBS color effort. The industry would not be switching from radio directly to UHF color that year. In October 1947, the FCC chairman, having blocked the CBS color system, suddenly resigned his enormously influential position and immediately took a new job—as vice-president and general counsel of the National Broadcasting Company. Sarnoff had learned to play the game in Washington at least as well as CBS had in the days of the old FRC. The move, as a rather blatant example of conflict of interest, aroused much criticism, and in 1952 the Communications Act was amended to prohibit a former commissioner from pleading his company's case before the FCC for a full year after resigning. Considering the circumstance, the restriction was rather mild, as it still permitted commissioners to use their government posts as launching bases into private industry. The rightness or wrongness of Denny's decision, however, was unimportant in the face of its irrevocableness. The FCC had cast the die, for better or worse.

With its high hopes for color scuttled, CBS now had to scrounge around for some television station licenses. Having put its eggs in the UHF basket, the company appeared in danger of having no television network whatsoever. To make matters worse, the FCC in 1948 ordered a freeze on the building and licensing of new television stations, and the situation remained in limbo for almost four years. The FCC cited the Korean War and the shortage of materials it had created as the major reason for the freeze, but the suspicion remains that the war at home, the rapid swing to the right, and resulting investigation of the supposedly subversive entertainment industries kept the freeze from thawing any sooner. With television stations in short supply, CBS had to pay vastly inflated prices to acquire the five stations a network was permitted to own. CBS's new president, Frank Stanton, attempted, in desperation, to purchase ABC for $28,000,000 just to lay his hands on its young rival's TV outlets.

The CBS executives, sophisticated and stylish as they were about programming and selling advertising time, were proving singularly inept in the business of creating a television network. Demoralized, Goldmark believed he was suffering unjustly from Paley's wrath at the sudden reversal, and he bridled at the thought of playing the role of scapegoat. "Since Paley's cash register was not clanking at that instant," he wrote, "we had been sentenced, shackled, and beaten down without a chance to enter our plea." He knew he had worked wonders in the field of color television, bringing forth a system in only months, where Sarnoff had struggled with Zworykin and others for years to come only half as far. But this was one race that would not go to the swift. All the delays—the Second World War, the freeze, the FCC equivocations—had operated in RCA's favor, giving the company time to develop some kind of system. Facing reversals, Sarnoff responded by redoubling his efforts to achieve victory. Paley did not give his ace inventor similarly lavish support.

Emboldened by the FCC's decrees, Sarnoff now prepared to swamp the marketplace with RCA television sets. In 1946 the company began mass-producing television sets, which, significantly, were not equipped with UHF receiving capacity. The sets received up to Channel 13 and no higher. The timing reveals that even if the FCC had approved the CBS color system, RCA-built or -licensed sets would never have been capable of receiving it. The move did not reflect but rather anticipated the FCC strategy. Sarnoff had prematurely introduced television twice before, in 1939 and 1941, and he was willing to risk it once again for the privilege of being first. His strategy, however, was cunning rather than foolhardy, for he knew the government agency had a history of reacting to situations in the marketplace rather than attempting to create them. He guessed, correctly, that the FCC would not initiate a new television system but rather legitimize one already in widespread use, taking its popularity as proof that it was serving the public's needs and interests. With the exception of Fly's attack on NBC's dual network structure, the FCC had a history of approving developments after the fact. CBS, in contrast to NBC, kept its nose clean and requested permission in advance of consumer acceptance. Such a strategy was certainly more logical, but not in keeping with typical FCC behavior.

At last the time was right. The black-and-white sets with which RCA flooded the market met with gleeful acceptance. In 1946, only 6,000 television sets were in use. By 1949, the number had increased to

3,000,000, and none of them were capable of receiving a CBS color picture. The popular response clinched Sarnoff's victory. When, in 1949, the FCC again opened hearings on color (not black-and-white) systems and this time found in CBS's favor, the decision came too late to allow consumer acceptance of CBS color. The public, well pleased with the RCA-type black-and-white sets already on the market and in homes, was not about to discard the sets in favor of a newer model. They were hungry for television now, any television, and David Sarnoff was happy to oblige.

For its part, CBS, despite the eleventh hour victory, had allowed itself to be outmaneuvered. The company attached the greatest importance to the 1949 decision, considering it absolute and vital, even though the real decision was being made in the marketplace. For example, when the CBS contingent, consisting of Goldmark, Richard Salant, later president of CBS News, and network vice-president Adrian Murphy traveled to Washington to lobby for support, they took devious, indirect routes through Ohio and Baltimore to throw the opposition off the scent. RCA, in contrast, simply did not attach the same importance to the hearings. Sarnoff gambled that eventually the FCC would recognize commercial realities, that the RCA television system was already established in dealerships and homes around the country.

These new, ultimately inconsequential hearings dragged on for eight interminable months and generated forty volumes of testimony. Both Stanton and Sarnoff testified, and the latter did not hesitate, in the process, to put down his rival: "The mechanical scanning wheel now belongs to the ages. As an expedient, it merely gave laboratory technicians something to play with." CBS proudly demonstrated its impressive color system. When RCA showed its wares, "the monkeys were green, the bananas were blue, and everyone had a good laugh," in the words of David Sarnoff. His flippancy revealed the trifling importance he attached to the elaborate charade taking place in Washington. And even when the FCC, in a document known as the First Report, selected CBS color (though not at the expense of, but in addition to, RCA's black-and-white system), the RCA General replied, "We may have lost the battle, but we'll win the war." He knew that 9,000,000 RCA-type television sets had been purchased at the time of the decision, making it irrelevant.

Coming at this late date, the CBS color victory was indeed hollow. The network could broadcast all the color programs it liked, but if no sets were on the market to receive it, and if there was no audience to watch it, no sponsor would consider purchasing time. To further strengthen his position by stalling for more time, Sarnoff challenged the FCC decision in the courts. He remained cocksure of himself throughout the tedious procedures. Goldmark even heard him twit Paley during the proceedings. "Bill," he said, "we could have avoided this headache if I had hired Peter in the first place."* Even though the Supreme Court upheld the FCC decision, the delay, extending from November 1950 to June 1951, permitted the number of RCA-type black-and-white sets sold to top the 12,000,000 mark. CBS color was more incompatible than ever.

Enjoying the fruits of this sales boom, television-set manufacturers and dealers became adamant supporters of the RCA black-and-white system. Loath to tamper with success, they proved positively hostile to the introduction of CBS color. Allen DuMont, at the time selling black-and-white sets and operating a small-scale television network, went so far as to appear on television to attack CBS color. One manufacturer sued CBS and another placed a full-page newspaper advertisement declaring the pro-CBS FCC decision "a threat to the American way of life"—presumably life with a patriotic black-and-white television set.

Clearly, if CBS were to succeed in this venture, it would have to enter the manufacturing side of the business itself. Paley, Stanton, and others in their circle should have realized that the chances of overtaking RCA in the set manufacturing game were practically nil. But Paley could not resist the challenge. In Goldmark's estimation, his boss "secretly admired Sarnoff's propensity for empire-building, his Horatio Alger adeptness."

At the time, the move might not have seemed as foolhardy as it does today, for, thanks to Goldmark, CBS had already come up with a highly successful technological innovation which completely scuttled a competing RCA system. The field, however, was not broadcasting but recording. In 1938, CBS had acquired none other than Columbia Records, the company that briefly owned the network in 1927. In addition to his color television system, Goldmark devised a long-playing (thirty-three-revolutions-per-minute) record, which rendered the standard RCA Victor seventy-eights obsolete. Paley and company figured they could accomplish the same feat, on an even larger scale, in the field of television-set manufacturing. To begin, they required a factory.

Adrian Murphy, the CBS vice-president responsible for looking after Goldmark, asked the inventor to inspect a Brooklyn-based tube manufacturer, Hytron Radio and Electronics. Goldmark liked what he

---

* Goldmark had in fact first turned to RCA for a job, but, meeting with a rebuff, resorted to his second choice, CBS.

saw—high-quality products and, to sweeten the deal, a set-manufac-
turing subsidiary called Air King Products. Impatient CBS planned to
purchase the facility as a shortcut toward manufacturing its own television sets. Time was short. RCA sets were selling at a phenome-
nal rate. Hurriedly, chairman Paley and president Stanton convinced
themselves that Hytron and Air King would be just what CBS needed
to mount a color campaign equal to RCA's. In June 1951, the company
acquired the manufacturer, which it renamed CBS–Columbia, for
$18,000,000 worth of CBS shares. To deflect attention from his true
motives, Paley at the time declared that the acquisition had nothing to
do with the FCC approval of CBS color. Meanwhile, the owners, two
brothers named Bruce and Lloyd Coffin, were installed in the CBS
board of directors. The entire affair became as solemn as a marriage.
But the marriage never worked: the bride turned out to be much too
costly to maintain.

The Hytron venture stalled within a matter of months. CBS heavily
promoted its sets and color programs, but to no avail. The public was
confused, unwilling to invest in a color set that would receive but a
single network's programming and might become obsolete at any moment. RCA did what it could to torpedo the acceptance of CBS color
by creating publicity aimed at discrediting the system. The company
even gave its executives RCA color sets plus the funds to throw parties at home to show them off to the potential advertisers.

Finally, in 1953, the FCC caught up with the reality of the marketplace, and, swayed by noticeable, though hardly breathtaking, improvements in RCA's color system, reversed its pro-CBS color decision. It approved RCA's color system primarily because it would be
compatible with the millions of RCA sets then in use.

Having succeeded in forcing CBS out of the color market, RCA proceeded at a less frantic pace to refine and introduce its own system.
RCA color sets went on sale in 1954, but with the exception of certain
special programs and sports events, which tended to appear at
Christmastime, when the temptation to purchase a color set presumably peaked, regular color programming did not become a reality for
NBC until 1964.

Without competition, the pace of developments slowed. It was not
until 1968, for example, that color sets outsold black and white, a full
twenty-one years after CBS had first begun to broadcast in color.
The development cost to RCA had run as high as $130,000,000. This
was hardly a triumph, but rather a concealed disaster. The company
ran the risk of going under in the process of bringing color onto the
market. Any more "triumphs" of this sort and RCA would have been
done for.

For its part, CBS lost an estimated $50,000,000 in its television mis-adventure, making it the largest financial disaster in CBS history. By 1961 Paley could no longer put off the inevitable and was forced to sell the now obsolete Hytron Company. Curiously, CBS did not learn from experience. It subsequently undertook other financially disap-pointing acquisitions in publishing, sports, musical instruments, even toys, all of which diluted the corporate commitment to network broadcasting.

Times had changed indeed. Where technological advances had come fast and cheap in the nineteen twenties, refinements in this in-creasingly complex industry now consumed decades and cost dear. Radio was paying for television's sins. Goldmark, at the very center of the struggle, harbored profound doubts about the entire effort. "Sarnoff offered his engineers prizes as high as $10,000 for any break-through in the color field," he wrote. "Some men are said to have suffered nervous breakdowns because of it. I wonder if it was worth it?"

War and Peace at CBS

As THE WAR RAGED toward its conclusion, the CBS-nurtured news and drama enterprises went out in bursts of glory. Though apparently operating in opposed areas—fiction and reality—the two divisions were in fact closely allied. Not only did the members of each mingle under one roof, but they shared a common point of view about American involvement in an overseas war. Playwrights dramatized what reporters later found to be true, and at the war's conclusion they even pooled their talents to produce dramatic-documentary works, otherwise known as propaganda.

After the 1941 Waldorf banquet, Murrow returned to London, where his broadcasts made the sound of war ring loudly in American ears. In 1942, William Paley, now on leave of absence from CBS and acting as a colonel in the U. S. Intelligence Corps, left the network in the hands of Paul Kesten and Ed Klauber (who resigned in 1943 following a heart attack) and followed Murrow to Europe. In London, Paley's appreciation of his young and talented European director continued to grow, for a number of reasons. Paley had always longed to mingle with the powerful outside his own sphere, and Murrow had the contacts and savvy to facilitate an entrée into government circles. But above all, Paley was aware of Murrow's value as a war correspondent.

On December 3, 1943, despite Paley's strong warnings, Murrow went on a predawn bombing mission over Berlin aboard a plane named *D for Dog*. Observing the raid from the air, he gathered material for what is generally considered to be the finest broadcast of his career, as well as the riskiest. His account, transmitted the following afternoon, forcefully conveyed the terror and helplessness of men at war. The absence of specific details about names and places, a security precaution, only served to increase the expressive power of the account:

Jock was wearing woolen gloves with the fingers cut off. I could see his fingernails turn white as he gripped the wheel. And then I was on my knees, flat on the deck, for he had whipped the "Dog" back into a climbing turn. The knees should have been strong enough to support me, but they weren't, and the stomach seemed in some danger of letting me down, too. I picked myself up and looked out again. . . .

The clouds were gone, and the sticks of incendiaries from the preceding waves made the place look like a badly laid out city with the street lights on. . . . As Jock hauled the "Dog" up again, I was thrown to the other side of the cockpit, and there below were more incendiaries, glowing white and then turning red. The cookies—the four-thousand-pound explosives—were bursting below like great sunflowers gone mad.

After *D for Dog* completed its bombing mission, Murrow remained with the crew.

When we went in for interrogation, I looked on the board and saw that the big, slow-smiling Canadian and the red-headed English boy with the two weeks' old moustache hadn't made it. They were missing. There were four reporters on this operation—two of them didn't come back. Two friends of mine—Norman Stockton of Australian Associated Newspapers, and Lowell Bennett, an American representing International News Service [Bennett parachuted and survived]. There is something of a tradition amongst reporters that those who are prevented by circumstances from filing their stories will be covered by their colleagues. This has been my effort to do so.

Murrow concluded the broadcast with a summary of his impressions of the raid:

Berlin was a kind of orchestrated hell, a terrible symphony of light and flame. . . . Men die in the sky while others are roasted alive in their cellars. Berlin last night wasn't a pretty sight. In about thirty-five minutes it was hit with about three times the stuff that ever came down in London in a night-long blitz. This is a calculated, remorseless campaign of destruction. Right now the mechanics are probably working on "D-Dog," getting him ready to fly again.

Reporting for Murrow was not simply a career but a passion, and flying a bombing mission was a logical extension of his method and interests. In London, he had described the reign of terror as bombs fell across the cityscape before his eyes. Now he was in the planes. Where other commentators and reporters labored to tell listeners something they did not know, Murrow strove to make them *feel*. Besides, he liked to hear the sound of his own voice: "I would hear the BBC playing back things I said and nothing has ever made me feel as good as that."

Meanwhile, CBS moved heavily into propaganda activities. Lewis and the rest of the "Columbia Workshop" fraternity underwent a transformation as they became part of the Office of War Information. In this atmosphere, distinctions between news and drama broke down; both were enlisted to serve identical patriotic purposes. In the heat of the moment, the normal considerations of free speech and an independent press did not apply. Corwin and Murrow, whose efforts had run parallel, finally united to create an ambitious series called "An American in England." Corwin wrote and directed; Murrow appeared in the show, which starred Joseph Julian. The large scale production, featuring a sixty-two-piece orchestra performing music composed for the occasion by Benjamin Britten, went out live, as was still the practice, beginning at 4 A.M. London time to reach American shores late the previous evening. All networks cleared their schedules to carry it. The eight programs, scripted in Corwin's breezy style, which mixed high-flown patriotic sentiments with vernacular humor and insight, proclaimed Anglo-American solidarity. Following on the heels of this series, Corwin directed "An American in Russia," based on CBS correspondent Larry LeSueur's experiences in the U.S.S.R.

By the end of 1944, when it appeared that an Allied victory was assured, CBS asked its poet laureate to prepare a celebratory work for the anticipated triumph. Corwin turned from his work in progress, a CBS-commissioned drama hailing the newborn United Nations, to complete his last large-scale piece, "On a Note of Triumph," a sprawling, pugnacious verse oratorio, first broadcast May 8, 1945, and again on May 13. It is entirely possible that no other program has enjoyed the prestige accorded to "On a Note of Triumph." CBS issued the broadcast in a recorded version; Simon and Schuster, in book form. Letters and phone calls of praise poured into CBS. Among the honors showered upon Corwin was the Wendell Willkie One World Award, which enabled him to fly around the world and record his impressions for broadcast.

He took off accompanied by a CBS engineer and a newfangled piece of equipment, a wire recorder. This recording device, crucial to the success of the mission, broke down so frequently that engineer Lee Bland was forced to patch the wire with a burning cigarette. Corwin nonetheless managed to conduct interviews in sixteen countries, and, beginning in January 1947, CBS broadcast a thirteen-part documentary series based on those interviews entitled "One World Flight." The series' theme was simple enough: All men in all nations, whether kings or commoners, are brothers. "One World Flight," incidentally, helped to shatter the network taboo against broadcasting prerecorded material.

Postwar euphoria, as well as Corwin's dream of universal brotherhood, was tragically short-lived. With relations between the U.S.S.R. and the United States rapidly chilling, the networks sensed a new political drift in Washington, and they quickly aligned themselves with it. Commentators known to be left-wing gradually disappeared from the airwaves. They were not fired, exactly, but demoted. When CBS moved Shirer to a less popular time period, he resigned. The shift even affected Corwin, who began to sense pressure from Paley to write more popular, less committed works. When the playwright sought to renew his contract, CBS made a demand he considered impossible to fulfill, namely that the network would receive fully half the earnings generated by the translation of his radio works to other mediums such as books or films. Sensing the inevitable, Corwin resigned, and with him went the driving force behind "The Columbia Workshop." This estimable endeavor never regained its former preeminence as Paley's attention turned to strictly commercial programming and to television.

Similarly, news, with which sustaining programming was closely allied, also withered in the postwar business-as-usual climate. CBS News's most visible symbol, Edward R. Murrow, did not return to broadcasting, where he might stir up trouble, but joined the administration as a vice-president in charge of news. Murrow and other old hands in the news operation lost further ground by resisting the introduction of television. They elected to confine their activities to radio, still considered an intellectual medium. They looked upon television news as an insubstantial picture show, a mere newsreel.

Finally, the social commitment Corwin, Murrow, and others like them called for was suddenly considered dangerously subversive. Their attitudes did not undergo a sinister transformation, but the shifting political climate caused perceptions of it to change.

It was increasingly evident to anyone who cared to listen in that not only network politics but also network programming was undergoing serious changes. At the outset of the war, the networks had managed to sell only a third of all their airtime. By the war's end, that figure reached two thirds and continued to climb. This gratifying increase did not cause the networks to feel still more generous toward sustaining programming, now that they could carry the burden more easily than ever before, but rather less, since every time period was potentially profitable. Sustaining programming was, paradoxically, the stepchild of relative poverty, not affluence. Adding to the commercial trend was the introduction of television, which promised to be a great expense. Networks would have to prove its effectiveness as an advertising medium as they once had with radio. They would now be looking for new comedians or possibly recycling the old ones. They would not be telling Corwin, or anyone else for that matter, to go ahead and write as he pleased because CBS did not care how many people did or did not watch. Finally, with the birth of ABC in 1943, each network faced competition from two networks instead of one. The wartime moratorium on full-blown network competition had come to an end, a casualty of both commercial and political pressures. High-quality programming, once a genuine network commitment, if only for reasons of vanity, now became identified with an earlier era of endurance and self-sacrifice.

When Colonel Paley came marching home, he found that the executive who had been responsible for CBS in his absence, Paul Kesten, was showing signs of strain. In an era when prominent network executives are accorded celebrity status, Kesten, who had ridden to his influential position on the strength of his shrewd promotion of broadcast advertising, was not, even at the time of his retirement in 1946, a particularly well known figure outside the industry. This elegant, quietly eccentric poet of advertising lingo left two important and related legacies. The first was a CBS commitment to developing its own television system, and the other was his chosen successor, the youthful Frank Stanton, Ph.D., a man at least as obsessed with style and image as Kesten. One potential legacy, however, Kesten could not pass on. Before taking his leave, he proposed to Paley that CBS become what it appeared to be on the verge of becoming: an elite, minority-oriented network, one appealing to more sophisticated (and more affluent) audiences. But Paley would have none of it.

Stanton came to the CBS presidency at a time of managerial crisis. Time had thinned the executive ranks. Many of the old guard who had been with CBS at its inception had retired, passed away, or moved on. Even Paley was noticeably absent, embroiled in a personal crisis involving his divorce from Dorothy Hart and remarriage to socialite Barbara ("Babe") Cushing.

Paley's personal troubles created a power vacuum at CBS, one Stanton struggled to fill adequately. There is reason to believe that Paley's view of himself and his role at CBS began to change around this time. Having become chairman of the network at the hardly advanced age of forty-five, he sought to play a caretaker role in the company's affairs rather than plunging directly into the fray. The time for the wholehearted commitment and risks of the Depression and war years was past. Paley's hope was that CBS would somehow learn to run itself. Partly as a result of personal stress, age, and the unrelenting competition, he gradually evolved into a more arrogant boss than he had previously been. Executives in the postwar era found Paley difficult to work for, indecisive, remote, often reversing himself. He gradually shifted from leader to despot. Much of the burden of running CBS on a day-to-day basis fell to others. Needless to say, Paley perennially found fault with their efforts. As the pressure to succeed grew, the pace of departure from the network accelerated to a level unthinkable in the halcyon years of the Depression. One heir apparent to Paley after another appeared and suddenly vanished, exiled from the industry or relegated to peripheral activities. In the process, CBS wreaked more damage on itself than any competitor could have.

This is not to say Paley abdicated all responsibility for the company and went to live happily ever after on his Long Island estate. Veterans of the CBS executive suites are quick, perhaps a little too quick, to point out that the chairman remained active in programming, picking the pilots and the stars, and making impressive appearances at the ritual stockholders' meetings. Yet his semiretirement from the active direction of the company created a slow-moving but ceaseless state of turmoil. Paley displayed a penchant for handing the company reins to an executive he knew little about, allowing him to make the best of the situation, then dispensing with him at a time of the chairman's choosing. The pattern began in earnest with the appointment of the thirty-eight-year-old Ph.D. to the CBS presidency.

Whatever duties Paley cared to assume at CBS, the burden of seeing that it was well run fell on Stanton's shoulders. For twenty-eight years he would be the network's chief operating officer, a kind of magnificent mandarin who functioned as company superintendent, spokesman, and image-maker. As far as the public was concerned, Stanton ran CBS, and would eventually be named Paley's successor. At the height of Stanton's influence, it was common to think of Paley and Stanton as a pair of complementary opposites, "the connoisseur philanthropist and the well-ordered mind," according to one description.

It was true that Stanton's fanatical attention to detail provided a needed asset to the company. Stanton was the technocrat CBS had always lacked, the nuts-and-bolts man raised to a high degree. But the sense of fun and bonhomie prized by Paley was lacking in Stanton, a factor that goes far in explaining the lack of rapport between the two men.

Just seven years younger than his boss, Stanton was not Paley's protégé but rather Kesten's. When the time came to find a successor to Kesten, Stanton was the obvious choice, even though he was basically an unknown quantity. Of Paley's decision to make him president, Stanton recalls, "The day he offered me the job was the second time in my life that I'd ever sat down across the table from him. I didn't know him at all."

Stanton's career at CBS was built on the foundation of research, a passion he had acquired while studying for his doctorate in psychology at Ohio State University. There Stanton became interested in examining why and how people perceive various stimuli. His research culminated in his 1933 Ph.D. thesis, "A Critique of Present Methods and a New Plan for Studying Radio Listening Behavior."

Stanton sent several copies to the management of CBS, who were duly impressed. But it was another study of his that really hit the mark. Entitled "Memory for Advertising Copy Presented Visually vs. Orally," it claimed that people remembered facts they had heard significantly better than those they had read. This was precisely the argument CBS was, at the time, advancing in the hope of luring advertisers away from print media and onto the airwaves. Stanton's study demonstrated what CBS had been saying all along, that broadcast advertising worked better than print, that the spoken voice is more effective than the written word.

Kesten had been engaged in commissioning surveys, the best known of which was Professor Elder's, to prove the point. Now here was this young Ph.D. coming up with precisely the same findings, which Kesten called "good red meat for my grinder." Stanton's research amounted to an uncommissioned survey bearing out CBS's beliefs. As such it was even more valuable than a commissioned project, for it appeared to be more objective, an independent confirmation of the company's line. Kesten fired off a telegram to the young scholar: "I don't know of any other organization where your background and experience would count so heavily in your favor or where your talent would find so enthusiastic a reception." Stanton promptly arrived in New York to accept a fifty-dollar-a-week position in CBS's tiny but crucial research department.

Throughout the nineteen thirties and forties, Stanton continued to apply his passion for research to CBS goals. With Dr. Paul Lazarsfeld of Columbia University, he developed what he thought would be an effective means of determining an audience's response to a program. The result, called the Program Analyzer, turned out to be the original programming-by-the-numbers device. The Analyzer, as distributed to members of a listening audience, consisted of two buttons, red and green. Pushing the green denoted a positive response to the program material, and the red a negative response. Pushing neither button indicated a lack of a definite response. The Analyzer then combined and tabulated the responses. Presumably these impersonal reviews of programs would let producers know just what people really liked to hear. While CBS programs were extensively tested, it cannot be said that the Analyzer had the last word in determining programming. Too many other variables were involved. Programming's inexact, occasionally mystical elements lay beyond the Analyzer's yes-or-no answers, yet its presence did increase producers' sensitivity to separate components within a program: a character, a joke, a sound effect. As a result, the Analyzer raised the level of caution—or inhibition—at the network, for who would wish to risk a red button, even in a good cause?

Stanton's duties at CBS eventually came to involve much more than problematical research. He moved from being third in a three-man research organization to the sales department, the prime "consumer" of the research department's findings, then on to management of the network-owned stations, and ultimately to the presidency of the company. Stanton even dabbled in programming and was responsible for grooming a new breed of radio personality, the supersalesman Arthur Godfrey.

In addition to his purely practical pursuits, Stanton also devoted a great deal of his energies to what had become an obsession around the corridors of CBS: style. Paley had it, so did Kesten, but Stanton raised it to a fine art. Dress, office decor, and attention to countless minor visual details became visible signs of a particular CBS élan. A 1946 description of the flaxen-haired president of CBS noted, "One of his favorite ensembles includes an ecru shirt, a tie of robin's-egg blue with splashes of saffron, and a slate-blue suit with pin stripes," an outfit that made Stanton, in the mind of one CBS vice-president, "the greatest argument we have for color television."

Despite his successes in various fields, Stanton's first five years in the presidency of CBS were marked by a number of serious setbacks. Contending with Sarnoff over the color television issue, he experienced the sometimes overwhelming strength of RCA's vast manufacturing enterprise, and, on more than one occasion, he simply allowed

CBS to be outmaneuvered in the television race. Furthermore, by making exactly the wrong guess as to how the FCC would apportion television frequencies, Stanton was faced with the worrisome prospect of having no more than a single network-owned television station. Such initial reverses stemmed from Stanton's admitted "naïveté." After all, it was a long way from designing audience-measurement machines to contending with both Paley and the awesome Radio Corporation of America. As time went on, Stanton would make or tolerate few outright blunders.

In 1951, after five trying years of fighting a losing battle over color television with RCA, Stanton announced a plan that bore his characteristic imprint: a radical reorganization of CBS. In the process of restructuring the company (a move that had Paley's support), Stanton strengthened his own position and simultaneously removed Paley from the inner workings of the network. All divisions would now report to Stanton, and he to Paley. The only other executive at this all-inclusive level was vice-president Joseph Ream, whose primary function was to purge the network of left-wing influences. The table of reorganization divided CBS into six separate fiefdoms: Research and Development, Television Manufacturing, Electronics Manufacturing, Television Broadcasting, Radio Broadcasting, and Records. The coming of television and CBS's ambition to rival RCA's manufacturing capacity made some subdivision necessary, but the manner in which it was carried out proved rather rigid, even counterproductive. Of the reorganization, Fred Friendly, Edward R. Murrow's protégé and the eventual head of CBS News, wrote, "Until 1951, the company had all the advantages and disadvantages of a small family business; thereafter it had all the advantages and disadvantages of a corporate enterprise."

The acquisition of Hytron, though temporary, opened the way to vast changes in CBS's structure. Never again would the company be exclusively in the broadcasting business. Instead, it would become increasingly subdivided and fragmented, a trend Stanton's reorganization accelerated. In the process, the company lost major assets such as flexibility, informality, and the familiar *esprit de corps*. Though years of ratings success lay ahead, the sense of CBS as a family business in which everyone seemed to know pretty much what everyone else was doing would become little more than nostalgia. As Stanton engineered rigid lines of authority, Paley found himself to be ever more remote from the company he had built in his own image. Suddenly it was a question of who was reporting to whom and deferring to someone on a higher level who would deliver the final, unequivocal maybe.

One CBS figure made distinctly uncomfortable by the new corporate environment was Edward R. Murrow. He resented Stanton's interfering with his prized direct access to Paley. After a short, unhappy period as a corporate vice-president, Murrow decided to return to radio in 1947 with a daily news program sponsored by Campbell Soup. Soon, Murrow would take up the subject of the House Un-American Activities Committee and begin a campaign that would further sour his relationship with Stanton. Ultimately, CBS would not be big enough to hold them both.

Part III

THE LAST FRONTIER

12

Prelude:
Rise of the Programmer

OUR ATTENTION NOW TURNS from those inventors, performers, and entrepreneurs who designed and built the networks to those who simply ran them. But merely running them turned out to be appallingly complex as well. As the technological revolution of the early part of this century came to an end, networks matured and approached the limits of their growth and influence. They were regulated now, and their individual territories pretty well delineated. But as the stakes dwindled, competition among networks became even more intense, and a new kind of network executive, the programmer, assumed crucial importance.

The role of the programmer is deceptively simple. He chooses which programs his network broadcasts and when. Like the practice of warfare, the practice of competitive programming is absurd, wasteful, and of compelling interest. Programmers, like generals, thrive on conflict. They cannot win unless the enemy, a rival network, loses. Typically, they are not pioneers, nor are they fired by an intensely personal conviction. Instead, they are men who ardently seek power and are occasionally strangled by it. In this highly competitive, volatile climate, a programmer's tenure can be breathtakingly short—a year or two or three—but the effect can be felt for a generation. As often as not, they become their own worst enemies.

Television programmers have no direct antecedents in radio, where advertising agencies assumed the burdens of production, except in the privileged areas of news and sustaining broadcasts. This responsibility remained with agencies until the anticipated cost, complexity, and risk of television forced them to yield their programming power to the networks, which had previously served for the most part as common carriers. In gaining this new power, however, the networks lost precious flexibility. Entrusted with programming responsibility, they had to do the thinking for the sponsor, devising programs they hoped a sponsor would want to associate with. Having taken commercial programming under their roof, they would have to be more commercial than ever to survive. Indicative of the new trend was Sarnoff's disbanding of the lauded NBC Symphony Orchestra in 1954 on the grounds that it was an unjustifiable expense. By that time, it was indeed an anachronism, a holdover from Sunday afternoon sustaining radio.

In the area of programming, all networks, however, took their lead from William Paley's postwar emphasis on talent. It was in fact Paley who had put the networks into the programming business back when CBS had unsalable airtime to fill and NBC's vaudevillians held sway over the Red network. Let the General fiddle with color television, Paley knew the play was the thing.

After the color television debacle, CBS tried to make light of the costly struggle by suggesting that it had never been completely serious about taking on the RCA giant. "It was something we did with our left hands," Stanton remarked when the struggle was finished, but that hand had been badly burned. Yet Paley the showman found a way to gain revenge on Sarnoff the technocrat. He would ransack NBC's lineup of stars, then withdraw into the dignified silence befitting a company chairman. Throughout the color war and talent raids, the balance of power appeared to shift wildly between CBS and NBC, each network threatening to smother the other. By the end of the struggle, each network, though altered from the experience, remained very much the same.

For all its worthy sustaining projects, now largely a thing of the past, CBS had never managed to develop an array of stars equal in popularity to the vaudeville-trained comedians who made the Red network (now NBC's sole network) consistently the most popular, if not the most profitable, of all. The biggest CBS radio name to have emerged by the end of the war turned out to be a comedian of a different sort, one who made the likes of "Amos 'n' Andy" seem almost Shakespearean by comparison. His name was Arthur Godfrey, and he was the brainchild not so much of Paley (although the two were close) as he was of Frank Stanton. He could, in fact, be considered the incarnation of Stanton's philosophy of broadcast advertising, because

Godfrey was, above all else, a comedian who could sell, and not only mount a popular program but do the selling himself. To a network, he was a walking, talking gold mine.

Shortly before the outbreak of the war, Stanton had found Godfrey, a former cemetery-lot salesman, banjo picker, cab driver, and sailor, working as an announcer at WJSV (later WTOP), the CBS Washington, D.C., outlet. So taken was he with Godfrey's freshness that he moved the relatively unknown announcer to New York and arranged for him to have a daily early morning program. Godfrey, Stanton felt, had the makings of a first-rate broadcasting salesman, a man with the potential for turning a previously marginal time period into a steady earner. He would be proved correct over and over again, in a variety of time periods, and not only on radio but on television.

But the man whose very voice had bare feet, as Fred Allen observed, was hardly an overnight success in the big city. After a thirteen-week trial period, the sponsor pulled out. "He was a little bit—somebody once said—like learning to drink a martini," Stanton recalls. "The first sip of a martini is bitter sometimes, and then you learn to like them." The audience learned to like Godfrey, whose growing importance to CBS programming paralleled that of Stanton to CBS administration.

While continuing with his morning radio program, Godfrey launched not one but two television programs in the late nineteen forties, on Monday and Wednesday evenings. All Godfrey programs consistently received high ratings, and their combined revenue contributed as much as 12 per cent of CBS's total earnings. By 1948, the network was paying him half a million dollars a year.

The secret of Godfrey's extraordinary pull stymied orthodox radio performers. "The traditional comedians in Hollywood did not understand Godfrey's style," Stanton says. "They were very contemptuous." Jack Benny, for example, told Stanton, "I can't understand what the hold is that this man has on the audience." And Steve Allen has written, perhaps more diplomatically but even more tellingly, "Godfrey doesn't make you think; he *relieves* you of the responsibility." These comedians combined a raft of traditional comedic skills with a highly developed sense of audience rapport. Godfrey, a phenomenon unique to broadcasting, retained just the rapport. That artlessness was the key to his appeal, for he was terribly easy to identify with. When television came to Godfrey, for example, he handled it in characteristic fashion, mopping his brow, complaining of the lights, the heat, all those newfangled things that made him uncomfortable. To Godfrey, the modern miracle of television was just another obstacle that his easygoing manner would surmount. In the postwar era, with the nation's growing fixation on material things, Godfrey furnished just the required tranquilizer, and his very lack of specialization or training enabled him to administer it in large doses.

Spurred by the Godfrey example, Paley now eyed the entire NBC Red lineup. Many of these top-rated comedians had been established as household names ever since 1932. Despite two decades of Depression and war, they continued their pre-eminence as television entered the scene. Rather than build new stars out of unknowns, as CBS had once done with Bing Crosby and Kate Smith, and as it was now doing with Godfrey, Paley preferred to snatch away these well-tried if somewhat tired names. His strategy did not depend on the coming of television for its success. The millions Paley was prepared to invest testified to his belief in the durability of the network radio system. His *modus operandi* reveals much about his formidable powers of negotiation as well as the importance he attached to the swift, bold execution of a plan. Paley was not a patient man.

The groundwork for this scheme had been laid in the late nineteen thirties when Paley lured away the cornerstones of NBC's popularity, Freeman Gosden and Charles Correll. "One day while we were writing," Gosden remembers, "I opened the door and it was Bill Paley." Gosden wondered what the CBS tycoon was doing interrupting his network's arch rivals in the midst of a script-writing session. Paley introduced himself. "I recognize you from your pictures," Gosden said. "Come in. What can we do for you?" Then Paley made his pitch.

"If you are free and can legally do it, regardless of what you are getting now I will give you twice as much."

"That was the beginning of a very beautiful friendship," according to Gosden.

But once Paley had "Amos 'n' Andy," he had to make sure he kept them. Paley settled on a financial scheme which would give such stars as he could lure to his networks higher take-home pay than they currently received and CBS an unassailable hold on their performing names.

Until the postwar era, stars were paid on a conventional salary basis. High as they were—Jack Benny received $12,000 a week—the salaries placed the performers in a punishing tax bracket. To alleviate this lamentable state of affairs, Paley proposed that the stars sell the network their professional names as a property in return for a large lump sum and a salary. Under tax laws then in existence, the performers would be able to keep more than twice as much money as they would have from their straight salaries. And CBS would exert greater control over the stars, protecting them from an NBC counterattack, because it would own the performers' names.

Among the first major performers to try the scheme were Gosden and Correll, already with CBS, who planned to sell the network their performing names, "Amos 'n' Andy," for well over a million dollars each. The success of the deal sparked the drive to acquire other comedians from NBC, but legal snags interfered. Unlike Gosden and Correll, Jack Benny, Edgar Bergen, and the other comedians Paley considered for recruitment performed under their own names, playing characters who were clearly themselves. Of this group, Paley first made overtures to Benny, the kingpin of NBC's Sunday night comedy lineup and well known as the star of radio's single most popular program. Paley assured the comedian that CBS would appreciate him more than NBC ever had. He set about fostering a personal relationship with Benny, one which stood in stark contrast to Benny's relationship with Sarnoff. The General had never even met his network's number one attraction. Not only did Benny agree to switch to CBS, but also he promised to encourage his colleagues to do the same.

But there was still that legal question to clear up. Benny and CBS fought all the way to the Supreme Court for a performer's right to sell his own name as a property. Benny won. CBS paid out $2,600,000 for Benny's company, Amusement Enterprises, and the deal led the way for Bing Crosby (an early CBS star who had defected to ABC), Red Skelton, Edgar Bergen, and Burns and Allen to make the switch, joining Gosden, Correll, and Benny.

Considering that these talent raids came on the eve of the networks' inauguration of regular commercial television programming, there is some question as to how Paley's coup fit into the scheme of things. Since none of the comedians were getting any younger, no one ventured to predict how they would go over with the television audience. The evidence points to Paley's luring them to CBS primarily to boost the radio network to pre-eminence. He was not interested in developing new forms of comedy so much as in reproducing the old Red network's success on CBS. The main anxiety of the moment was whether these precious comedians would succeed on another network. Benny again took the risk of being the first to test the audience's loyalty.

His sponsor, the American Tobacco Company, had come to CBS with him, and they were terribly concerned about staying with radio's number one salesman. To induce the company to stick with Benny, Paley went to the extraordinary length of agreeing to hand over $3,000 a week to American Tobacco for every single rating point that Benny fell below his usual NBC mark. The arrangement demonstrated CBS's good faith. They did not intend simply to buy out a rival and then drive him into obscurity, but were committed to maintaining Benny's popularity. The comedian's highly promoted debut on CBS took place on January 2, 1949, and the industry awaited an answer to the question of whether listeners accustomed to finding their favorite entertainer in the same place at the same time would follow him to another place on the dial. They did. Benny rated substantially higher on CBS than he had on NBC. Here was a resounding triumph for Paley, one that caused shock and consternation at Radio City.

Considering the magnitude of NBC's loss, Sarnoff reacted with surprising indifference. Never quite adjusted to the fact that NBC had become as thoroughly commercial as it had, the General remained remote from his comedians, symbols of that commerciality, and instead chose to lavish his attentions on the development of color television. NBC made a token effort to retain some of its lineup, offering fat deals to Bob Hope and Fred Allen, but in the main the General's indifference bordered on arrogance.

Fortunately for his company, the impending transition from radio to television helped cushion the blow. If television had been delayed for another decade, NBC would have been in very serious trouble, but now all networks had to start from scratch, find or adapt new performers, and capture new audiences. Some tried-and-true performers made more successful transitions than others. Benny, the consummate offstage operator, survived; Fred Allen did not. He would fall victim to a new craze in television programming—the game show.

In sum, Paley's talent raids neither helped CBS as much as they might have nor did they damage NBC beyond repair. In fact, the shortage of comedians allowed a new generation, beginning with Milton Berle and Sid Caesar, to emerge on NBC. Even the cloud created by Paley's talent raids proved to have a silver lining.

As rivals, Sarnoff and Paley continued to complement each other as if by tacit agreement. Where Sarnoff played the role of pioneer, Paley was content to play leapfrog, because he was so good at it.

In 1949, CBS finally succeeded in capturing the ratings lead for the first time, on the strength of the comedians imported from NBC. CBS managed to maintain that lead in radio and, subsequently, television, for the next twenty-five years, long after the comedians who had begun it retired from the airwaves.

Now, at mid-century, as the networks approached their thirtieth year, they were still under the control of the men who had built them. But the world was changing. There were hints that the networks were reaching the limits of growth. As early as 1958, for example, the number of television sets in use reached the saturation point: 48,000,000. Future increases in the size of the market would come only as the population itself increased. From now on, things would be merely good, instead of fantastic. More alarming, new technological developments—the ones that promised to open up new markets—took place beyond the network reach. The FCC did what it could to keep things that way, laying down regulations prohibiting networks from invading new fields, especially cable television.

As a result, the network structures turned their energies from creating new markets to competing against one another within the existing ones. There were no new worlds to conquer, only advertising minutes to sell. The networks retained significant opportunities for innovation in but one sphere, television programming. In the shrinking marketplace, programming relied ever more heavily on formulas, and the quest for success in that arena boosted a new kind of network executive to extraordinary prominence, and that executive was the programmer.

Of all the people who have embarked on that harrowing quest for programming (i.e., ratings) superiority, five stand out: Pat Weaver, Lou Cowan, Robert Kintner, James Aubrey, and Fred Silverman. Taken together, they can be considered Paley's professional descendants. Taken separately, they are about as different as any five men can be.

13

Operation Frontal Lobes

To ONE PROGRAMMER, at least, television was the greatest thing to hit Western civilization since the Gutenberg printing press. This man of boundless optimism was, in all likelihood, the only network executive to have written two (unpublished) books of philosophy or, for that matter, to have invented a substitute for smoking.

The most inventive and resourceful, not to mention the most verbose, of all programmers, his brief career as president of NBC television was marked by monumental ambition. "Let us dare to think and think with daring!" ran a characteristic exhortation to the NBC corps. Sylvester Laflin (Pat) Weaver, Jr., was the kind of man who could not so much as schedule a documentary without attempting to locate it in the intellectual history of the world.

In 1953, when he ascended to the presidency, the management of NBC television was in trouble. Sarnoff's protestations to the contrary, Paley's talent raids had hit the network hard, for NBC was well aware that the presence of stars would be just as crucial to the acceptance of television as it had been to that of radio. In the wake of the talent raids, NBC's president, Niles Trammell, who had made an unsuccessful eleventh-hour bid to retain Benny, stepped down in 1949 after a nine-year reign. Hailing from a Southern background, Trammell was a gentleman of the old school. He was unprepared to contend with the rough-and-tumble atmosphere now swirling about the networks.

Trammell's successor, Joseph McConnell, oversaw a subdivision of the network paralleling Stanton's reorganization of CBS. But Sarnoff remained concerned about how NBC would enter the television era. He knew well the importance of setting precedents. Who among the executive ranks would combine the managerial stringency of a Stanton with show business flair? The General commissioned the management consultants Booz, Allen & Hamilton to study the issue. A decade before, such reliance on an outside agency to settle an internal problem would have been unthinkable, but the television network was too complex, too sensitive, it seemed, for a casual resolution. In light of the study's recommendations, Sarnoff appointed Frank White, a man who, as former president of Columbia Records and the Mutual Broadcasting System, had sound credentials, but lacked the stamina for the job. Toiling in a most difficult position, White succumbed to exhaustion within seven months of taking up the position. After handing in his resignation, he went on to head the Kenyon and Eckhardt advertising agency. Sarnoff then appointed himself interim president.

In the meantime, his son Robert, known throughout 30 Rockefeller Plaza as Bobby, had joined the company and begun moving up the ranks. Bobby had not endured the same harsh struggle for survival that his father once had. He was of a milder, less domineering disposition than the General, faintly supercilious, yet eager to make his own mark on the company. As a student at Harvard, he had not planned to join the RCA hierarchy. After the war and a stint at *Look* magazine, he took a job in NBC's sales department, but not at his father's behest. Rather, he was contacted by the department chief who made it clear that *he*, not the General, was doing the hiring. From there he moved into the infant television programming department, where his specialty became a new NBC children's program entitled "Howdy Doody."

Soon thereafter he moved up to become series coordinator of a respected documentary, "Victory at Sea," which had originated with a college classmate, Henry Salomon, Jr. Narrated by Alexander Scourby, the series featured stirring music composed by Richard Rodgers and served as a forerunner of NBC documentary units. It also marked the only time Bobby Sarnoff would receive a credit for the making of a series. With his father's grudging support, he rose out of this sphere and into the labyrinthine company administration. It became apparent that he would be network president one day, when the General deemed him ready.

Pending that day, Sarnoff appointed Pat Weaver, at the time an NBC vice-president, to the top position. "I knew I was just warming up the seat for Bobby," he subsequently remarked, but the self-deprecation stood in contrast to the grandeur of his aspirations for the new medium. He displayed a knack for combining the most far-fetched ideas with practical, businesslike concerns, or even disguising these practical concerns as revolutionary concepts. He was a great salesman, presenting a facade of eternal optimism about the wonders television would bestow upon society. "Here in full color is the art of all mankind," he wrote in 1955, not forgetting to plug RCA's chief technical concern of the moment, color television. "To tell you what an informed, intelligent citizen can find in broadcasting," he claimed, "calls not for a speech but for a rhapsody." This was, for Weaver, a relatively understated and straightforward assessment. A decade before McLuhan, Weaver perceived and proselytized on behalf of the transforming effect of television on society. He took to saying things like, "Our telementaries [a Weaverism for programs] would range in subject matter from explanations-in-depth of current events to historical surveys. The whole march of mankind would be converted to telementaries with an impact and sweep such as we've never seen, and it would have an effect that would be almost traumatic on people."

Though he invoked some of the language of the by now discarded service concept of network broadcasting, he was, in fact, first and foremost a creature of advertising culture. He knew television could sell as nothing before ever had. His so-called revolutionary pronouncements were not the credo of a visionary, but reams of inspired, inflated advertising copy promoting the new medium. His brainstorming about telementaries camouflaged shrewd advertising and programming strategies. After he left the network, the boasts quickly died down, but his innovations in the art of integrating advertising and network broadcasting remain influential to this day. He was, in short, a combination of philosopher manqué and supersalesman.

Weaver's early career explains to some extent this apparent contradiction. The son of an advertising executive, he was graduated from Dartmouth and took a year-long fling as a writer in Paris. In 1932, he went to work for KHJ in Los Angeles, writing, producing, directing, and even acting in local programs. His older brother was the comedian Doodles Weaver. One of Pat's earliest efforts was a humor program known as "The Merrymakers." Later he moved to KFRC in San Francisco, then came to New York, where he wrote for and produced an NBC variety program called "Evening in Paris." Since advertising agencies produced most programming, he left the network for Young & Rubicam, the advertising agency producing Fred Allen's "Town Hall Tonight." By 1937, at the age of twenty-nine, he was supervising all the agency's radio programs.

The following year, the American Tobacco Company, a mainstay of

broadcast advertising, hired the young man away from Young & Rubicam and made him advertising manager. This was a position that had
more to do with broadcasting than advertising. In it, the ebullient
Weaver struck up a rapport with the company's president, George
Washington Hill, the notorious and, to some, demonic figure who had
been responsible for promoting those endlessly repeated Lucky Strike
slogans such as L.S.—M.F.T. To Hill, advertising was propaganda,
pure and simple. In this milieu, Weaver learned to view programming
as an adjunct of advertising, a commodity largely subservient to the
advertiser's needs. Weaver would later take this knowledge with him
to NBC and use it as the basis for his television programming innovations.

Hill died in 1946, and as a result, Weaver did not receive the promotion he had been expecting to company vice-president. Not only
did he leave his job, but he quit smoking his customary four packs of
cigarettes a day. To take their place, he invented what he called a
new "pleasure product"—an inhalator that offered the user a choice
of essences to inhale. To this activity he gave the ghastly name
"smacking."

Weaver passed through Young & Rubicam once more and then, in
1949, returned to his first love, broadcasting, as the NBC vice-
president in charge of television programming. At last he found himself in the right position at the right time. Circumstances conspired to
push him into the limelight. The sudden dearth of comedic talent,
thanks to Paley's raids, threw responsibility for developing new performers and programmers into his lap, and he welcomed it. And when
previous candidates for network leadership fell by the wayside,
Weaver became the obvious choice. In February 1953, at the age of
forty-four, he was appointed president of the television network.

It was a tumultuous year. All networks frantically groped toward
some stable formulation of network programming. Weaver, as it happened, turned out to be a man of as many words as the inveterate speechmaker David Sarnoff, but where Sarnoff was sedentary,
Weaver often balanced on a Bongo Board as he dictated. In prolix
memoranda which eventually filled forty bound volumes Weaver developed NBC's programming strategy. At the time he came to power,
the networks considered that the future of television programming lay
in live production emanating from New York. Film was still a rarity,
more often used for news and documentary programs. The Hollywood
establishment, seeing in television a dire threat, at this stage refused
to co-operate with the broadcasters. Yet live production in New York
posed serious problems. Television required far more technical support and more elaborate studios than radio. NBC's facilities at Radio

City, for instance, had been designed in the late nineteen twenties, with no thought of television; they were small, hot, obsolete. Building new television studios in Manhattan skyscrapers would prove costly and cumbersome.

As its solution to the problem, CBS enlisted the services of California-based architect William Pereira to design a self-enclosed production facility. By 1953, CBS had a shiny new Television City in operation on a lot adjacent to the Farmer's Market in Los Angeles. In addition, the network had already seized the initiative in television programming with its roster of shows broadcast from New York. These included "Arthur Godfrey's Talent Scouts" and a new Sunday night variety show emceed by *Daily News* columnist Ed Sullivan.* As a result of this activity, some NBC affiliates threatened to desert the network in favor of CBS's stronger lineup, which would attract larger audiences and enable the stations to charge higher advertising rates for their local commercials, or spots.

As Weaver analyzed NBC's problem, "the programming just had no direction. Programs landed next to each other by mere chance, with each agency building its show in a way that was aimed at nothing more than keeping its client happy." To make the NBC schedule coherent, Weaver took a leaf from Paley's book and began to devise network-originated programming which various sponsors would share. The idea was that the network could spend a great deal more money and try much more risky ideas than any single advertiser-producer would.

As a first step, Weaver scheduled comedy at 7 P.M., when he figured children were watching, and drama at 9 P.M., when, presumably, the adults took over control of the dial. Weaver had ample precedent for the decision to schedule as much comedy as he did. The Red network had achieved its popularity on the strength of Benny, Cantor, et al., and the pattern now appeared to repeat itself on television. As early as 1948, Milton Berle, appearing in the hour-long "Texaco Star Theatre" on Tuesday nights captured fully two thirds of the viewing audience with his frantic, hammy, intermittently hilarious sketches. To many viewers, Milton was the first taste of television, as Gosden and Correll had been of radio a generation before. But Berle's program had been based on the radio model of sponsor control, as evidenced by the show's title. Weaver's network-originated comedy programs included "The All Star Revue," "The Comedy Hour," and "The Saturday Night Revue," one component of which was "Your Show of

* The premiere of Sullivan's "Toast of the Town" presented the practically unknown comedy team of Dean Martin and Jerry Lewis.

Shows," featuring Sid Caesar and Imogene Coca. The Weaver strategy worked; Caesar and Coca were so popular that audiences began to resist going out to the movies on Saturday nights in favor of staying home to watch the mirthful parodies of popular films.

Weaver also explored ways of presenting higher-quality programming on television, to expand broadcasting's definition of culture beyond symphonic music and Shakespeare. Behind this strategy lay an appealing, elaborate, pretentious mixture of acute perception and absolute balderdash. "I believe," ran one of his pronouncements, "the great trend of mass media, certainly of broadcasting, has been upward, as against those who think that mass man has been ruining class man." To bring more class to the mass, Weaver launched something called Operation Frontal Lobes, a catch-all description for news and other documentaries, and something called Operation Wisdom, a series of filmed interviews with notable figures such as Wanda Landowska and Bertrand Russell. Neither of these concepts changed the course of history or television programming, but they gave Weaver ample opportunity to display his salesmanship, his talent for hyping a product. NBC was not presenting an interview or a documentary. No, Ed Murrow at CBS would do that. NBC was presenting nothing less than a revolution in mass media. Behind Weaver's airy claims were savvy decisions about what kind of programming NBC should present for maximum commercial advantage. Nonetheless, he remained entirely sincere about his theory of programming, as if he needed to inspire himself with the dream of crossing an ocean to justify getting his feet wet.

Operations Wisdom and Frontal Lobes did not long survive. Educational and minority-oriented in nature, they went against the grain of network television, which preserved few oases for the high-prestige, low-audience program. In contrast, two other Weaver innovations were so eminently commercial, that is to say advertising-oriented, that they have lasted twenty-five years without showing any signs of flagging. Both drew strength from the immediacy of live television, but survived virtually intact into the film and videotape eras.

The first was the spectacular, these days called the special, a one-time-only event, usually of a lengthy, expensive, and highly popular nature. Pre-empting regularly scheduled programming in favor of one-time-only events was nothing new to an industry that had presented several thousand hours of coverage of World War II, not to mention political conventions. In fact, NBC's 1926 debut program could be classified as a spectacular.

The Weaver version of a spectacular was a direct outgrowth of the newfound network control over programming. In the past, one-time-only pre-emptions involved clumsy rebates to the advertising agencies which produced the programs, but now, with the networks themselves in control, the matter was simplified. It was easy for a programmer to exercise his prerogative to pre-empt an entire evening's programming and in the process gain an even larger than usual audience. Weaver's most successful spectacular became an NBC perennial. A musical adaptation of J. M. Barrie's *Peter Pan* starring Mary Martin attracted one of the largest audiences of the era, over 60,000,000 viewers. Weaver hardly invented the spectacular; he simply sold it very effectively as a programming strategy to attract the attention of both audiences and advertisers to NBC. Because ratings for spectaculars were unpredictable, their sponsors were forced to abandon the strict cost-per-thousands-of-homes-reached formula on which rates were traditionally based. The network tried to convince sponsors that what they might be losing in audience they were gaining in prestige and identification with a spectacular.

Weaver's other lasting innovation, the magazine-format program, was also geared toward strengthening the network's hold on sponsors. As the name suggests, the magazine format took its cue from the multiple sponsorship in print media. No single advertiser sponsored the program or, as a result, could exert control over its content. The network sold the advertising minutes to a variety of sponsors, the way a magazine sells space in the same issue to numerous advertisers. The end result was a neat program formula combining maximum network control over programming with total subservience to advertisers' aggregate desires. In addition, the magazine-format programs recruited many new advertisers, for the programs ran outside of high-priced prime time. For a relatively small financial risk, then, a company could test the waters of network advertising by buying a few minutes here and there on a magazine-format program; no need to spend $30,000 on a half-hour show week after week, hire talent, fight with musicians over fees, or cope with all the other headaches of mounting a program. NBC would be glad to do it all for the sponsor attracted to, but still wary of, television.

Under Weaver's supervision, NBC launched three magazine-format programs. The first, "Today," made its debut on January 14, 1952. The program's star, Dave Garroway, was a former radio talk show host out of Chicago with a gift for disarming gab. Mixing harmless chatter, weather, news, and magazine-type features, the early morning program hit its stride with the appearance of a chimpanzee, J. Fred Muggs. The formula, borrowing heavily from techniques Arthur Godfrey had introduced several years earlier on CBS, proved eminently successful, at least from a commercial point of view. In 1954, NBC's single most profitable program was "Today." Only slightly less successful was its late night entry, "Tonight," which relied on traditional NBC comedy as its focus. "Tonight" began on July 27, 1953, with Steve Allen as its host. Eventually he was succeeded by Jack Paar and later Johnny Carson, all of whom lent a chatty show business gloss to the program. The sole clinker was NBC's midday magazine-format program, "Home," which lasted from 1954 to 1957. The program faced heavy competition from soap operas and was further hampered by appearing on the air at a time when many potential viewers were nowhere near a television set.

Taken together, the magazine-format programs demonstrated the disproportionate influence advertisers wielded over the networks, despite network control of programming. In practice, the networks, in their drive to sell every available advertising minute at the highest possible price, proved to be even less adventurous than the sponsors had in the days when they controlled programs. The new system had a leveling influence, eliminating distinctive approaches to programming in favor of bland, sure-fire concepts designed to offend no sponsor. Advertisers, in short, had proven to be more responsible and innovative as programmers than the networks. Network-originated programming now was set on a course to become ever more rigid and standardized, enslaved to ratings. Visions of revolutionary telementaries aside, then, the magazine-format programs turned out to be a formula designed first and last to accommodate advertising. At its worst the format amounted to little more than commercials in search of a program.

Yet the three years Weaver presided over NBC proved to be the best of times as well as the worst. While McCarthy threatened to wreck the entertainment industry, certain segments of broadcasting developed innovative programming which accorded with the live, anything-goes spirit of television that Weaver professed to espouse. Television was still not a national phenomenon equal to radio, not yet. Many smaller communities lacked complete television service. Since sets were expensive at a time when the economy was recovering from the effects of war, television first tended to fall in the hands of urban, upper-middle-class audiences. Programmers were not so acutely aware of what they considered to be the unsophisticated tastes of the rural audience.

Furthermore, the television networks were not yet full blown. Linkups were proving to be hideously expensive. Bell Labs had developed a coaxial cable capable of transmitting the complex television signal over long distances, but cost restricted its use to connections between New York, Philadelphia, and Miami. A linkup with the West

Coast, allowing simultaneous transmission across the nation, would have to wait until 1951, when Bell Labs perfected an alternate system of land-based transmission, microwave repeaters. Technically, this system employed the radio transmission method which AT&T had always shunned, since it could not control its use, but microwaves were different. Highly directional, they were, in practice, as easy to control as wire transmission. The much-lauded coaxial cable, then, existed more as a creature of publicity than of reality. In practice, it was soon supplanted by the microwave repeaters, still in AT&T's iron grip. Thus another change only brought more of the same.

In the charmed interval before the television networks became truly national, then, a flurry of dramatic anthology programs of unusually high quality flourished and then died. As exceptions, they eventually proved some hard and fast rules about the nature of commercial network broadcasting. CBS presented "Playhouse 90" and "The U.S. Steel Hour." NBC had on its roster "Kraft Television Theater," "Studio One," "General Electric Theater," "Du Pont Show of the Month," and "Goodyear Television Playhouse," which in March 1953 presented Rod Steiger starring in Paddy Chayefsky's drama of a butcher, his mother, and his desire to break loose and get married: *Marty*. While many of the dramas were adaptations of classic American fiction by the likes of Fitzgerald, Faulkner, and Wharton, many of the original works, reflecting the tastes of the shows' makers and audiences, concentrated on projecting a certain urban pathos characteristic of a post-war society. One CBS discovery, Rod Serling, portrayed in *Requiem for a Heavyweight* the desperate lot of a washed-up prizefighter, played by Jack Palance, whose own manager bets against him. The shows were live, of course, and open to moments of both spontaneity and heart-stopping blunders: lines forgotten, cues missed, all under the scrutiny of 30,000,000 viewers. Preservation of the dramatic anthologies was haphazard. Sponsors often made filmed records called kinescopes (not to be confused with the television picture tube Zworykin invented), which were filmed records of the slightly blurry, low-contrast screen image. Videotape would not be commercially introduced until Ampex brought out its first model in 1956.

Unlike the radio dramatic anthologies, CBS's "Mercury Theatre on the Air," for example, the television dramatic anthologies were not presented on a sustaining basis and so were forced to compete for audiences on the same terms as Ed Sullivan, Arthur Godfrey, or Lucille Ball. Though hoping to benefit from the prestige of associating with a high-toned dramatic anthology, advertisers grew increasingly nervous about some of the messages the young, untried, and ambitious playwrights were sending to the American public.

A classic confrontation occurred over Reginald Rose's drama *Thunder on Sycamore Street*. The author of *Twelve Angry Men* wished to delve into the traumatic effects of a black family's moving into a white suburban neighborhood. However, the network, CBS, and the sponsor objected to the play's use of a black family. Southern affiliates would never stand for a sympathetic treatment of a black hero. It was said that some Southern stations even refused to show black faces on local screens. Rose considered their objections and came up with a new plan. He decided to enlarge the theme. Viewers would not know why the neighborhood wished to reject the stranger. Throughout the play, suspicions loomed. To what ethnic group *did* he belong? At the end, it was revealed that he was an ex-convict. By then, Rose had made his point. The sponsor, Westinghouse, found, to its dismay, that it had presented a controversial drama after all.

The extreme caution went beyond social prejudice and revealed disturbing truths about sponsored television. "Most advertisers were selling magic," wrote the media historian Erik Barnouw in a bitter, persuasive analysis of the situation. Commercials presented straightforward answers to simple problems. In contrast, the playwrights "were forever suggesting that a problem might stem from childhood and be involved with feelings toward a mother or father." In this context, the commercials simply appeared "fraudulent." By seeking sponsorship for the dramatic anthologies, the networks had attempted to mix oil and water. Sponsorship had worked well in certain kinds of programming because comedians such as Jack Benny had labored to integrate material and message to the satisfaction of both parties. Off limits to advertising, the sustaining program was free to roam, to take stands, to express personal opinions and feelings which did not have a place in a comedy-variety show. Still grappling with their new-found power over programming, networks were discovering they could not successfully combine personal vision with the hard sell; one negated the other. With its visual component, television aggravated the division, for it portrayed pathos and grit with more realism than radio had ever been capable of. As fantasy became harder to suggest, the disparity between commercial and program was especially jarring in the dramatic anthologies. In any case the competition was too intense, the costs were too high to sustain the luxury. In the end, either the commercials or the anthologies would have to go.

Yet another important series which fell uncomfortably between the commercial and sustaining sectors was "Omnibus," an enthralling anthology of cultural and intellectual activity that brought unaccustomed reach and depth to network broadcasting. Though not the handiwork of Pat Weaver, but rather of producer Robert Saudek,

"Omnibus" amounted to a regularly scheduled spectacular whose only
constant was the televising of activities broadcasting had hitherto neglected to consider. Watching the series on Sunday afternoons became
an experience akin to attending highly engaging, anecdotal lectures
given by a popular college professor. Education and entertainment,
fascination and concentration, stimulation and guesswork all happily
coexisted in a ninety-minute format.

The program's unorthodox ambitions were rooted in its unique origins, which hinted at the first stirrings of an organized response to the
networks' abandonment of public-service programming. The program
began not with one of the established networks, but with the Radio
and Television Workshop of the Ford Foundation, which had undertaken to create the high-quality, minority-oriented programming that
the networks in their competitive frenzy found to be expendable. The
Foundation then contrived to find willing sponsors and a network for
such a program. The scheme turned out to be a precursor of the Foundation's even more ambitious plan to organize an entirely new national network devoted solely to the concept of public service. But the
bold stroke of creating the Public Broadcasting System still lay fifteen
years in the future.

Producer Robert Saudek, who had previously been ABC's vice-
president for public affairs, approached the series as would a magazine editor of discriminating taste. He found ways to squeeze excerpts
of various artistic forms—dance, music, drama—onto the small black-
and-white screen with a minimum of frills. The selection of features
reflected the aspirations of those who, as H. G. Wells once had, approached broadcasting with high hopes and went away bitterly disappointed. CBS scheduled the series in a low cost time period, Sunday
afternoons. There the series, narrated by BBC correspondent Alistair
Cooke, made its debut on November 9, 1952, and in time began attracting surprisingly loyal audiences.

Viewers watched an unorthodox parade of able and interesting individuals displaying their wares or experimenting with new ideas. On
Sunday, March 5, 1956, for example, "Omnibus" presented an interview with the humorist James Thurber at his Connecticut home, and
later in the program Joseph Welch, the Boston attorney who had succeeded in unmasking McCarthy during the Army-McCarthy hearings,
interpreted the United States Constitution. In other programs, Leonard Bernstein explored jazz, William Saroyan presented plays, Orson
Welles starred in a production of King Lear, staged by Peter Brook.
"Omnibus" took its cameras to the editorial offices of the New York
Times, and to Harvard, where the junior senator from Massachusetts,
John F. Kennedy, spoke to the viewers.

Since the series flourished at the peak of the McCarthy scare, its apparently nonpolitical contents were in fact occasionally considered controversial. While "Omnibus" was thought to be exempt from blacklisting (along with CBS News), Saudek often had to contend with pressure aimed at keeping such blacklisted performers as Welles and Bernstein off the air. The "Omnibus" three-part presentation of the Constitution by Joseph Welch, for example, could be construed as a muted political statement or affirmation.

"Omnibus" appeared as a weekly series for five seasons at a total cost of approximately $8,500,000, of which advertising revenue offset about $5,500,000. Though the program is closely identified with its first landlord, CBS, it ran for one season on ABC and finally three on NBC before making its last appearance in April 1961. The program spawned no real successors, at least not on the commercial networks, much as it was admired by the industry.

The lack of worthy successors to the enlightened programming of the early and mid-nineteen fifties was apparent in many prominent programming genres, not just the high-flown areas of cultural, dramatic, and news programs. Even commercials broke new ground in the early years of television. Their producers discovered clever uses for a variety of animation techniques, both live action and illustrated. Packages of Old Golds danced in geometric patterns, the animated figure of Speedy Alka-Seltzer promised fast relief, animated gremlins representing Ajax the foaming cleanser scoured an actual bathtub. Some commercials were live, and their length, typically a minute, permitted the salesmen and -women to become well known in their own right. Betty Furness gained notoriety demonstrating Westinghouse freezers during breaks in "Playhouse 90" dramas. Children's programming, in contrast, displayed mixed results. "Romper Room," "Ding Dong School," and "Howdy Doody" attempted to mix education and amusement, with noticeably bland results. Only NBC's "Kukla, Fran, and Ollie" managed to connect directly with a child's imagination through the varied personalities of its puppets. This program, one of the first to be broadcast in color, originated at Chicago's WGN. It would be years until another children's program, "Sesame Street," rediscovered the magic of puppetry.

If all these varied genres of programming, ranging from the ridiculous to the sublime, had anything in common in this era, it would have to be a fascination with the new medium of television and a delight in the discovery of its possibilities. Though it was visual, television still maintained strong resemblances to radio in that it was still largely live and open to almost any kind of programming. Not the least consideration was the importance of filling up time, building a full schedule for the networks to present to their affiliates each day of the week. Some efforts were amateurish and smacked of desperation, and at least one comedian took the resulting chaos as his creative license.

His name was Ernie Kovacs, and he was as much a product of this era of experimentation and fascination with the medium as were "Today" or "Omnibus." As a former columnist and disc jockey, Kovacs' roots did not go back to the vaudeville traditions of most other broadcasting comedians. As a result, he was not desperately committed to pleasing audiences by generating a certain number of surefire laughs per minute. Rather, his comedy sprang from the technology and idiosyncrasies of the broadcasting studio. On camera, his characteristic pose was in a control room, surrounded by monitors, and not on a stage like Burns and Allen or Milton Berle. Kovacs did not crack jokes so much as stage elaborate, often surreal scenarios whose humor, if there was any, came only after a good deal of thought and appreciation on the part of the viewer. Kovacs delighted in playing tricks, manipulating the medium. On one occasion, he started his program at the end of a sketch. The viewer saw dogs leaving the stage, people saying good-bye. Apparently an animal contest was coming to an end. Kovacs never bothered to explain. Fascinated with the dancing abstract patterns of a sound track, he displayed it on screen along with the music. His favorite composer, incidentally, was Béla Bartók, whose music inspired and often accompanied miniature mime dramas devised by Kovacs. Whether setting a bathtub full of water on fire or parodying panel shows, Kovacs' humor was visual, and it was about television. For this reason, his humor exerts a strong fascination for those young enough to have grown up imbued with television's conventions and absurdities, of which Kovacs displayed a preternatural grasp. His work, however, was not of a piece. Confused, uneven, it reflected the driven man who created it.

Born in New Jersey in 1919, Kovacs broke into television in 1950. He had made up his mind to be a sports announcer, but Philadelphia station WPTZ hired him to narrate a cooking show. The following year, he came to New York, where "The Ernie Kovacs Show" began as a summer replacement for "Kukla, Fran, and Ollie" on NBC. In this era of programming turmoil, Kovacs quickly found vacancies on the air to call his own. He had two CBS programs, "Kovacs Unlimited," which ran in the daytime from 1952 to 1954, and yet another "Ernie Kovacs Show" in 1953. Everything was live, of course, exacting a terrible toll on Kovacs, whose fund of invention raced to keep up with the daily demands of the medium. Through it all he attracted considerable attention, which reached a peak in 1957, when he presented a half-hour color special on NBC in which not a single word was spoken. In one compelling stunt, water he poured from a jar appeared to flow out at an oblique angle. In reality, the stage on which he worked was tilted.

By the end of the decade, Kovacs' brand of anarchy had fallen out of fashion on the two predominant networks, which were committed to ever more standardized programming, but he continued his career on ABC with a series of videotaped black-and-white comedy programs in which he presented gags perfected over the years. When he died in a car accident in January 1962, he was still in the process of mastering his wild comic gift.

Though this brief flowering of imaginative, if self-conscious, television programming died a lingering death through the second half of the decade, the unequivocal sign that it was not to last came as early as December 1955, when the General replaced Pat Weaver with his son Bobby, who he had decided was at last ready to run the television network. Like other volatile influences, Weaver did not fit snugly into Sarnoff's well-ordered universe. The influx of filmed series from Hollywood appealed to him as the safest path to lucrative programming, rather than the Weaver-inspired live New York production extravaganzas. Weaver did not vanish all at once, however. While Bobby was appointed network president, Weaver became chairman, though the General continued to reign supreme over the entire RCA empire from patents to programming. When Weaver finally left the network, he joined a new subindustry, cable television, which at the time threatened to cause the networks nothing more than a bit of static.

After Weaver ceased programming NBC's television network, the feverish creation of programs in New York wound down. All networks were looking for specialists in the filmed series emanating from Hollywood studios, old and new. ABC, the unhealthily lean and hungry newcomer, had taken a sudden lead in the field and spread the influence of filmed series far and wide by supplying highly influential programmers to both of the other networks. Robert Kintner departed ABC amid a bitter dispute to assist Bobby Sarnoff in running NBC. James Aubrey left for CBS, where he was instantly considered Paley's heir. The optimistic theorizing of the New York impresario gave way to the sharp decision-making of executives who emphatically did not take to writing philosophy in their spare time.

Quiz Kids

IF PAT WEAVER WAS AN ADVERTISING EXECUTIVE who occasionally masqueraded as a philosopher, then Louis Cowan, the CBS television president from 1958 to 1959, could be compared to a professor moonlighting as a riverboat gambler.

Wealthy, educated, progressive, maintaining a host of philanthropic and educational concerns, he nonetheless came to be known for—and ultimately was undone by—his Midas touch in creating outlandishly popular game shows. In another era, Cowan could have reaped the rewards—largely financial—of this ability, and gone quietly about his business. But in the McCarthy era, the game show came to assume an importance completely out of proportion with its aims. To the networks, game shows offered just the panacea, the materialistic catharsis, that their schedules needed in the midst of political turmoil. In the end, this seemingly innocuous genre would contribute to the demise of the most respected figure in broadcasting, Edward R. Murrow. Cowan would have been horrified.

In the radio era, the quiz program had been a respectable enough component of programming. It was, so to speak, broadcasting's equivalent to the parlor game. In 1938, for example, NBC's Blue (educational) network began carrying a quiz show called "Information Please." Here a panel of "experts" answered questions posed by the audience. The stakes were low: two dollars for each question asked,

Dr. Vladimir Zworykin holding his iconoscope, the television pickup system he developed in the nineteen twenties for David Sarnoff. *Courtesy RCA.*

Another television pioneer, Peter Goldmark, displays the color system he developed for CBS. *Courtesy CBS.*

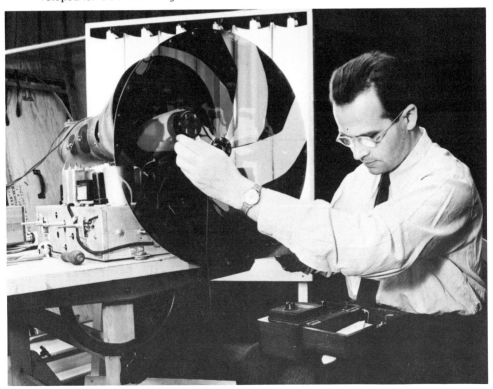

SEE IT NOW: Edward R. Murrow, Fred Friendly, and Carl Sandburg. The poet appeared on the program on October 5, 1954. *Courtesy CBS.*

Ernie Kovacs in "Kovacs Unlimited," in 1953. *Courtesy CBS.*

Lee J. Cobb, E. G. Marshall, and Jack Klugman appeared in the film version of Reginald Rose's 1954 television drama, *Twelve Angry Men. Courtesy Museum of Modern Art/Film Stills Archives.*

Keenan Wynn, Jack Palance, and Ed Wynn in Rod Serling's "Playhouse 90" drama, *Requiem for a Heavyweight*, 1956. *Courtesy CBS.*

BREAKING THE TABOOS: "All in the Family" probed the roots of national prejudice and family unity. *Courtesy CBS.*

RED AND GREEN BUTTONS: An enlarged version of Dr. Frank Stanton's Program Analyzer, called Big Annie, in use at CBS studios in New York. *Courtesy CBS*.

THE CORPORATE IMAGE: CBS headquarters at 51 West Fifty-second Street in New York City, better known as Black Rock. *Courtesy CBS*.

CBS president Dr. Frank Stanton and the chairman of the board, William S. Paley, in 1960. *Courtesy CBS*.

five if it stumped the panel. Under the deft guidance of moderator Clifton Fadiman, the program centered not so much on the questions as on the personalities of experts such as New York *Times* sports columnist John Kieran and humorist Oscar Levant. Puns and sophisticated chitchat were the order of the day. The appeal of "Quiz Kids," another game show, lay in the novelty of the "experts" being precocious children. They received compensation in the form of $100 U. S. Savings Bonds. It was all good, clean fun.

Lou Cowan had developed "Quiz Kids," and at the time it was just one facet of a varied, promising career in broadcasting. Born in Chicago of a wealthy family, he graduated with a bachelor of philosophy degree from the University of Chicago, and, rather than entering one of the standard professions, began his professional life as a press agent, then moved to radio, at WGN, which had served as a seedbed of so many influential network forces from "Amos 'n' Andy" to Fred Silverman. He married Pauline Spiegel, whose father had begun a well-known mail-order company. In addition to his academic leanings, Cowan early on manifested a knack for dreaming up successful quiz show formulas, but they were only the most lucrative among the other sustaining, public information programs he produced. Yet on the strength of his knack he would find himself boosted to the presidency of CBS and subsequently tied to the largest and most public scandal to afflict the industry.

After World War II, Cowan launched a new quiz show on radio, "Stop the Music." The idea was simplicity itself. The emcee played a snatch of a tune. The first phone caller to correctly identify it could win a vacation, a television set, a refrigerator. A program like this would have been unthinkable during the Depression, but the new emphasis on large material rewards caught the postwar public's obsession with acquiring the trappings of peacetime prosperity. Furthermore, Cowan's formula marked an innovation in commercial radio's constant search for ways to intertwine program content and products. Here, products, provided by the manufacturers for free in return for a mention of their name, became an integral part, indeed, the point of the program. "Stop the Music" had its premiere in January 1948 on ABC. A year later, its competition on NBC, Fred Allen, perhaps the most respected of all radio comedians, suffered from a catastrophic drop in his ratings, which slid from 28.7 to 11.2. Meanwhile, "Stop the Music" jumped to 20.0 and began spawning imitations. Driven off the air, Allen never succeeded in making a successful transition to television.

But radio, of course, was on the way out. Cowan next began developing a quiz show for television. As a starting point, he pondered the stakes offered by the radio quiz show "Take It or Leave It." The program's $64 question had become a part of the language. For television, Cowan decided to multiply the stakes a thousandfold and make the compensation prize nothing less than a Cadillac. He also decided the staging would be extravagant, intense, dramatic, featuring an isolation booth in which contestants would endure agonizing mental workouts behind soundproof glass.

Cowan approached Charles Revson, president of Revlon, about sponsoring the program, and Revson agreed. CBS then made a fateful decision: it scheduled "The $64,000 Question" Tuesday nights at 10 P.M., immediately preceding "See It Now," the television forum in which Edward R. Murrow had been laboring to rescue CBS from anti-Communist hysteria. The irony behind the juxtaposition of "The $64,000 Question" and "See It Now" was that a relatively innocuous quiz show would eventually silence broadcasting's strongest anti-McCarthy voice.

At the time, CBS found itself to be the victim of two kinds of anti-Communist pressure. The first emanated from Washington, D.C., where in 1947 the House Un-American Affairs Committee instigated an investigation of the film industry. Meanwhile, Senator Joseph McCarthy waged his erratic campaign against what he thought was the Communist infiltration of the government. The second kind of pressure, even more potent and uncontrollable, came from self-appointed vigilantes. Preying on the networks' fear of investigation, they offered to assist in flushing Communists from their concealed lairs in the network hierarchy.

Take, for example, the case of Theodore Kirkpatrick, John Keenan, and Kenneth Bierly. These ex-FBI men started a weekly publication called *Counterattack: The Newsletter of Facts on Communism.* Working out of an office at 240 Madison Avenue, the staff of *Counterattack* solicited jobs investigating "questionable" individuals. The idea was that any organization which submitted to their scrutiny could then rest easy. *Counterattack* spread additional fear by adopting a stance that those who were not with it must be against it. To criticize or even balk at a *Counterattack* slur could be construed, in this scheme of things, as an admission of Communist sympathy. In time, major companies such as General Motors and Du Pont submitted to investigations, and CBS, now haunted by the ghosts of its departed left-wing sustaining programming, went along as well. The network made no secret of its self-investigation, for it wished to make a clean breast, in public.

In 1950, *Counterattack,* tightened the screws of fear by publishing a compilation of citations against alleged Communists in broadcasting. The pamphlet, entitled *Red Channels: The Report of Communist*

Influence in Radio and Television, displayed on its cover a macabre illustration of a red hand about to grasp a precariously tilting microphone. Within, an introduction railed against the day that "the Communist party will assume control of this nation as the result of a final upheaval and civil war."

The bulk of *Red Channels* consisted of a list of the supposedly Communist affiliations of 151 artists associated with the broadcasting and film industries. These were not unknown network functionaries but rather highly visible performers and writers, many of whom were prominently associated with CBS. The list included Leonard Bernstein, Aaron Copland, Norman Corwin, Ben Grauer, Dashiell Hammett, Nat Hiken (a CBS television producer), Alexander Kendrick (a CBS newswriter), Gypsy Rose Lee, Joseph Losey, Burgess Meredith, Arthur Miller, Zero Mostel, Edward G. Robinson, Pete Seeger, Irwin Shaw, and Orson Welles. In the case of Welles, for example, the twenty-one citations drew primarily upon a suppressed appendix to a HUAC report. In addition to this questionable practice, signatures from petitions appearing in newspapers provided another prime source of supposedly damning evidence. And some citations had no basis in fact whatsoever.

The most heavily bruised network, CBS, responded rapidly, installing Joseph Ream as executive vice-president directly beneath Stanton and introducing the highly publicized loyalty oath. In time, responsibility for policing the network fell to Daniel O'Shea and his assistant Alfred Berry, an ex-FBI agent. John Cogley, author of the Fund for the Republic's 1956 study of blacklisting, found that "all seemed to agree that O'Shea was, if nothing else, candid. He believed in blacklisting (though undoubtedly the word offended him), and he tried to practice it as judiciously as possible." CBS had managed to be first in war, first in peace, and first in the Cold War.

These were different times, factionalized, pressurized, scandalized. A struggle was under way, but the conflict was buried, exploding like an underground atom test, spreading tremors of anxiety throughout network bureaucracies. It was an era of symbolic warfare, a battle fought with words and gestures. In this polarized atmosphere language took on special values, and apparently innocuous words became euphemisms for stigma. "Questionable," "security," and "sympathizer" carried with them the weight of blunt instruments. It was a conflict fought not on the battlefield, but in the stuffy offices where concealed copies of *Red Channels* ruled the actions of men and women. In this period of rumor-mongering, whispering, and unexpressed fears, well-dressed individuals struggled to salvage their careers. Aggression held in check, or turned against the self, suicide became a hideously prevalent reaction to the investigations.

At CBS, all 2,500 employees on the network's payroll, including writers and performers, were required to answer yes or no to the following three questions. The first began, "Are you now, or have you ever been a member of the communist party, U.S.A., or any communist organization?" The second began, "Are you now, or have you ever been, a member of a fascist organization?" and the third, "Are you now, or have you ever been a member of any organization, association, movement, group, or combination of persons which advocates the overthrow of our constitutional form of government?" If an employee had trouble with any of these questions, he could approach Berry and O'Shea for assistance, and, if lucky, could achieve "rehabilitation" through a combination of credible recanting and the right connections.

Murrow passed the test with flying colors, but the network's top-rated television star could not. In 1953, HUAC got wind of a story that Lucille Ball, star of "I Love Lucy," had been a Communist in the nineteen thirties, joining the party in order to earn her grandfather's favor. In 1951 CBS had scheduled a domestic comedy featuring Ball and her husband Desi Arnaz. Despite the rudimentary sets and low production budget (only $38,000 an episode) of "I Love Lucy," its ratings began to soar, on the strength of the star's clowning and suspense surrounding a pregnancy which progressed both onstage and in real life. As the pregnancy continued, attention mounted, climaxing on January 19, 1953, the day Ball gave birth in reality and the day the episode relating the event aired. The story made fluffy front-page news, and the episode won a startlingly high rating. Now a hot property, Ball was cleared in a hurry of the charges.

The conflict intensified when still another group entered the Communist-conspiracy field. These self-appointed vigilantes proved just as effective as HUAC, McCarthy, or *Counterattack* in bringing the industry to heel, because they went after advertisers.

In Syracuse, New York, Laurence Johnson, owner of several supermarkets and an officer of the National Association of Supermarkets, objected to CBS's hiring of actors mentioned in *Counterattack*. Johnson did not take his grievance to the network or government, but to the Block Drug Company, sponsor of the series in which the actors performed. (It was titled, appropriately enough, "Danger.") Johnson threatened to display signs in his supermarkets calling attention to the "fact" that the Block Drug sponsored a program employing Communist actors. Johnson's organization also corresponded with Stanton, proposing to the master researcher that a poll be set up at supermarkets asking consumers, "Do you want any part of your purchase price of any products advertised on the Columbia Broadcasting System to be used to hire communist fronters?"

Johnson had selected his pressure point well. He guessed the ultimate threat to the networks lay not in shackling their freedom to speak out, the silencing of respected commentators and performers, or even the emasculation of independently minded new divisions, but in the intimidation of highly cautious advertisers, especially those manufacturing products sold in supermarkets. With 60 per cent of network revenues coming from this group, Johnson exerted surprisingly strong leverage.

Stanton, however, did not respond to Johnson's threat.

Eventually, the responsibility for saving CBS not only from its critics but also, given the network's overpowering urge to co-operate with them, from itself, fell to Murrow. While the Johnson, McCarthy, and *Counterattack* campaigns against the network gained momentum, Murrow made the delicate transition from radio to television. He exchanged the so-called intellectual medium for the more popular and influential forum. But appearing on the screen involved much more than simply talking into a microphone while on camera. He would have to master a new craft, documentary filmmaking, so that he could show as well as tell. His assistant in this arduous process was Fred Friendly, a younger news producer with whom Murrow had earlier collaborated on a successful record album, *I Can Hear It Now*, a compilation of historic speeches made during Murrow's era, linked by his graceful and forceful narration. In 1948, Murrow launched a new radio series, "Hear It Now," and, in 1950, a visual adaptation retitled "See It Now."

The deceptively simple title revealed the strengths of the television medium. The title promised an emphasis on direct visual presentation and a corresponding absence of florid commentary and description, those earmarks of radio journalism. The new method of presentation would allow the viewer to make up his own mind, without having to rely solely on correspondents' descriptions. The title promised as well the spontaneity that had been broadcasting's touchstone. The viewer would see things as they were in reality, as they were happening. On the basis of Murrow's reputation, "See It Now" attracted as its sponsor Alcoa, which was, significantly, not a company relying on supermarket sales. Nonetheless, Alcoa's sponsorship did not afford the program full protection even within the commercial framework, because the average cost per program ran much higher than the amount Alcoa paid. By making up the difference, CBS in effect partially subsidized the program. The support came with strings attached. Murrow complained, "They come to me, the vice-presidents, and say, 'Look, there's so much going out of this spout and only so much coming in.' And I say, 'If that's the way you want to do it, you'd better get yourselves another boy.'"

Using "See It Now" as his new pulpit, Murrow zeroed in on his target by gradual stages. He undoubtedly sensed that McCarthy was an enemy he was destined to face, and it would be only a matter of time until they locked horns. A trial run took place on October 20, 1953, when "See It Now" took up the case of one Lt. Milo Radulovich. Here was a young man who had been dismissed from the Air Force because of suspicion surrounding his family's political sympathies. Radulovich protested that his only real "offense" was that he had maintained a "close and continuing" relationship with his family. In an understated way, the program demanded to know how this kind of guilt by association could be condoned in our land.

After a period of equivocation, Murrow and Friendly decided to lunge for the heart of the beast. For a year and a half their staff had patiently assembled a filmed record of the senator in action. Murrow and Friendly first thought of setting up some kind of debate, but, studying the clips, they realized McCarthy turned out to be his own worst enemy. Rather than attempting to directly attack, expose, or otherwise humiliate him, they proposed simply to edit the clips together to reveal the man's reprehensible practices. In this they were abetted by the fact of McCarthy's exceedingly untelegenic appearance. He was paunchy and balding. Clownlike wisps of hair sprang from his pasty-looking forehead. And the voice was clearly that of a bully, slurring words, badgering witnesses in a contemptuous monotone. Television mercilessly exposed these shortcomings. Had there been only radio still in use at the time, McCarthy might well have flourished awhile longer.

Finally, Murrow deemed that on March 9, 1954, the time would be right for a report on Senator Joseph McCarthy to appear. Reaction to the forthcoming program around the corridors of CBS was ambivalent, approaching the bizarre. While Paley knew of the program's existence, he chose not to preview it. However, he did convey to Murrow the message, "I'll be with you tonight, Ed, and I'll be with you tomorrow as well," when, presumably, a storm of controversy would break loose. This was a nice sentiment, but hardly a ringing affirmation. With the advantage of hindsight, it becomes apparent that while Murrow and Friendly enjoyed Paley's personal, nearly tacit approval, they did not have the official support of CBS as a corporation. This strange relationship was revealed in a New York *Times* advertisement for the McCarthy program. Nowhere in it did the usual CBS trademarks appear. Murrow and Friendly paid for it with $1,500 of their personal funds. The layout and wording of the advertisement suggested that Murrow and Friendly were undertaking this report at their own risk.

And risks they were, but only insofar as Paley allowed them to be. McCarthy posed a threat to Paley's interests as well as Murrow's. He even posed a threat to Paley's friend President Eisenhower, and no one had as yet dared to speak out. Back in November 1953, for example, the President had passed up a significant opportunity to denounce McCarthy during a televised "Dinner with the President," attended by heads of all three networks. Everyone, then, was adopting a hands-off attitude toward the junior senator from Wisconsin.

Beginning his report on McCarthy that March evening, Murrow was obviously wracked with tension. His proximity to the camera had the effect of elongating his already prominent forehead, as if to emphasize the cerebral nature of this conflict. After a brief introduction which gave little hint of the fireworks to follow, most of the program was devoted to the patiently assembled filmclips of McCarthy in action, remorselessly revealing his shoddy practices and demeanor. Here was McCarthy in his full, foul glory, browbeating frightened witnesses, waving about sheafs of papers supposedly containing lists of Communists in the State Department, deciding on the spur of the moment that the American Civil Liberties Union was known to be a Communist front when the false assertion suited his purposes in interrogating a witness. If McCarthy had begun the broadcast with a lingering reputation as a crusader for democracy, he ended as a villain and a bully. As Murrow stated succinctly, "His mistake has been to confuse dissent with disloyalty."

Compared to the nightmare of German bombs falling across London, McCarthy must have seemed a considerably less awesome threat to Murrow. Like his broadcasts from London fifteen years before, his closing remarks amounted to another call to arms. "This is no time for men who oppose Senator McCarthy's methods to keep silent, or for those who approve. We can deny our heritage and our history, but we cannot escape responsibility for the result. There is no way for a citizen of a republic to abdicate his responsibilities." Murrow's long face seemed ready to burst forth from the television screen.

"The actions of the junior senator from Wisconsin have caused alarm and dismay amongst our allies abroad, and given considerable comfort to our enemies. And whose fault is that? Not really his. He didn't create this situation of fear; he merely exploited it—and rather successfully. Cassius was right. 'The fault, dear Brutus, is not in our stars, but in ourselves.' Good night and good luck," he said, swinging away from the camera almost before the words were out of his mouth.

The next day the storm did break. Though the right-wing Hearst press lashed away at Murrow and his "pink-painting" cronies, most letters, phone calls, telegrams, and newspaper columns approved of Murrow's position. Even the aloof General Sarnoff associated himself with Murrow by appearing on "Person to Person" several days later. At home he introduced his wife Lizette, now grown stout and reticent, and displayed the telegraph key he had used in the *Titanic* disaster as well as his awards and diplomas. Murrow and Friendly were hoping for a stronger show of solidarity.

The lingering effects of McCarthyism were capable of generating a pervasive backlash. The struggle was not over yet. Just a week after the report on Senator McCarthy, Murrow and Friendly drove the dagger home with an examination of McCarthy's handling of a single case, that of Annie Lee Moss. In his zeal to show how the State Department had been infiltrated by Communists, McCarthy suspected that Moss, a clerical worker, was a master code-cracking spy. Under his crude, bullying questions, this patient, docile witness revealed that she did not know who Karl Marx was. The spectacle of the senator picking on a bewildered and defenseless woman further damaged his reputation.

Both Paley and Stanton had advised Murrow to offer McCarthy time to reply to the charges, and so he had at the beginning of the report. McCarthy naturally accepted the challenge. At first he proposed that William F. Buckley, Jr., carry his standard. Buckley was the co-author of a 1954 book, *McCarthy and His Enemies*, which undertook to defend McCarthy's actions on the grounds that they fulfilled a legitimate need for enforcing national security. But it was McCarthy to whom Murrow had offered sufficient rope to hang himself, not Buckley.

McCarthy prepared a reply for an April 6 broadcast. CBS subsequently paid the $6,336.99 it cost to produce. Previewing the reply, Friendly noted that McCarthy was "caked in makeup that attempted to compensate for his deteriorating physical condition" and that "his receding hairline was disguised by a botched mixture of false hair and eyebrow pencil." In the broadcast itself, McCarthy did his level best to pillory Murrow as a Communist. "Murrow is a symbol," he declared, "the leader and the cleverest of the jackal pack which is always found at the throat of anyone who dares to expose individual Communist traitors." McCarthy lived up to Murrow's advance reviews; attempting to redeem himself, he employed just those shoddy tactics to which Murrow had drawn attention several weeks earlier.

McCarthy's reputation continued its downward spiral throughout the month of April. ABC, casting about for some inexpensive way to fill up its daytime schedule, began broadcasting the Army-McCarthy hearings during the latter part of the month. While McCarthy attempted to find Communists in the Army, a Boston attorney, Joseph Welch, succeeded in rattling the senator in prolonged, tense, face-to-face confrontations. As a by-product, ABC called attention to itself, in the process picking up some much-needed television affiliates.

In 1954 the Senate voted to censure McCarthy, who died of hepatitis three years later.

Murrow and Friendly, however, had not been attacking McCarthy so much as the pervasive climate of fear. Even after it was apparent they had won their hazardous skirmish with McCarthy, they continued to probe. The following year they wrestled with the problem in quite another manner, presenting an interview with J. Robert Oppenheimer, the physicist who had played a key role in the development of the atomic bomb and was subsequently denied full security clearance. The interview revealed not some mad, irresponsible scientist, as popular prejudice feared, but a highly moral, articulate, even delicate thinker who argued cogently for less secrecy surrounding scientific investigations so that the public would be better informed and better equipped to control the fruits of scientific discovery. Previewing the program, Paley was so entranced that he proposed to allow it to run a few minutes beyond the normal half-hour period. However, editors trimmed it to fit the conventional schedule. Murrow and Friendly again had to dig into their pockets to pay for the ad in the New York *Times*.

Part of the reason for the continuing ambivalence stemmed from the fact that the same program which received Paley's endorsement incurred security officer O'Shea's wrath. Clearly, the CBS attitude toward the climate of fear was still shot through with inconsistencies. On one hand, it kowtowed to professional fearmongers. On the other, it wished to speak out as freely as it had in the heyday of the New Deal.

No network was big enough to hold both an O'Shea and a Murrow. O'Shea left the network that same year. The coast was clearing. Nonetheless, this was not an era of celebration. There was plenty of hell to pay for the confrontations. There were, for example, several suicides. Don Hollenbeck, a CBS reporter who had appeared on the air with a local news program following "See It Now" and acclaimed the Report on McCarthy, was subjected to a series of attacks in the Hearst press. In the midst of a personal crisis, he died in June 1954. Philip Loeb, the actor who played Gertrude Berg's husband on "The Rise of the Goldbergs" and had been among *Red Channels* entries, was another casualty. And Laurence Johnson, the vigilante of the supermarkets, was discovered dead of a drug overdose in a hotel room in 1962. A few hours later, a jury would award a discharged CBS disc jockey, John Henry Faulk, record damages in a suit CBS had brought against Johnson's organization. Murrow had helped the unemployed Faulk with legal fees.

Finally, Murrow did not have much of a chance to savor his triumph, though it was a vindication of the network and, by extension, the entire industry. He quickly became disillusioned by the network he had risked so much to defend. Alcoa's sponsorship of "See It Now" lapsed even before the conclusion of the 1955 season. According to Friendly, the program's inquiry into a Texas land scandal threatened Alcoa's interests, and the company therefore dropped the program. But this was merely a pretext. The end was clearly in sight for "See It Now." Murrow's associate producer, Fred Friendly, has commended the network and Alcoa for their noninterference during the program's lifetime, but the situation might not have been as benign as that. By making the program beholden to any sponsor, even an enlightened one, CBS was, in effect, holding a Damoclean sword above Murrow's head. According to the sensible precedent established by the networks in the nineteen thirties, a program with a strong point of view such as "See It Now" should have been sustaining. The fact of sponsorship exerted an implied form of censorship, at the same time relieving the network of having to take responsibility for any restrictions. Let Alcoa take the heat, the strategy ran, while CBS collected kudos.

"See It Now" had been charged with a mission to defend the network's honor and independence, but without a common enemy, Murrow and a thoroughly commercialized CBS were at variance. Mission accomplished, Paley moved to phase out Murrow's influence over CBS. He urged the commentator to run for senator from New York, to no avail. Their relationship suffered further damage in a dramatic confrontation over the future of "See It Now." Friendly has reconstructed the climactic encounter thus:

"Bill, are you going to destroy all this?" Murrow demanded to know. "Don't you want an instrument like the 'See It Now' organization, which you have poured so much into for so long, to continue?"

"Yes," Paley replied, "but I don't want this constant stomachache every time you do a controversial subject."

"I'm afraid that's a price you have to be willing to pay. It goes with the job," Murrow said.

Paley was not willing to pay the price any longer. Murrow, for his part, helped to hasten the end. Many "See It Now" programs were deliberately provocative, if not downright self-destructive. The program's last regular season, for example, contained not one but two installments examining the health hazards of smoking. These, of course, posed a direct challenge to the morality of one of the mainstays of broadcast advertising. Such an investigation was not merely uncommercial, it was anticommercial. Think of all the revenue from cigarette advertising it might place in jeopardy. The Murrow who presented these programs was indirectly displaying his contempt for advertising. He sensed its continued supremacy would threaten his own stake in broadcasting, and with good reason.

Murrow's well-noted reaction to the debut of "The $64,000 Question" in June 1955 was, "Any bets on how long we'll keep this time period now?" He naturally felt revulsion at the acquisitive fever the game show generated, and he knew that it would upset the delicate balance between sponsor and network which had permitted "See It Now" to exist. If this game show were successful, as it appeared destined to be, CBS could command higher advertising rates not only for its time period, but for adjacent periods as well, when the large audience would carry over. The prestige of sponsoring "See It Now" would, then, cost more than ever. By scheduling "See It Now" and "The $64,000 Question" in adjacent time periods, CBS effectively made the decision to drive Murrow off the air.

At its high point, the game show drew 85 per cent of the television audience. As Wendy Barrie demonstrated Revlon's Loving Lipstick, and Gino Prato, a shoemaker, won $32,000, Murrow and his tradition became an anachronism. Indeed, to emphasize the new mood around CBS, Stanton appointed the creator of "The $64,000 Question," Louis Cowan, as CBS vice-president in charge of "creative services." Stanton did not summarily yank Murrow off the air—that would have been too obvious—but instead allowed him to drown in a commercial programming ocean. "See It Now" struggled through several more years on an irregular schedule. According to one headline, the program would be "Seen Only Now and Then."

Yet, surprisingly, it turned out that Murrow, too, knew how to play the commercial game. In 1955, he banded together with associates from his radio program, Jesse Zousmer and John Aaron, to create a program designed to cash in on his celebrity. Murrow actually owned 40 per cent of the program, "Person to Person," which he sold to CBS as a package. In this he approximated arrangements top comedians, not journalists, would make with the networks. Though Murrow earned substantial money, no doubt well deserved, in the process he sullied his reputation. It became an open question as to which Murrow was the real Murrow, the correspondent or the celebrity.

No matter what he did, though, Murrow did it well. Some segments of "Person to Person" were charming and thought-provoking. There was, for instance, the interview with Harpo Marx at the comedian's home in Palm Springs. Harpo refused to speak, and the program turned into a live Marx Brothers movie. Then there was the program of February 6, 1959, in which a young and earnest Fidel Castro, dressed in pajamas, talked with Murrow while bouncing his son on his knee. "Person to Person" demonstrated that Murrow had succeeded in making the difficult transition from radio to television, a transition which not every newsman but certainly most established radio performers wished to make. Like the entire network, he tried to work both sides of the street, earning some cash out of the show business aspects of broadcasting even while undertaking the serious business of helping to destroy the climate of fear.

Murrow's last broadcast for the network, part of a successor to "See It Now," called "CBS Reports," examined the plight of migrant farm workers. "Harvest of Shame" (1960) was a report so harsh as to be completely out of step with the determinedly escapist programming the network was offering at the time. CBS had made its point. Murrow was obsolete.

Though "See It Now" and "The $64,000 Question" seemed to come from different worlds, these two programs, both produced live in New York, did have much in common. The game show served as a bright commercial reflection of the profound anxieties which Murrow found lurking just below the surface of the popular consciousness. If Murrow revealed anxiety, "The $64,000 Question" promised to relieve it, to allow contestants, and through them, millions of viewers, to vent their frustrations with the acquisition of material goods. The game show employed the imagery of the McCarthy era. Contestants under interrogation agonized in a dramatic "isolation booth" in which they wracked their brains to answer questions. Names of subsequent game shows carried echoes of McCarthyism: "Let's Make a Deal," "Truth or Consequences." The tortured consciences of the McCarthy era now served as the premise for a game. These shows have remained a perennial programming genre, but only at this juncture, for an interval of about two years, did they achieve the status of a national mania.

NBC, needless to say, entered the game show field with all possible haste. In September 1956, "Twenty-one," produced by Jack Barry and Dan Enright, promised that contestants could win unlimited amounts of money. Scheduled opposite CBS's hit series "I Love Lucy," it languished in the ratings until the following spring, when Charles Van Doren, a charming and apparently earnest young English instructor at Columbia University vanquished Herbert Stempel, a successful contestant who found himself cast in the role of the heavy. As if participating in an electronic fairy tale, Van Doren quickly became a television celebrity. He won $129,000 on "Twenty-one," married, bought a house, and received a promotion at Columbia from instructor to assistant professor. His popularity appeared to further the cause of scholarship and enhance the image of intellectuals in the public mind. Guest appearances on "The Steve Allen Show" led to Robert Sarnoff's offering Van Doren a $50,000-a-year contract with NBC. He became Dave Garroway's summer replacement on "Today."

Meanwhile, Van Doren's nemesis, Herbert Stempel, claimed that "Twenty-one" was fixed, that Van Doren had received answers in advance of questions and was coached in histrionics like lip-biting and stuttering to increase the aura of tension. Rumors of widespread fixing abounded, but the press, fearing costly libel suits brought by the prosperous networks, was slow to take up the accusations. Barry and Enright resigned, they said, to devote themselves full time to vindicating their names. While not directly involved in the potential scandal, Lou Cowan grew nervous. From the remove of his executive suite, he conducted his own investigation, seeking not the truth so much as the reassurance from CBS game show units that nothing dishonest was going on. Ultimately, such selective blindness would not prove sufficient to salvage his reputation.

As scandal brewed, quiz-show ratings plummeted. Rigged or not, they had outlived their usefulness as a programming novelty, and the networks began dropping them from their evening schedules one by one. CBS, fresh from the trauma of McCarthyism, again found itself in difficult straits. Stanton had rushed to place the television network at the disposal of Cowan, hoping to avoid any semblance of unprofitable controversy associated with Murrow. But now Cowan's formula for success was turning out to be a liability. The apparently harmless fun of the game shows was not so innocent after all.

New York District Attorney Frank Hogan commenced a protracted investigation into the matter, but he found himself on shaky ground. If the quiz shows were rigged, exactly what law had their producers broken? Had the rigging actually hurt the public? The entire scandal took on an element of unreality, of a hypothetical crime committed in the imaginary land of television. Eventually, the true nature of the abuse was determined. The quiz shows were guilty of deception, passing off prerehearsed events as spontaneous reality. Hogan questioned 150 witnesses in the course of his investigation and estimated that two thirds of them committed perjury. At last, the press began running stories by contestants about how the quiz shows, by now a dying breed, were fixed.

Enter Congressman Oren Harris, a Democrat from Arkansas, who in late 1959 initiated an investigation into the matter by the House Committee on Legislative Oversight. Now CBS suddenly began taking the quiz-show problem much more seriously. The threat the investigation posed to the network's integrity and credibility loomed as large as McCarthyism. The two, in fact, were not unrelated; one was a com-mercial distortion of the other. Heretofore CBS had acted innocent; now it acted guilty and contrite of a crime no one had accused it of— yet. Stanton endeavored to send signals to Washington that it would discipline itself, thank you. On October 16, he spoke to the Radio-Television News Directors Association and announced that CBS would cancel all the high-stakes quiz shows. "Whoever may produce pro-grams," he said, trying to deflect blame from the network, even though Cowan was now a CBS vice-president, "it has now been made crystal-clear that the American people hold the networks responsible for what appears on their schedules." That Stanton would even sug-gest that someone else might be responsible for the deception (which had yet to be proved) was a neat little bit of disingenuousness.

Eliminated programs included "Top Dollar" and "The Big Payoff." Cowan's "The $64,000 Question" and an equally successful spin-off, "The $64,000 Challenge," which had started the whole phenomenon, were already off the air. While CBS appeared to be manfully dis-ciplining itself, it did not have much at stake any longer. By implica-tion, Cowan's position was insecure, for he was a symbol of the quiz shows, despite his involvement with other types of programming. Nothing else made the same impact. Stanton's comments did not suc-ceed in altering the course the congressional committee had set. Hear-ings would resume November 2, when Charles Van Doren himself was scheduled to testify.

The stress of the moment exposed the smoldering conflict between Stanton and Murrow. In the course of a telephone interview, Stanton lumped Murrow's "Person to Person," in which participants were asked prerehearsed questions, in the same general category of misrep-resentation as coaching quiz-show contestants and even adding canned laughter to a situation comedy sound track. Stanton could hardly deliver that thrust with Murrow in the next room, able to dash in and confront him. The latter, in fact, was in London, on sabbatical, while Charles Collingwood stood in for him on "Person to Person." The parochial controversy took on a transoceanic dimension. "I am sorry Dr. Stanton feels that I have participated in perpetrating a fraud on the public," ran Murrow's rebuttal from London. "My conscience is clear. His seems to be bothering him." That Murrow, symbol of CBS integrity lo these many years, was now being called a liar by no one less than the network president demonstrates how low his stock had fallen at CBS. In years gone by, Paley had fêted the reporter at the

Waldorf, given his programs pride of place. Now Stanton was trying to discredit him.

As Murrow's star declined, Stanton's rose. He began to assume the mantle of statesman or spokesman for the entire industry. Rivaling Murrow for Paley's good graces, Stanton and the commercial broadcasting philosophy he represented won out. The executive supplanted the maverick, the man of peace took over from the man of war, moral or otherwise. Stanton's salary at CBS was now second only to Paley's.

"I would give almost anything I have to reverse the course of my life in the last three years," ran Van Doren's prepared statement to Harris's committee on November 2. "I cannot take back one week or action; the past does not change for anyone."

Thereupon, this latter-day Candide proceeded to narrate a fascinating tale of skullduggery which confirmed everyone's worst suspicions of low practices by quiz-show producers. The confession had been a long time coming. Subpoenaed by the committee, Van Doren drove around New England with his wife for several days before returning to Washington to testify. "I was involved, deeply involved, in a deception," he confessed upon his return. "The fact that I, too, was deceived cannot keep me from being the principal victim of the deception, because I was its principal symbol."

Van Doren continued, "Before my first actual appearance on 'Twenty-one,' I was asked by [the show's producer Albert] Freedman to come into his apartment. He took me into his bedroom where we could talk alone. He told me that Herbert Stempel, the current champion, was an 'unbeatable contestant' because he knew too much. He said that Stempel was unpopular, and was defeating opponents right and left to the detriment of the program. He asked me if, as a favor to him, I would agree to make an arrangement whereby I would tie Stempel and thus increase the entertainment value of the program." Freedman employed a variety of arguments to persuade Van Doren, that by defeating Stempel he "would be doing a great service to the intellectual life" and to teachers and educators in general. But, Van Doren concluded, "I have done a disservice to all of them. I deeply regret this, since I believe nothing is of more vital importance to our civilization than education."

In the course of his articulate confession, Van Doren metamorphosed from an affable celebrity to a symbol of the innocent seduced and abandoned by the moneygrubbing, deceitful men who ran the networks. The quiz-show scandals became a national obsession to the extent that Van Doren's confession was front-page news. Even the normally noncommittal Eisenhower commented on the affair, calling it a "terrible thing to do to the American public."

As the scandal reached a crescendo, Stanton traveled to Washington to testify, maintaining that until August 1958, he had been "completely unaware" of "any irregularity" in CBS's quiz shows. Cowan, more directly involved, could not testify. He was confined to a hospital bed with phlebitis. Returning to work, he was told, in effect, to clean out his desk. He had held his position at CBS little more than a year.

Had there been no quiz scandal, however, it is doubtful that Cowan would have lasted much longer. The game show had run its course as a hot property, and Cowan had not impressed as an administrator. It was clear to all networks that filmed series—predictable, easy to control, habit-forming—were the wave of the future. To this end, Stanton had, as early as April 1958, hired a potential Cowan replacement, James Aubrey, who had made a reputation as a filmed-series specialist at ABC. Now a vice-president at CBS, Aubrey awaited the opportunity to edge out Cowan and the live programming he stood for. The quiz-show scandals provided the perfect chance. Cowan could be offered to the public as a "sacrificial lamb," evidence of CBS's determination to go straight, even though he was not directly implicated in any rigging. "As you yourself have said many times, administration is not your forte," ran Stanton's reply to Cowan's letter of "resignation." A few days later, in December 1959, Stanton appointed Aubrey the next network president. Seeking someone to administer a surefire philosophy of programming, he had enlisted Cowan as a safe choice, but he brought scandal down on CBS's head. But this time, both Paley and Stanton knew they could not go wrong with Aubrey. They were even planning to leave CBS in his hands one day.

From initiation to confession, the quiz-show scandal was a purely public phenomenon. Its significance resides more with the history of network public relations than with the history of the networks themselves. They were a set piece illustrating some of the tawdry aspects of the business. Yet the fixing of the quiz shows was not the real injury the networks wreaked on the public; it was the removal of valuable programs such as "See It Now" that constituted the more subtle and chronic damage. The quiz shows were symptoms, more important for what they revealed about the dynamics of the industry than for what they were in themselves, which amounted to little more than an exercise in trivia.

In certain ways the quiz show scandal resembled the uproar surrounding Orson Welles's "War of the Worlds" broadcast twenty years earlier. Though not at all comparable in quality or intention, they each relied heavily on the manipulation of reality, and in each case the program played heavily on the anxiety surrounding a political issue of the moment, whether it was impending war or McCarthyism. The scope and vehemence of the public reaction to the distortion, whether well-intended, as in Welles's case or purely avaricious, as in the case of the quiz shows, was testimony both to the suggestibility of an audience in the grip of political fears and the extraordinary persuasiveness of broadcasting.

And the quiz scandals would not be the last time the networks would be hit with the misrepresentation issue. In 1971, during the waning days of American involvement in Vietnam, a gruff and perturbed Frank Stanton would testify before a Senate subcommittee and refuse to submit outtakes, or discarded scenes, from a recent CBS News documentary, "The Selling of the Pentagon." Well-intentioned though the program was, it contained deceptively edited interviews with and speeches by government and military figures in order to make its already valid points even stronger. Though the occasional misrepresentations put forth by the networks have been widespread, they have, typically, not been long-lived. They have been as insubstantial as a bad dream, but ones rooted in the anxieties of political realities.

In terms of the history of network public relations, a conventional interpretation of this swiftly moving era has it that the networks disgraced themselves in 1959 with the quiz-show scandal, then redeemed themselves in the fall of 1960, when all three cleared their schedules to broadcast four presidential debates between Richard Nixon and John Kennedy. Unsponsored, they attracted huge audiences ranging from 60,000,000 to 75,000,000 viewers. Undertaking such selfless, public-spirited activity could only serve to eradicate the ill will and mistrust the networks had acquired in the public mind, and, more important, in any government agency which might have been tempted by the recent scandal to launch another painful investigation.

Curiously, the chief obstacle to the Great Debates was Congress itself. Before the networks could broadcast the confrontation, they had to overcome a legal obstacle, Section 315 of the 1934 Communications Act, also known as the Equal Time Law, which specified that stations must provide equal airtime, if requested, for all political candidates. This provision proved to be difficult to enforce. Intended to guarantee free speech, the provision had the effect of stifling it.

Here was an issue Stanton could sink his teeth into. He could be seen cleaning up CBS's image while making his mark as a champion of network news at the time CBS dumped Murrow. He spearheaded a drive to persuade Congress to repeal Section 315, to allow broadcasting the same latitude print media enjoys under First Amendment guarantees of free speech. But to Congress's way of looking at things, the stations made use of a limited public resource, the airwaves, and were thus liable to regulation in the public interest. Furthermore, networks or stations had not traditionally been editorially oriented, as were many publications, but rather advertising-oriented. In fact, they had a history of suppressing political statements or controversy in favor of appealing to the widest possible audience for the sake of reaping the greatest possible advertising revenue. Congress sidestepped the issue by simply suspending Section 315 for the Great Debates.

As recently as 1976, the FCC was still wrestling with the problem, finally deciding to exempt live debates from the provision on the grounds that they qualified as a bona fide news event, to which Section 315 did not apply. The fancy footwork with terminology, however, did not resolve the issue, but merely pushed it into the background.

The history of free speech and the networks, incidentally, is quirky indeed. Both the industry and the FCC have reversed their positions on several occasions. In 1939, for example, an industry code frowned on editorializing. Along much the same lines, a 1941 FCC decision unequivocally banned editorializing. "The broadcaster cannot be an advocate," ran the "Mayflower Doctrine," so called because the decision concerned a Mayflower Broadcasting Corporation. This cozy arrangement, which permitted networks and stations alike to abdicate public-service programming over the years, held sway until 1949, when the FCC enunciated a "Fairness Doctrine," which reversed the trend. Now, the FCC was saying, stations should indeed engage in the presentation of various sides of public issues. However, the networks took the position that any doctrine—Mayflower, Fairness, or otherwise—interfered with their right to free speech. In contrast, the FCC maintained that as long as the airwaves were limited, it had the right to enforce the free speech it felt the networks and stations, in the grip of their commercial obsessions, would otherwise ignore.

The solution to the problem had a nasty way of shifting according to the angle from which it was seen. Furthermore, technological improvements have made the notion of limited airwaves obsolete. Media scholar Frank Kahn notes that "there is little practical difference between the technological scarcity that permits approximately 10,000 broadcasting stations and the economic scarcity that limits daily newspapers to fewer than 2,000." Is the FCC right, then, to try and *enforce* free speech? Can it legislate it into existence on the basis of the First Amendment? Or, as Kahn puts it, "Can the river run higher than the source?" Since 1949 it has.

As heavily publicized as the Great Debates and Quiz-Show Scandal were, neither significantly altered the course of the networks' development; what they did do was expose to public scrutiny the pressure and contradictory impulses under which the networks labored. The public was afforded an unusual glimpse into both the grotesque commercialism and the aspiration toward responsibility that characterized the networks. Despite threats of investigations, there was little the FCC or any other government agency could do to enforce a higher standard of behavior. That opportunity had been lost years ago, in the nineteen twenties. When networks embarked on public-service programming binges, as did CBS in the nineteen thirties and forties and ABC in the mid-fifties, the impulse stemmed not from government pressure but from internal needs. Some of these were altruistic, and some were expedient. Occasionally, a network just had to fill the airtime with something inexpensive to produce. But those days were clearly at an end. The networks were too prosperous to be generous. In time, a disillusioned Murrow and an activist Congress would make one last attempt to ensure public service a place in the broadcast spectrum.

Cowan, as much a victim as an instigator of network greed, never did find his way back to a position of power after CBS dismissed him. Such has been the lot of most programmers after an upheaval has forced them out of the executive suite. After devoting himself to writing, publishing, and teaching, Cowan and his wife, Pauline, a former civil rights organizer, perished in 1976 in a fire that ravaged their duplex apartment in the Westbury Hotel in New York. The other symbol of the era, Charles Van Doren, is today editorial vice-president of the Encyclopaedia Britannica.

It is now a felony to rig a quiz show.

CBS Plus Thirty

ROBERT KINTNER WAS ONE of the very few network programmers who did make it back after being fired. The feat suggests both his resiliency and the esteem he generally enjoyed within the industry. Victim of a bitter 1956 power struggle at ABC, then just emerging from obscurity with its first programming successes—ones which he had been instrumental in engineering—Kintner made a carefully orchestrated transition to NBC. In tandem with Bobby Sarnoff, he proceeded to run that network with a stringency and toughness that earned him respect until he again fell victim in another bitter dispute. The second time around, at age fifty-seven, he was not able to make it back.

Kintner was a blunt, bristling former newsman who looked like a Marine drill sergeant and spoke with a rasping voice. He was stocky, deaf in one ear (a war injury), and wore unusually thick glasses because of cataract operations on both eyes. Short on temper and long on willpower, he was a classic of his type. He possessed a newshound's analytical, detached, ferociously competitive approach to network existence combined with a thorough grasp of its economics. He forged a reputation as a staunch advocate of the sanctity of network news, managing for a time to boost NBC ahead of CBS both in the quality of its coverage and the popularity of its correspondents. The best known among these were Chet Huntley, David Brinkley, and

Barbara Walters, all of whom Kintner thrust into the limelight. As NBC president he insisted that the network devote as much time as CBS did to breaking stories, plus an additional thirty minutes' coverage. This policy became known around the corridors of 30 Rockefeller Plaza as "CBS Plus Thirty." No matter if the story required extra coverage or not, Kintner made his point simply by taking over the additional airtime.

Kintner first came to broadcasting in 1944, when he joined ABC. At the time, the network was little more than the remnants of the Blue, which Edward Noble had purchased from NBC. The network's mission was to provide diversity of opinion on the airwaves and to maintain the Blue network's strong commitment to public-service programming. Kintner himself was well suited for such a role. He was born in East Stroudsburg, Pennsylvania, the son of the superintendent of schools there, and graduated from Swarthmore College in 1931. Two years later he found a $17.50-a-week job with the New York *Herald Tribune*. At first he covered Wall Street, but then switched his field of attention to Washington, where in time he came to be the co-author of Joseph Alsop's column.

There, in 1944, he made the acquaintance of Noble, who at the time was undersecretary of Commerce and had just come into control of ABC. Would Kintner like to come along? It was not an easy decision. Unfamiliar with broadcasting, he dined with Sol Taishoff, owner of *Broadcasting* magazine, a trade publication, in the hope of gaining insight into the industry. Dinner extended into breakfast and still the meeting continued, even through lunch the following day, but by then, Kintner had found a new course for himself. Under Mark Woods, the NBC company man whom Sarnoff crowned ABC's first king, Kintner found himself in charge of news and special-events, which were practically all ABC had to offer at the time. In 1949 Kintner succeeded Mark Woods as network president, inheriting staggering problems.

ABC may have survived as a public service-oriented radio network, but with the advent of television it was clear that the network, if it was to continue, would have to turn away from its public-service mandate, the one FCC chairman Fly had tried so hard to ensure, and compete with the other two networks on their thoroughly commercial terms. As NBC and CBS rushed ahead with expensive, star-studded plans for television programming, ABC could brag of little more than the five television stations it owned. That was enough for Stanton at CBS, who made overtures to purchase the network to acquire those valuable stations and one valuable executive, Robert Kintner. When this deal broke down, Noble then came within a hair's breadth of selling ABC off to movie mogul Spyros P. Skouras, who at the time headed Twentieth Century-Fox. While ABC narrowly escaped being sold to the film corporation, the potential deal was a harbinger of the precedent-setting relationship the hard-up network would eventually establish with the film community.

With deals barely falling short of consummation, ABC faced an impossible task of getting started in the network television game. The sole bright spot turned out to be the network-owned television stations, which, like nearly all television stations, whether they were affiliated, network owned and operated, or independent, were enormously profitable. For years, they, rather than network programming, kept ABC afloat. Not until 1971 would the network begin showing profits on a regular basis. Since the network could not afford the New York-style showmanship of NBC's Pat Weaver or the talent raids pulled off by Paley for CBS, it had little appealing television programming to offer potential affiliates. The lack of affiliates and the lack of expensive television programming went hand in hand.

Furthermore, the FCC's 1948 freeze on the construction of new television stations continued unabated until 1953. While rivals snapped up affiliates around the country, ABC found that when it finally could offer a schedule, affiliates were indeed scarce. The majority of the nation's television markets had but one or two television stations, and they inevitably enlisted with bigger and better-established CBS or NBC. What few affiliates ABC could boast of tended to congregate in urban areas, where the greater number of stations competing in the same market meant stiffer competition for audiences. In time, ABC's predominantly urban audience would lead the network to create a special breed of programming, but for the moment, the network found itself saddled with one commercial penalty after another, all because it had entered the field five years later than the competition.

Television, even in its infancy, was never the carefree hobby that radio had been in its early years. Throughout the radio era less than half of all stations were associated with one of the three primary commercial networks, but for television the figure amounted to 95 per cent. When CBS had entered the radio field in 1927, on the heels of NBC, it found affiliates plentiful and was able to grow rapidly. But television stations were in far shorter supply, amounting to but 1250 in the early nineteen fifties, as compared with 10,000 radio stations. Not only was the number of available affiliates smaller, but the number of competing networks had grown by 50 per cent with the entrance of ABC into the market.

Network television promised to become much more monopolistic than radio had ever been. In the beginning networks had served primarily as distribution agencies of centralized programming produced by advertising agencies. Now, they would both monopolize an affiliate's most valuable airtime and supply it with network-originated programming. Twenty-five years before, CBS had entered a growing market, and after three or four years of travail began to earn a profit. But upon entering network television, ABC found it was having the life squeezed out of it by a shrinking market. It was an open question as to whether the industry could sustain as many as three competing national television networks.

Prospects for ABC's survival would have been slight indeed, were it not for the unforeseen consequences of a 1950 antitrust action against the film industry. Wishing to curb the motion picture studios' monopolistic practice of both making movies and owning the theaters in which they were exhibited, the Justice Department ordered them to sell off the bulk of their theaters. One of the affected companies, Paramount, set up a young company vice-president, Leonard Goldenson, as head of a newly independent movie theater chain called United Paramount Theatres. A lawyer by training, Goldenson quickly mastered the trade of movie exhibiting. Here an entrepreneur flourished or withered according to his ability to gauge popular taste, trends, and fads—in short, to know his audience.

The Hollywood establishment regarded the advent of television with fear and loathing, since its sudden popularity, combined with the antitrust ruling, was writing *finis* to the studio-system script by which the industry had lived. But Goldenson did not run with the pack. He had the unusual notion of trying to join forces with the enemy rather than fighting it. As the poorest and most disorganized of the networks, ABC was the logical place to gain a foothold. It was known that Noble needed cash for his network if it was to be able to compete with NBC and CBS. Goldenson commenced negotiations with Noble, who at the time held 53 per cent of the network's stock. In May 1951, ABC and United Paramount Theatres agreed to merge. Under the plan, Goldenson would control the company, with Noble holding only 9 per cent of the stock.

Here at last was the eventuality that FCC chairman Fly, in his zeal to force NBC to give up one of its networks, should have foreseen but was powerless to prevent. Though he questioned Noble and Woods about their intentions for ABC, he could not stop Noble from selling out to another individual who would not be operating under similar constraints, even if they were merely implied. Goldenson's commitment to public service was minimal. He did not have the orientation of either Sarnoff, who regarded commercial broadcasting as a necessary evil, or Paley, who learned early on the numerous advantages of maintaining a commitment to public-service programming. Goldenson brought to ABC the instincts of a motion picture exhibitor who saw no necessity beyond packing the house. The era, as it happened, was suited to his talent, because television programming remained the last area in which networks could make significant commercial strides. Goldenson's roots in the film industry would prove to be just what the network needed to present a standardized commercial product. Under Goldenson's control, ABC came to resemble in many ways the old film-studio monopoly before the antitrust decision. The company made the product and owned the houses in which it was exhibited, in this case the network-owned and -operated stations. Once upon a time, a small, struggling CBS had met the NBC competition head on by projecting a sophisticated image. ABC elected not to take a similar high road, but instead built from the bottom up.

The FCC did not give its blessing to the ABC–UPT merger for two long years, until February 1953. During the interim, the other networks overcame their initial difficulties in entering the industry, built their affiliate rosters, and beefed up their schedules. When, at last, ABC–UPT was off and staggering, it was a peculiar hybrid organization, a product of two separate divestitures. Part of the organization was a spin-off of NBC, part of Paramount. Would they find common ground?

The new, reconstituted ABC moved out of Radio City, where it had existed as a separate fiefdom since NBC had sold the network off, and took up headquarters in a building (previously a riding arena) on Manhattan's West Sixty-sixth Street. Studios were scattered throughout the neighborhood. Unlike CBS's headquarters at 485 Madison, by now as comfortable as an old shoe, or NBC's home fortress, ABC could boast of no impressive skyscraper to call its own.

Kintner, meanwhile, found himself in drastically changed circumstances. In 1954, the "old" Kintner, casting about for ways to fill up ABC's daytime schedule, hit upon the idea of his network being the sole broadcaster of the Army-McCarthy hearings. ABC began to make a mark and acquire affiliates with this inexpensive, important programming. Simultaneously, the "new" Kintner, along with Goldenson, cast his eye toward Hollywood as a source of competitive entertainment programming. While the major studios did not yet realize that television might become a major customer for their products, Walt Disney began exploring the possibility of breaking into network television. He first approached NBC, but the network was, at the time, committed to Pat Weaver's live, New York-oriented programming. Furthermore, it refused to meet Disney's demand that it assist with the financing of an amusement park he planned to build in Anaheim, California. Over at ABC, in contrast, Goldenson and Kintner were willing to sink half a million dollars into the venture in order to acquire Disney-produced programming. Disney agreed to provide twenty-six hour-long television programs for the upstart network at a price of $2,000,000.

Kintner set himself the task of recouping the sizable investment by selling time not to one principal sponsor, as was still the common practice, but to several, charging a premium rate to boot. Taking a leaf from Weaver's magazine format, he hammered out an unorthodox joint-sponsorship agreement with three sponsors. When "Disneyland" made its debut in the 1954–55 season, ABC found to its delight that it had two bona fide hits on its hands: the successful Disney series and the park itself, which made money for both Disney and ABC. The industry watched carefully as affiliates of other networks took the unusual step of clearing time on their schedules to carry the series. ABC quickly followed up with another Disney concoction, "The Mickey Mouse Club," and in 1955, the television network could boast its very first profit, $6,000,000 before taxes. Drawing strength from its momentum, ABC bolstered its schedule with two more made-in-Hollywood hits, "Ozzie and Harriet," a domestic comedy, and "Wyatt Earp," a Western. ABC became the first network to crack the majors by arranging with Warner Brothers to produce television programming derived from its library of feature films. Warner agreed to supply forty hour-long programs at a cost of $75,000 per installment. Out of this arrangement came another successful Western, "Cheyenne," starring the then unknown Clint Walker. Beginning in 1955, it ran for seven seasons.

As a result of these startling successes, the industry's perennial loser, ABC, now began setting precedents which all networks followed. In its desperation, the ragtag network had found the formula that was to dominate television network entertainment in the foreseeable future. NBC established a relationship with the Music Corporation of America, a powerful Hollywood representative, giving it *carte blanche* to fill the vacancies in its nighttime schedule. This was in 1957, by which date the network had turned away decisively from all vestiges of Weaverism, with the exception of the magazine-format programs. MCA obliged with such Westerns as "Wagon Train" and "Tales of Wells Fargo." CBS followed suit, acquiring "Perry Mason" from Twentieth Century-Fox, and "I Love Lucy" and "December Bride" from Desilu, which had taken over the defunct RKO studios. Following on the heels of series produced by the studios came the movies themselves, sold in blocks involving multimillion-dollar deals. Movies quickly replaced live drama as a television staple. At the same time the number of television stations—mainly affiliates—shot up from the mere 108 in operation during the freeze to over 500. The establishment of the coast-to-coast network broadcasting brought about a leveling influence and the end of live drama. Even while professing to despise their rivals, the film studios had learned ways to profit from the networks' insatiable hunger for standardized programming.

Ironically, the impetus for this crucial transition stemmed from upstart ABC, which had stumbled across the true direction in which future commercial network entertainment programming lay. It was not, as NBC under Weaver had supposed, in special events emanating from New York, and not even in retreading stars of network radio, as Paley had assumed. But ABC's efforts went beyond the simple fact of reliance on filmed series. The network also developed multiple sponsorship arrangements to enable networks to bear the burden of their great production costs. Furthermore, its programming tended to be youth-oriented, featuring younger, unknown actors and appealing to young, even juvenile, audiences. In time this approach would serve ABC well, for it was attracting and educating an entire generation of viewers who, twenty years hence, would become the primary television audience. Finally, the ABC-sparked reliance on Hollywood production meant that the networks' hard-won control over programming now passed out of their hands, after the briefest of intervals, and into those of a small, tightly knit group of Hollywood producers. These producers exerted an influence over network programming comparable to that of advertising agencies during the heyday of radio.

Despite these precedent-setting program strategies, ABC still lagged far behind the competition in respectability or profitability. By 1958, it mustered $103,000,000 in billings, as compared with NBC's nearly $216,000,000 and CBS's $247,000,000. ABC was fourth in a three-way race, went the running gag; if the Korean War had been on ABC, it would have been canceled in thirteen weeks. Internal dissension plagued the network. Kintner had come to work for and been promoted by Noble. Yet now he was responsible to a new master, Leonard Goldenson, who blamed him for a slump in ABC's profits following the first flush of success in 1955. Doubtless Goldenson wished to be master of his own house, but it was most unfortunate, from ABC's point of view, that he could not find a way to match his showmanship with Kintner's drive. Instead, he turned an asset into a ferocious competitor.

In late 1956, the ABC–UPT board, firmly in Goldenson's control, outvoted Kintner four to one. His forced resignation proved to be damaging to the company in its own right, since it involved $280,000 in severance pay and resulted in the departure of eight executives.

Now on his own, Kintner entertained overtures both from Stanton and the General himself. To Kintner's way of thinking, CBS already had sufficient administrative muscle. He determined that the prospects were better at a beleaguered NBC, which he joined first as co-ordinator of the network's transition to color. In July 1958 he was appointed network president, working in harness with Bobby, though the younger Sarnoff, as network chairman, actually ranked higher on the corporate ladder. Bob and Bob, as they were familiarly known, succeeded in coexisting for nine years, during which time NBC enjoyed a measure of stability after the upheavals surrounding Weaver's tenure. During Kintner's reign at NBC, ABC felt his loss keenly, especially in the area of entertainment programming. That network's original claim to fame, Walt Disney, moved to NBC in 1961, with "The Wonderful World of Color." CBS felt his presence even more sharply, as he succeeded in bringing supremacy in news coverage to NBC.

While at NBC, Kintner became the prototype of a new breed of network executive, the man who constantly watched television on a battery of monitors, nervously turning his attention from one network to the next. He rose early to watch NBC's "Today," selected one of his two hundred pairs of cufflinks for the day, and traveled by limousine to 30 Rockefeller Plaza from either his country home in Westport, Connecticut, or his city home in the fashionable Sutton Place neighborhood. His annual income went as high as $200,000. At the office, he habitually fired out as many as seventy memos a day to harried employees. His field of vision ran from preparing extensive coverage of the arrival of Pope Paul VI in the United States in 1965 to his noticing that a correspondent's socks sagged on camera.

As a network chief, Kintner came to epitomize the schizophrenic nature of television in the nineteen sixties. On one hand he pursued excellence in news coverage, taking a managing editor's delight at scooping a rival outfit. On the other hand, he oversaw the network's entertainment programming with a cynicism that abdicated all responsibility. The General had never grasped the essence of commercial programming, and neither did Kintner; in that sense he fit well into the NBC tradition. Responsibility for entertainment programming was, of course, not the work of one man, but of a committee, and in general this committee followed trends rather than started them. The word that best characterizes the entertainment programmers' attitude toward the shows they scheduled would be contempt. Their mix of Westerns and domestic comedies neglected the legitimate entertainment values of NBC Red's light programming: Jack Benny, or even "Amos 'n' Andy." It was programming designed not to attract an audience but to hold it. "TV is based on the principle of the least obnoxious," said Paul Klein, one of NBC's veteran programmers, "You don't sit down to watch a *show,* you just sit down to watch *TV.* Then it's just a matter of 'What's on?' You're turning on TV to eat up your life."

In time, Klein refined his theory of programming into what he called the "L.O.P." approach, according to which a viewer does not select a program on the basis of a positive desire to watch, but merely chooses the Least Objectionable Program offered at a given hour. This was the NBC strategy, then: to counterprogram what the other networks ran. In practice, this meant trying to capture segments of the audience the network thought would not wish to watch the CBS offering. ABC still lagged so far behind in number of affiliates that it did not have the potential for reaching as large an audience as its older brothers. Perhaps the most offensive element of the L.O.P. theory was its blaming the audience rather than the networks for the low quality of programming. Implicitly it said that even if a good program were available, people would not wish to watch. That programming theory would come to such a pass—condescending, insulting, ultimately self-defeating—was a direct result of the demise of a commitment to public service-oriented programming. In the nineteen thirties and forties, the balance between commercial and sustaining programming permitted the networks to program for a plurality of tastes. Now they were locked into achieving a consensus of the meanest sort.

Since television was a thoroughly network phenomenon, there was precious little programming emanating from other sources to rival the appeal of network concoctions. Among themselves, the networks effectively exercised a program monopoly. They had the affiliates and, through them, the heavily restricted airwaves locked up tight. As the only game in town, they reaped richly. Profits before taxes for all three went from $56,400,000 in 1963 to $78,700,000 in 1966, the year of Kintner's departure from NBC. Such were the rewards of a legally sanctioned monopoly, one which the FCC, in its desire both to control station licensing and to allow the networks free rein, only served to reinforce. There could be no escape from this stagnant, if profitable, situation until new technology circumvented the network stranglehold on television.

Both CBS and NBC tried to atone for their commercial sins by presenting ever more elaborate news broadcasts. Undertaken in the name of prestige, they were in fact bids for even larger audiences, for the era of the sustaining news broadcast was long gone. News could be profitable as well, the networks were discovering. In the dynamics of the situation, soaring profits from entertainment programming did not subsidize news operations so much as underwrite even more expensive entertainment programming.

NBC, for its part, had been for a long while content to lope along with John Cameron Swayze's "Camel News Caravan." Narrated by Swayze in his machine-gun style of delivery, the program, consisting of fifteen minutes of headlines five nights a week, began as early as 1947. In 1956, however, Swayze was replaced by a team of reporters, Chet Huntley and David Brinkley.

The dry, wry, acerbic Brinkley, born in 1920 in North Carolina, made the transition from United Press to NBC in 1943. For several years he delivered reports on Swayze's "Caravan." Huntley had made a name for himself as an NBC radio correspondent, in time becoming a television news analyst. During the McCarthy era, Huntley's criticism of the senator incurred the wrath of various right-wing groups that threatened to boycott his sponsor's products. But Huntley endured. Together, Huntley and Brinkley covered the 1956 Democratic Convention for NBC. Often their reportage proved to be more in touch with the goings-on than CBS's. Furthermore, viewers found the chemistry between the two men appealing in its own right and good reason to tune in NBC. On the strength of their performance, "The Camel News Caravan" gave way to "The Huntley-Brinkley Report."

At first, the fifteen-minute-long program did not make much of an impression. Groping for a distinctive style, the then director of NBC News, Reuven Frank, wrote what he thought would make for a distinctive closing line: "Good night, Chet. Good night, David. And good night for NBC News." Huntley and Brinkley complained the gambit was corny, embarrassing, and yet it became their trademark, much as "Good night and good luck" belonged to Murrow.

When Kintner found the program, it was largely sustaining, though not as a matter of policy. It simply had not succeeded in attracting a sponsor on a regular basis. Finally, Texaco Oil took it on, and in the process, the program gained a certain gloss and appeal it had previously lacked. From 1958, when the Texaco association began, through the 1960 conventions, the program's prestige swelled.

Meanwhile, the troops over at CBS News were demoralized. Cowan's successor, James Aubrey, considered network news a drain on corporate profits, pure and simple. Kintner rubbed salt in the wound by running one simple and overwhelming statement of fact at the end of each Huntley-Brinkey report: "This program has the largest daily news circulation in the world."

Both networks attached considerable importance to coverage of the 1960 political conventions. It was a time for making and breaking reputations, for the passing of the old guard. The nation would be looking to new men, younger men, for leadership, and the networks to some extent reflected this aspiration. At the conventions, Huntley and Brinkley went from strength to strength, not only bettering CBS in terms of critical esteem, but also in straight popularity. Jack Gould, television critic for the New York *Times*, wrote that "Chet Huntley and David Brinkley swept away the stuffy, old-fashioned concept of ponderous reportage on the home screen. They talked as recognizable humans, sprinkled their observations with delightful wit, and were easily the TV hit of the week." The acclaim launched them into unassailable leads in the by now intense race for news pre-eminence. They had caught the spirit of the times. Sincerity was out of fashion; irony was in. CBS News would take seven long years to effect a decisive comeback.

The first step in the rebuilding of the prestige of CBS News began with the removal of Douglas Edwards from the evening news program. His replacement was Walter Cronkite, but today's grand old man of network news took a long while in finding himself. Furthermore, the entire operation was hampered by news chief Fred Friendly's continual battles with Aubrey. By installing Murrow's friend and protégé in the top news spot in 1964, the network hoped to retain the Murrow touch, but Friendly lacked Murrow's self-assurance or his close rapport with Paley. Every bit as tough-minded, Friendly displayed a tendency to become verbally aggressive, engaging Paley in debates on the primacy of news and, on one occasion, charging from the chairman's office in a huff straight into the men's room.

Cowed by Huntley and Brinkley's success, Friendly violated his own instincts by replacing Cronkite with CBS's answer to a two-man news team, Roger Mudd and Robert Trout. Cronkite's stock plummeted; a low-level scandal erupted. Was Cronkite being fired? The man in question suddenly disappeared to California for a few days, then surfaced in New York, where at a news conference he accepted the shake-up with grace. In the meantime, Aubrey fulminated against the network's lavish, expensive coverage of the 1964 Republican Convention in San Francisco, storming out of the city even before Barry Goldwater received the nomination. Huntley and Brinkley repeated their 1960 performances to even greater acclaim and popularity. The momentum carried over into their evening news broadcasts, which maintained a decisive lead over Cronkite until 1967, a year after Kintner left NBC.

By the time of Kintner's departure, the rivalry between the two networks had altered the face of television news. In 1963, for example, both networks expanded their fifteen-minute nightly newscasts to half an hour, and talk of increasing them to a full hour began to circulate. News budgets shot up, reflecting not only the increasing importance of news programming but also the drive to earn a buck out of its popularity. NBC's news budget went from a $10,000,000 expenditure in 1958 to $52,000,000 a decade later. Of this amount, no less than $6,000,000 went to "The Huntley-Brinkley Report." But income increased as well. By 1968, the half-hour news program generated over $100,000 in advertising revenue each night. The program's annual gross approached $30,000,000, the second largest of *all* NBC programs, including entertainment. As Kintner had earlier brought news into the big-business climate of network broadcasting, he now introduced big business to network news.

Yet he could not last forever at NBC. The time bomb of Bobby Sarnoff's advancement continued to tick away, unnoticed. In 1965, Kintner was appointed network chairman, anticipating Bobby's accession to RCA throne, following the General's gradual retirement. This apparent reward for services rendered only masked a breakdown in the relationship between the two Bobs. The following year, Kintner resigned from a network for the second time in his career, but this time, he did not make it back.

16

The Aubrey Dictum

James L. Aubrey, Jr. The name still rankles, still arouses admiration and envy. No one ever enjoyed a higher reputation as a programmer, not even Fred Silverman, and no one ever fell out of favor faster. If Kintner struggled to hold the realities of network programming at arm's length, Aubrey wholeheartedly embraced them. As the head of CBS, he was known as a cold, ruthless, calculating executive with superb judgment, and nobody wished to cross him because it appeared that one day he would succeed Frank Stanton as the network strong man, and after that, William Paley himself. In all respects he gave the impression of being the complete television programmer. Indeed, one might say he was born to it.

Aubrey was the son of an advertising executive. He grew up in the Chicago suburb of Lake Forest and acquired his education in the East, at Exeter and Princeton. In 1944, at the age of twenty-six, he married an MGM starlet, Phyllis Thaxter, and began working as a space salesman for magazines. In 1948, he moved to broadcasting, finding a job as a time salesman for the CBS radio and television stations in Los Angeles. Rising through the ranks at KNXT, by 1956 Aubrey was managing the network's Hollywood programming. He was making progress, but he was not yet on the fast track.

Blocked in his drive for power at CBS, Aubrey found a berth at ABC, as vice-president for programs and talent. In practice, this position was a mandate to generate some commercially successful series for the network, which, at the time, had little more to its name than "Disneyland." The network was, in fact, struggling to meet its weekly payroll. Financial crises were relieved at the last possible moment when satchels of cash earned by ABC's Los Angeles station, KABC, were flown to New York. Nonetheless, ABC's commercial potential was enormous. As an executive in charge of filmed series, Aubrey found himself poised for takeoff. At ABC his powers widened appreciably. "He went from a little nothing down the hall at CBS to vice-president in charge of programs at ABC," recalled a colleague. He earned $35,000 a year.

Working with Oliver Treyz, the network president Goldenson installed after Kintner's departure, Aubrey made a reputation for himself as a specialist in the filmed series with which ABC, learning from its success with "Disneyland," unnerved the other two networks. Typical products of the era included an offbeat Western, "Maverick," a rural comedy, "The Real McCoys," and an urban adventure series, "77 Sunset Strip." With each of these series, ABC built its constituencies, both urban and rural, and usually on the young side. It was but a hop, skip, and jump from such standardized series to a Least Objectionable Program philosophy of television. Aubrey spent just two years at ABC, long enough to make a reputation for himself as the kind of competitive animal a network would need to survive in the increasingly restricted arena of commercial rivalry. If Aubrey had gambled that by moving to ABC he would attract sufficient attention at CBS to create an offer to bring him back in a new and more powerful role, then his gamble paid off handsomely, for when Stanton did hire him away from ABC, he saw in Aubrey more than just another able young executive.

At the time Aubrey took over the management of CBS television from Lou Cowan in late 1959, executives considered him the greatest piece of executive manpower they had ever seen. Indeed, Stanton went so far as to believe, "I thought he would succeed me as president of CBS." Paley shared his enthusiasm. CBS, they figured, had at last found a winner. Both men looked forward to retiring one day and leaving the network in Aubrey's capable hands. He seemed to have everything required—the polish, cool judgment, background, and easy grace befitting a top network executive. Above all, he appeared to be decisive. No creative dithering here. Aubrey made decisions without the merest hint of reflection. Paley and Stanton found all these traits marvelously reassuring.

In 1960, Aubrey's first full year at the helm of CBS, he lost no time in bringing the network up to date, ridding it of all vestiges of the nineteen fifties. He canceled the single remaining live drama series, "Playhouse 90," which by now emanated from Hollywood, and committed the network to a schedule of filmed series for most evenings of the week. "The Ed Sullivan Show" remained one of the very few exceptions. Now viewers witnessed a programming phenomenon that would have been inconceivable in the radio era: virtually no live programming in prime time. The filmed series had gained a stranglehold on the schedule.

The difference between live and filmed television programming amounted to far more than a difference in technique. They represented two different cultures, New York and Hollywood. The live programs from New York, espoused by Weaver and Cowan, were characterized by an involvement with contemporary life, even in comedy or light entertainment formats. They reflected cosmopolitan, pluralistic values. By saturating the airwaves with filmed series produced in Hollywood, the networks ultimately cast their lot with the more restricted, escapist values of the motion picture studios both major and minor. Such an observation would be all too obvious were it not that the networks for a time held out the possibility of pursuing the alternative, riskier course of live programming. But the filmed series proved too safe and too successful to resist. To an industry cowed by McCarthyism and locked into an internecine war over ratings, they appeared to be just the right weapons to carry on the fight. With the center of program production located a continent away in Hollywood, the networks were, once again, relegated to the status of common carriers. Companies producing filmed series simply licensed networks to carry programs for a specified number of weeks. Often the networks paid for the pilot, then shared in the eventual profits. The arrangement gave rise to any number of odd, trivial series whose low quality obscured the economic sense they made.

To paraphrase Edward R. Murrow, Aubrey did not create this situation, he merely exploited it, and very successfully, too. Winning a ratings race with programs of this type meant very little indeed, although the networks attached desperate importance to the numbers. And of all executives of the era, Aubrey appeared to be the most capable of satisfying that insane craving. He represented the new breed of executive coming to power in the early nineteen sixties, aggressive, young, calculating, and possessed of a seductive combination of charm and arrogance.

Aubrey began his reign with a boast. He would double CBS's profits, which, at the time he came to power, hovered around the $25,000,000 mark. To this end, he cleared away older network executives who infringed upon what he regarded as his territory. Only

Paley and Stanton could tell Aubrey what to do, and he took little instruction from either of them. An early victim of the Aubrey purge was Hubbell Robinson, the programming vice-president. Only a few years before, Robinson had done Aubrey the singular favor of scheduling the very first program Aubrey promoted for CBS, a filmed series starring Richard Boone called "Have Gun, Will Travel."

Before long, Aubrey's ruthless, single-minded approach to programming generated sparks in the executive suite. He clashed repeatedly with CBS News president Fred Friendly, who demanded the airtime Aubrey resented turning over to profit-draining news specials. Friendly recalls Aubrey telling him, "In this adversary system, you and I are always going to be at each other's throats. They say to me, 'Take your soiled little hands, get the ratings, and make as much money as you can'; they say to you, 'Take your lily-white hands, do your best, go the high road and bring us prestige.'" At budget meetings, Aubrey routinely tormented Friendly by making such statements to Paley as "You can see, Mr. Chairman, how much higher our profits could have been this year if it had not been for the drain of news." Perhaps Aubrey did not state the conflict as eloquently as Friendly recalled, but nonetheless, the two men were now competing for money and attention rather than co-operating. The conflict was an unforeseen consequence of Stanton's 1951 table of reorganization. By walling off divisions of the network, he had placed them in a position of vying with each other for pre-eminence.

Aubrey usually got his way, often against the better judgment of Paley and Stanton, for the simple reason that he was making good on his promise to double company profits. The source of all these riches, the filmed series which Aubrey so vigorously championed, happened to be puerile and banal, often flavored with strong rural themes. Sexuality was everpresent but diluted to the point of sterility. Aubrey dictated a memorandum concerning the kind of program he was looking for, and, in the words of one executive, it specified that the ingredients for a successful prime-time series included "broads, bosoms, and fun." When word got around that the charming, sophisticated, Ivy League president of CBS television was advocating such hokey fare, Aubrey denied responsibility for the memo. Yet the revelation struck a chord, and the memo became known as the Aubrey dictum.

In contrast, ABC hatched a so-called Treyz trend, named after programmer Oliver Treyz. The Treyz trend called for plenty of violence. As such, it proved to be a risky proposition. One episode of the ABC series "Bus Stop" featured the popular singer Fabian portraying a lunatic who murders a storekeeper and his lawyer, then rides with his married girl friend to their own deaths. As a result, Treyz found himself hauled before a Senate subcommittee investigating salacious programming. Treyz resigned in the face of public criticism.

Paley was not exactly pleased with the fruits of the Aubrey dictum: the programming negated the sophisticated image CBS had projected ever since the network had come under his control. He at first resisted, but in the end he acquiesced to such Aubrey-backed series as "The Munsters," "Gomer Pyle," and "Petticoat Junction," all of which performed well in the ratings race. The Aubrey dictum reached its apogee with the premiere of "The Beverly Hillbillies," a rural comedy which shot to the top of the ratings and became a rallying point for television critics. In their eyes, the series epitomized the utter vacuousness of network television in a time of social upheaval.

That was just the point. Aubrey-era programming was meant as a habit-forming tranquilizer. In direct contrast to Weaver, Aubrey contended that the viewer preferred to watch the same programs in the same time periods week after week, season after season. News and entertainment specials only served to disrupt viewing patterns. The viewer would be disappointed not to find his favorite characters engaged in the harmless nonsense of the week. Because it could be more completely controlled, and repeated, film proved to be the ideal medium for such an approach. So committed was Aubrey to film as a cheap programming source that he engineered an agreement to purchase a package of Paramount's pre-1948 feature titles for a bargain price of $56,000,000, but to his anger and disappointment, Paley vetoed the deal. It was the first setback Aubrey had received while running the network.

In part, CBS's rapid growth under the Aubrey regime reflected a boom in the national economy. All Aubrey needed to do was ride the wave skillfully, and he did, with more cunning than his rivals. By 1964, all leading daytime programs were part of the CBS roster, and most prime-time programming belonged to the network as well. Whereas NBC charged about $41,000 for a minute of prime-time advertising, and ABC $45,000, CBS could command $50,000, a figure amounting to $1,000,000 in revenue each night. Soon Wall Street took note of the network's robust financial condition. In 1962, the company reported about half a billion dollars in net sales, with the television network contributing fully 60 per cent of the total. CBS stock began climbing steadily. A 1963 trade report attributed 886,000 shares of CBS to Paley, worth nearly $48,000,000 at the time. Paley's personal fortune, then, grew fat from the effects of the Aubrey dictum. (Not that Aubrey was the sole source of CBS financial success. Paley's decision to finance the musical *My Fair Lady* had meant a return to the network by 1964 of $33,000,000.) Paley continued to enjoy his by now traditional status as the highest paid executive in the industry, earning $325,000 in 1964. Frank Stanton fared well also: his earnings nearly equaled Paley's and he owned about 300,000 shares of CBS. In addition to owning a round 20,000 shares of CBS, Aubrey enjoyed the benefit of stock options, or the opportunity to buy shares at a fixed price, plus a salary that in 1964 amounted to $225,000. As a result, any programming decision he made which increased CBS ratings had the effect of lining his pockets with money. He would not get richer by pre-empting "The Beverly Hillbillies" in favor of a live news special.

In the abstract, at least, CBS had a variety of ways in which it might dispose of its newfound wealth. It might improve the quality of its programming, for instance. Or widen its news coverage. It could revive more substantial entertainment fare or pioneer new forms of programming, as it had done in the early nineteen thirties, when the network enjoyed a similar boom. CBS did none of the above. The network did not see fit to pass on its good fortune to the viewer, only to the shareholder.

The cash-rich company, following the trend of the times, began to buy up other companies. Stanton undertook diversification in the name of easing the tax bite into corporate profits and lessening the company's reliance on broadcasting as the primary profit center. This arrangement raised the unpleasant specter of the television network's becoming but another profit center within the company, competing with a host of alien concerns.

Though diversification has rarely been a happy venture for CBS, it has been a crucial one, affecting the company more profoundly than any other event during the six decades of its existence. Moving ever further from its base in network broadcasting, the glossy CBS image and esprit de corps upon which the company had prided itself became something for a public relations department to maintain rather than a self-evident reality.

The visible symbol of this new, diversified, anonymous CBS was its bold new headquarters located at 51 West Fifty-second Street, occupied in the fall of 1961. Where the old building exuded a ramshackle, casual charm, harboring many separate and illustrious desmesnes, the new one tended to reduce everyone to ciphers on a flow chart. Rising between ABC's New York headquarters at 1330 Avenue of the Americas and NBC's throne at 30 Rockefeller Plaza, the CBS edifice, known as Black Rock, completed the trio of skyscrapers comprising broadcast row. Along with much of the city's commercial activity, the networks had slowly moved uptown, away from the dungeonlike streets of lower Manhattan where AT&T and Western Union had their headquarters, and ever closer to the heart of the advertising industry.

If NBC's tower captured the network aspiration towards glamour and respectability in the mode of the nineteen thirties, then Black Rock epitomized the corporate image of the nineteen sixties.

The building was Stanton's abiding legacy to the network. For years he had hunted for a new site, even taking options in his own name so as not to arouse suspicions. Finally, when the company was flush with Aubrey-era profits, it plunged $40,000,000 into new headquarters intended to be the last word in sophistication. The result would be the architect Eero Saarinen's only skyscraper and his last work, one which he did not live to see finished. In this case, the architect had an unforeseen collaborator by the name of Frank Stanton. The CBS president became almost obsessively concerned with the minutiae of the building's appearance. According to Friendly, Black Rock is five hundred feet tall and all Stanton. "You dream about it at night," he remarked at the time. "You think about it in the morning on the way to the office. You spend time on the weekends, you spend time with the architect. I can't quantify it . . . you give everything you've got to making sure you get what you want."

The good doctor was carrying on a love affair with a black building. One of the things he wanted was that blackness. He was particularly pleased with a new process that allowed the granite exterior to retain a dark color after it was roughened. The building's color served as a partial inspiration for its nickname; the other inspiration had to do with the grim executive reckoning occurring within its confines.

To be sure, Black Rock exudes power. The dark granite slabs resemble giant vertical louvers. The windows, tinted gray, recall the dark windows of a large, sleek limousine. In fact, the edifice was a structural equivalent of those other accouterments of executive authority, the gray flannel suit and the black limousine. It is impressive yet forbidding, anonymous yet ominous.

So much for the exterior. The interior was a different matter. The architectural critic Ada Louise Huxtable dubbed it "a solid gold corporate cliché." That cliché was interrupted at the thirty-fifth floor, which was given over to Paley's offices and executive conference rooms. The seat of his power is distinctly unbusinesslike. The floors are covered with a plush dark green carpet, and the walls adorned with instantly recognizable examples of modern art. Paley's personal domain, then, defies the corporate anonymity. The long, hushed corridors punctuated by sculpture and paintings serve to create the impression of a palace of a modern-day doge. And Paley's office resembles a den, not the seat of a vast corporate enterprise. Perhaps the most revealing detail is the desk at which the silver-haired chairman of the board sits, a nineteenth-century *chemin-de-fer* table with numerals inlaid in pearl at each place. Paley naturally sits at position number one, the single most successful gambler in the network sweepstakes. The sole jarring note in the midst of this lavish tranquillity is the huge, ghostly ABC sign looming just beyond the picture window. Amid this extravaganza of quietly optimistic tastefulness, then, lies a contradiction. Paley, still the company's supreme arbiter, obviously displays values out of keeping with the network product. Though he and his network have grown rich, they have grown apart. The decor only serves to underscore his remoteness from the day-to-day operations.

Aside from Paley's exotic outpost in Black Rock, Stanton lavished an inordinate amount of attention on the building's appointments. He oversaw the design of a special typeface to indicate floors in the elevators, placed sensors in his secretaries' chairs to keep track of their comings and goings, and on Saturday morning prowled the hushed skyscraper, screwdriver in hand, making sure that grooves in the screws were parallel to the ground.

It was in these imposing quarters, then, that CBS pushed forward its diversification program. To this end, Stanton received inspiration from a memo prepared by Alfred Sloan, the guiding force behind General Motors, about that corporation's plans for decentralization. The omens for such a move, however, were mixed. While Columbia Records prospered, the $50,000,000 Hytron calamity loomed large. Nevertheless, CBS made a highly public plunge in 1964, paying out $11,200,000 for an 80 per cent interest in the New York Yankees. Sports writers cried foul. Stanton had to defend his decision to purchase the ball club before a Senate subcommittee on antitrust and monopoly. Worse, the purchase had a demoralizing effect on the team. CBS had obviously figured that the Yankees would maintain their outstanding winning record. During the ten years previous to the purchase, they had won the pennant nine times. But now key players and members of management began retiring. In 1966, only two years after the Yankees became part of the CBS family, they finished in the cellar. As public attendance fell, CBS went ahead with another $2,000,000 for complete control of the club. Stanton devoted ever more space to the Yankees in house publications. It looked as if CBS cared more about baseball than broadcasting. Eventually, it became apparent that these two highly specialized fields could not be successfully yoked together. Compared to Hytron, the Yankee misadventure amounted to a minor disaster; CBS sold the team in 1973 for $10,000,000. The Yankees slowly began to rebuild, but it was clear that Stanton had come to bat with the bases loaded and struck out.

There appeared to be no end to the mergers and acquisitions CBS did not consider making at the time. Reports circulated that Stanton was casting a covetous eye on Paramount, McGraw-Hill, *The New Yorker*, Time-Life. Chief stumbling block to these potential mergers remained antitrust considerations. Finally, in 1967, CBS did make another major acquisition, paying out more than $275,000,000 in cash and stock for the publishing concern of Holt, Rinehart, and Winston. The company looked like a safe bet, and much of its profit came from the lucrative textbook market. Soon after, the bottom dropped out of the market, and Holt profits slumped. Other CBS acquisitions of the era included Creative Playthings, a retailer of "educational" toys ($13,500,000); Fender Guitar ($13,000,000); and several specialized publishing and music companies. With each acquisition, the network dwindled in importance to the company.

At the same time, technological advances threatened to loosen the networks' grip on the public's airwaves. The growth of cable television, sometimes known as community antenna television (CATV), created the potential for local systems to generate programming exclusively for their customers, who would then be siphoned away from the network mainstream. It became apparent that the time-honored affiliate system, backbone of the networks, would one day have to vie with alternate systems of program distribution. The new cable industry gave signs of leaping ahead as swiftly as network broadcasting once had. CBS moved quickly into the CATV market, snapping up nine systems in Canada, which had preceded the United States in exploring cable applications, and four more in this country. But, in a crucial 1970 ruling, the FCC, concerned about the networks' monopolizing the burgeoning cable industry, ordered them to sell off their domestic cable interests. The networks reluctantly complied. The shadow cast by this regulatory wall would lengthen with every passing year as cable distribution continued to reach more viewers.

Apparently the latest thing in television technology, the cable harked back to the earliest days of broadcasting, the prenetwork era when AT&T advanced the concept of "toll broadcasting" and searched for ways to induce the listener to pay for receiving radio programs as he paid to use his telephone. In contrast, Sarnoff had argued that the listener, paying handsomely for his set, would not respond well to an additional charge for receiving programs. As a result, the networks came to rely completely on advertising as their source of revenue. The resurrected concept of point-to-point communications, as opposed to the networks' penchant for broadcasting through the public's airwaves for all to enjoy, promised to induce variables into a stagnant system. Cable offered the potential of sending programs to specially selected audiences identified by region, income, age, and other characteristics. Where network broadcasting strived to reach mass audiences with the lowest common denominator in programming, cable brought the possibility of programming for many different audiences.

For a long while, the possibilities for cable remained just that and no more. The networks stood at the apogee of their power. So pervasive was their influence that they seemed synonymous with broadcasting. However, a pressure from within—the drive to diversify —and a pressure from without—technological innovations—meant that networks would in time assume decreasing importance to their parent companies and to viewers, who could anticipate new sources of programming. The first faint signs of obsolescence were becoming apparent, and while networks were in no danger of going broke and in fact would continue to find the demand for advertising rising over the years to come, they could anticipate a waning of their relative influence as the broadcasting industry began to expand beyond their reach. Increasingly, networks girded for the prospect of competing not against each other so much as against a host of non-network broadcasting systems—cable, tape, discs, and, most threatening of all, communications satellites. Located in stationary orbits above the earth, these multichanneled satellites could act as giant relay systems, distributing to local stations or directly to homes. With the commercial networks wedded to AT&T's landlines, the satellite presaged an entirely new transmission system, one allowing stations to circumvent networks.

Despite such heady notions whirling through the minds of industry theorists, CBS plodded along a conventional path, eventually stumbling into another managerial crisis. For a company obsessed with public image, CBS did have a knack for blundering into scandal. Again, a programmer with a Midas touch was turning out to be a liability.

In the end, James Aubrey did himself in as no ratings-hungry competitor could have done. So convinced was he of the correctness of his decisions that he began treating established CBS stars with a ruthlessness that earned him the sobriquet the Smiling Cobra. Godfrey was one of the first to go. After recovering from an operation for lung cancer, he found himself restricted to radio. Next, Jack Benny departed the network to which he had brought new life in the postwar era for a farewell season on NBC. Though these and other dismissals raised eyebrows, for sheer shock value they could not match Aubrey's cavalier handling of the prime-time schedule. For all of his addiction to the habit theory of programming, Aubrey was a restless programmer, and his restlessness caused him to violate his own successful, if rigid, premises. For the 1964-65 season, he scheduled four completely unknown series. Neither "The Cara Williams Show," "The Baileys of Balboa,"

"The Reporter," nor "Living Doll" possessed a pilot, a known star, or, for that matter, even a script at the time Aubrey scheduled them.

As it happened, three of the four programs were produced by Aubrey's long-time friend, a none-too-successful actor turned producer named Keefe Brasselle, with whom Aubrey had been acquainted ever since his days at KNXT in Los Angeles. None of the Brasselle-produced programs lasted the entire season. Now Aubrey found himself in serious trouble with Paley, for in addition to all the other reservations that the chairman may have had about Aubrey's taste in programming, failing in his own terms was inexcusable. Aubrey's extravagant reliance on Brasselle also aroused the suspicions of the FCC, which instituted an investigation of a conflict of interest. CBS prepared a counterreport which attempted to exonerate Aubrey. Then the IRS chimed in, claiming Aubrey owed back taxes. Aubrey paid, though it was indeed odd that he, unlike other network executives, did not participate in the usual salary-deferment arrangement to ease the tax bite. Finally, his personal life became an issue. The industry was abuzz with rumors concerning his offbeat after-hours activities. From all quarters, then, the pressure mounted.

One weekend in February 1965, Stanton summoned Aubrey back to New York from Miami, where CBS was having an affiliates meeting. Paley flew in from his retreat in the Bahamas. Aubrey brought his lawyers to the meeting with Stanton. There the CBS president asked for Aubrey's resignation. When the news of Aubrey's departure broke, CBS stock skittered downward.

Even after Aubrey vacated his office, CBS felt the dismissal might cause tremors and proceeded to brace itself. As Aubrey hired a public relations concern to enhance his image, Paley charged a CBS vice-president, Kidder Meade, with the task of projecting a favorable public image for him. The expected blow finally landed the following fall, when *Life* ran an unusually hard-nosed exposé of Aubrey's career at CBS. One of the reasons *Life* ran the exposé was that the magazine itself was engaged in a losing battle with television for an audience and advertising revenue.

In the wake of the damage the article did to CBS's already battered reputation, Paley finally decided he had retreated just a little too far into the shadows. To the world at large, Stanton appeared to be the chief proprietor of the network and Paley a shadowy figure living in luxury. Yet there were signs that Stanton's days were numbered, that Paley would, in the end, hold him accountable for the company's errors. While the CBS vice-chairman—that was Stanton's title by now—presented a flawless facade, he had in reality been involved with any number of CBS fumbles, beginning with the television station debacle, the reversal on color, the Yankees, and now Aubrey. As for Hytron, Paley tended to place the blame for that one squarely on Goldmark's shoulders. While adept at maintaining CBS, Stanton's record in the admittedly risky area of development, innovation, and experimentation was unimpressive. CBS was not an innovative company, but a masterful follower of the trends of the times, whether they happened to be in technology, taste, or politics. With every shake-up in personnel—and they would continue at an accelerated pace after Aubrey's departure—speculation revived as to when Paley would finally retire and appoint Stanton chairman, but the old guard carried on. Paley, in fact, was finding reasons why Stanton should not continue.

Though he left New York embroiled in controversy, Aubrey's reputation as an executive remained intact. In fact, in Hollywood his personal image was enhanced as a result of the *Life* exposé. He found his way to the presidency of MGM, where he presided over the liquidation of that company's assets. Once, Hollywood had blamed television for its sorry state, yet now a major studio looked to James Aubrey for guidance.

17

A Student of Television

IN 1959, WHEN A TWENTY-TWO-YEAR-OLD GRADUATE STUDENT at Ohio State University was casting about for a worthwhile topic for his master's thesis in communications, he decided to turn his attention not to venerable NBC or august CBS, but to the scrappy newcomer, ABC. The graduate student judged the network not by its public service or prestige but by the same yardstick the network itself employed: the best programming strategy to capture the largest possible audience. In a thesis that amounted to over four hundred pages, the graduate student recorded with fanatical precision the minute moves and countermoves the network had made between the years 1953 and 1959 in pursuit of its goal. On the basis of his findings, he predicted a glowing future for ABC, in spite of the fact that the network steadily lost money. By the time the network finally finished a season with a decisive ratings lead, in 1975, he was president of its entertainment division and chief programmer.

The graduate student was, of course, Fred Silverman, and with an awesome and precocious grasp of the intricacies of network operations, especially the cutting edge of programming, he had dissected a bewildering array of actions made by ABC executives throughout the nineteen fifties as they labored to attain full competitive strength. He interviewed network employees, visited advertising agencies, noting everything. He liked what he saw about the fourth-place network in a three-way race, the continued rapid growth, the ability to attract major sponsors, such as tobacco and detergent manufacturers, whose participation in broadcast advertising had been long and successful. He noted ABC's catch-up efforts to provide affiliates with a full daytime schedule, and he especially appreciated ABC's $11,000,000 expenditure to revamp its Monday night schedule for the 1959–60 season. By the following season, Silverman predicted, ABC would find itself on equal footing with its rivals. He also detected a trend back to live programming. In this last prediction, Silverman was, of course, in error, but the most unusual element of his analysis was his faith in ABC's competitive strategy at a time when the network was generally demoralized within and scorned without.

As Silverman saw the situation, ABC's hidden strength lay in its emphasis on programming for youthful audiences. He even recommended that the network adapt and recycle a more juvenile version of its competitors' 1953–54 schedules. In this respect he was one of the first to advocate an alternative theory of programming that finally received full recognition in the nineteen seventies: the importance of reaching not the largest possible audience, as James Aubrey had tried to do, but specific segments of the population who, in the eyes of advertisers, would be most receptive to their messages and products. In this scheme of things, the core market consisted of teen-agers and young families in the eighteen- to thirty-four-year-old age bracket. To this end, Silverman called for a "balance of all program types" in ABC's future seasons, "specially conceived and plotted for the younger-larger family groups."

What the boy wonder of the Ohio State speech department had done was to hit upon a programming philosophy which even ABC had yet to articulate fully. For the moment, it was still groping toward the strategy of employing programming as a bait to attract those audience segments advertisers most wanted to reach, whether it be homemakers listening to a soap opera while they ironed or teen-agers tuning in situation comedies in lieu of completing homework assignments. But Silverman wanted to take the network a bit further. "For the 1960–61 and seasons which follow," he proclaimed, as if the network had hired him as a special consultant, "ABC should provide a balanced schedule, within the 'get-age' framework." It should be noted that there was a distinct lack of interest on the part of the young Silverman in news or other noncommercial programming. It was just not very high on his —or, it is safe to say ABC's—agenda.

In his appraisal of ABC's performance during the trying years of the fifties, Silverman came to these remarkably positive conclusions:

> The network was the first to reach an agreement with a major motion picture studio; first to broadcast feature films on a network basis; first to program the "adult western" in sizable numbers; first to originate a one-hour mystery program with continuing characters; first to recognize the value of the 7:30 pm time period; and first to originate a new breed of young, virile television personalities.

Nearly all the firsts which Silverman admired were programming decisions designed to capture youthful audiences. In commending ABC for its foresight, he was setting the course for his own career as a programmer-strategist.

If he had not become a network programmer, he might have been a chess master or perhaps a military theoretician, for in the world of Fred Silverman, strategy is all. The son of a television repairman, he was raised in the New York borough of Queens. Before receiving his master's degree at Ohio State, he attended Syracuse University as an undergraduate. Naturally, he sent copies of his *magnum opus* to all the networks, but ABC, muddled in its own problems, did not respond to the well-organized minutiae that went into the making of his thesis. If it had, the network might have attained its supremacy in the ratings race much sooner. Silverman instead found employment at WGN, the major independent station in Chicago. There he worked ratings wonders with those younger-larger family groups by recycling old movies in new formats. After a brief stint in New York with another independent station, WPIX-TV, CBS hired him to head its daytime programming department. He was twenty-six, and his thesis had paid off after all. His boss, program director Mike Dann, had seen the study and been highly impressed. "Reading it I could see the kid had instincts that were unbelievable," Dann recalled. At CBS, Silverman again demonstrated a flair for bringing previously marginal airtime to commercial life by paying strict attention to demographics, especially as they revealed viewing patterns of younger audiences in the daytime hours. To help sponsors reach homemakers, he scheduled new soap operas. And to help sponsors reach children, he replaced reruns of situation comedies on Saturday mornings with cartoons. When Mike Dann, a cocky adherent of the Paley approach to programming, left the network in 1970, he was replaced by none other than the young man he had hired seven years before.

Still young, Silverman rapidly became old in the ways of television programming. His career began to display strong resemblances to that of another older CBS executive, Frank Stanton. Like him, Silverman had begun his involvement with network broadcasting in a Midwestern academic setting, devoting himself to a great deal of research. Like Stanton, he had made an intensive study of a network's chief concern at the moment. In Stanton's case it was convincing advertisers that broadcast advertising sold more effectively than print, and in Silverman's it was the formulation of a programming strategy aimed at youthful audiences. Like Stanton he sent the fruits of his research to the networks, and sooner or later found a receptive ear at CBS. Both men displayed a command of the minutiae essential to operating a network, a command that presaged sound administrative ability, hard work, long hours, and a corresponding lack of originality.

Silverman came to play a dual role of *wunderkind* and Peck's Bad Boy at CBS, where executive style often outweighs the importance of executive substance. He did not function smoothly in the highly refined, bureaucratic atmosphere. Neither as innovative and articulate as Weaver, as cold-blooded as Aubrey, nor as flamboyant as Cowan, Silverman remained an anomaly among CBS executives. He did not attempt to shove a condescending program philosophy at the audience, nor did he feel the need to offset blatantly commercial programming with public-service or prestige offerings. He took programs at their own level, laughing or crying with them, getting emotionally involved with scripts, pilots, and performers that other executives disdained. In so doing, Silverman made his peers feel uncomfortable, because his passion for connecting or identifying with the programs made him appear to be more like one of "them," the vast, unseen audience, than one of "us," the elite, highly paid executive corps whose code of honor in part entailed a rigid segregation of personal preference from professional taste. As programmers, executives were forced to violate their own instincts about scheduling material that common sense told them was woefully inadequate in favor of adhering to the abstract, self-justifying rules of the programming game. Silverman, however, experienced no such disjunction; he liked what other executives disdained. This ability to identify was simultaneously the source of Silverman's strength as a programmer, in that he could in good conscience rely on his instincts, and of his weakness, in that he was incapable of seeing beyond a narrow programming spectrum. Silverman did not bother to concern himself with what the public ought or needed to know, only what he guessed it would watch.

Silverman's last four years at CBS witnessed a profound alteration in the network's approach to programming. When he inherited the position of vice-president from Dann, the network was still living off the Aubrey years. By the 1969–70 season, the CBS comedy series were a tired lot indeed, "The Beverly Hillbillies," "Gomer Pyle," "Mayberry R.F.D.," "Here's Lucy," etc. Robert Wood, the network's president, spearheaded the effort to deruralize the schedule, to eliminate the Aubrey-inspired fluff along with remnants of the earlier, New York-oriented programming era which had given birth to Jackie Gleason and Ed Sullivan as television stars. It is worth noting that these programs were still popular, but, as Wood, with a background in sales acutely realized, they were popular with the "wrong" people. They were popular with older audiences, with rural audiences, not with the young, urban homes that advertisers wanted to reach. It was, in Silverman's opinion, "absolutely essential to change the network's demographics."

Before he could act, Wood staked his career on convincing chairman Paley of the wisdom of the new course he envisioned for CBS. "A parade will be coming down the street," he said in a crucial pitch reported by New York *Times* television correspondent Les Brown, "and you may watch it from your rocking chair, collecting your dividends, and it will go by you. Or you might get up from that chair and get into the parade, so that when it goes by your house you won't just be watching it, you'll be leading it." CBS was "falling behind the times," not to mention the advertising community. Wood, in short, skillfully employed the "get-age" philosophy Silverman had espoused so many years before.

Wood got his way, overseeing the cancellation of thirteen series in an effort to clear away the rural dead wood from the 1970–71 season. The most important replacement appeared on the air midseason. It was an apparently rudimentary, abrasive situation comedy produced by the team of Norman Lear and Bud Yorkin. By the time "All in the Family," the sitcom which would set the tone of entertainment programming for the rest of the decade, aired for the first time on the evening of January 12, 1971, the series had already suffered a long, tortured history. Lear, a veteran comedy writer and producer, had written the original pilot in the late sixties, adapting a hit English series, "Till Death Do Us Part," produced by the British Broadcasting Corporation. Written by Johnny Speight, the British original took as its protagonist a lower-middle-class bigot and scored its points about the nature of social prejudice through the use of heavy, mordant satire. Lear, professing to base his version of the bigot on his own father, stumbled across an infinitely adaptable vehicle for satirizing and ventilating the prejudices of a nation polarized along political and ethnic lines. Lear's Archie Bunker displayed a knack for uttering the unspeakable on television, shattering its repressive ignorance of all social issues. The racism and hypocrisy that had been implicit in television

Leonard Goldenson, ABC chairman, right, with company president Elton Rule. *Courtesy ABC*.

The General's son, Robert W. Sarnoff, in 1972. *Courtesy RCA*.

Fred Silverman, formerly of CBS and ABC, now of NBC. The programmer *par excellence* who brought ABC from "fourth in a three-way race" to number one.

Newton Minow, former chairman of the Federal Communications Commission and now chairman of the Public Broadcasting System. *Courtesy PBS.*

Julia Child as "The French Chef." *Photo by Paul Child, courtesy WGBH.*

Dr. Jacob Bronowski, writer and narrator of the highly acclaimed series "The Ascent of Man." *Courtesy PBS.*

The British invasion of PBS began with the BBC adaptation of John Galsworthy's *The Forsyte Saga* and continued with...

...the highly popular tale of an Edwardian family, "Upstairs, Downstairs." *(Both photos courtesy WGBH)*

Mikhail Baryshnikov in a PBS telecast of Balanchine's "Prodigal Son." *Courtesy WNET.*

programming for nearly a decade were all at once unmasked and ridiculed.

CBS, however, hardly rushed to embrace Lear's iconoclastic sitcom. Interestingly, it was the younger and more competitive ABC that had financed two earlier versions of the pilot, which they found too risqué to air. Any network would be afraid of the public reaction to a scene in which Archie intrudes upon his daughter and her boy friend, who struggles to pull up his fly. Even worse, Archie uttered the most taboo word in the network lexicon, "goddamn." When Lear agreed to tone down the pilot, eliminating the fly incident and some "goddamns," CBS agreed to schedule the program. After its debut, the airwaves did not sizzle, and neither did television sets melt, but the program did meet with some dismay on the part of critics. However, "All in the Family" gathered strength as the season wore on, especially during summer reruns, climbing to the very top of the ratings on the evident strength of its characterizations. A decade after its debut, a modified version of the series continues to hover near the top of the ratings, nourished by an inexhaustible supply of national prejudice.

Lear cleverly exploited the success of the series, using it as a springboard from which he launched similar sitcoms. Characters appeared on "All in the Family," where they gained popularity and audience exposure, then graduated to their own series. Notable examples included "Maude" and "The Jeffersons," both on CBS.

The Lear comedies, unlike the standardized tedium of filmed series, crackled with spontaneity. They reintroduced the authentic, raucous values of classic radio comedy: warmth of humor, reliance on sharp script writing, wordplay, and immediacy. Lear managed to strike a balance between the electricity of live performance and the technical demands imposed by television. Much of this was due to the use of videotape and a live audience. In the writing as well, "All in the Family" marked a return to traditional but discarded techniques. Its humor sprang from character rather than action, eliciting some degree of response and reflection on the part of the viewer. Mind-numbing car chases were absent. In the manner of "Amos 'n' Andy" and "Easy Aces," the series relied heavily on malapropisms and ethnic humor, in this instance employing it to demolish rather than reinforce damaging stereotypes.

CBS bolstered its revamped schedule with other programs reflecting or exploiting social concerns, adapting old formulas to new themes. A cops-and-robbers series, "Kojak," explored the difficulties of an inner-city police department. Even the prominent exception to the urban bias, a rural family drama series called "The Waltons," was set in the Depression era, emphasizing a relevance to the present. The strategy worked again and again. In 1973–74, nine of the ten most popular programs were on the CBS schedule, and the presence of the majority of them was due largely to Fred Silverman.

The influx of urban-oriented programs was abetted by a subtle but crucial change in the nature of network advertising. After a decade of debate, the FCC finally decided to ban cigarette advertising on television, beginning January 2, 1971, the day after the usual New Year's glut of cigarette-sponsored football games and ten days before "All in the Family" went on the air. Ever since Congress Cigar had advertised the La Palina on WCAU, right through George Washington Hill's successful advocacy of cigarette advertising on NBC, the tobacco industry had been a broadcast advertising staple. At the time of the ban, more than $200,000,000, or almost a fifth of all network revenue, was derived from cigarette advertising. To stave off the sudden dip in revenues, CBS instituted thirty-second commercials, thus opening up the field to new sponsors who could now advertise on network television for half of what it cost in the days when sixty-second commercials predominated. With the number of sponsors of a given program now nearly doubling, whatever vestiges of sponsor-program identification remained were now obliterated. Network revenues skidded slightly in reaction to the ban for the first time since the Depression. Pretax profits fell precipitously from a 1969 high of $92,700,000 to $50,000,000 the following year and $53,700,000 in 1971, the first full year of the ban. By 1972, however, profits again shot up to $110,900,000 and more than doubled that extraordinary figure only two years later as the demand for the fixed amount of broadcast advertising time available continued to increase. But costs also were staggering: a ninety-minute episode of a Western like "The Virginian," for example, consumed as much as $285,000. Such was the high price of mediocrity.

Silverman, for his part, was doing quite well, earning about a quarter of a million dollars in 1974, but after twelve years with CBS he had yet to attain full-fledged executive status. Compared to the revenues he helped CBS earn, his salary was insignificant, the equivalent of several minutes of advertising time on the network. He had reached the limit at CBS. One evening after work, a disconsolate Silverman was approached by ABC president Fred Pierce, who began delicately sounding out the boy wonder of television programming as to his future plans. Pierce offered the terms Silverman had desired but never achieved at CBS, $300,000 salary, a $1,000,000 life-insurance policy, stock options, limousine service, a co-operative apartment, and a fancy title, president of the entertainment division. Silverman defected. The severity of his loss to CBS can be compared to the long-lasting damage Kintner's departure had inflicted upon ABC when he left that network in 1956 to take over the presidency of NBC television. Once again an invaluable asset had been turned into a ruthless competitor.

Silverman could hardly have chosen a more auspicious time to switch. Under the patient doctoring of executives like Pierce and Elton Rule, the network was poised for a takeoff which would have come about whether or not Silverman was in a position to preside over it. The network which had lost a total of $100,000,000 between 1963 and 1971 suddenly found itself turning a handsome profit. So in demand was advertising time that even the third place network could at last support itself. The economy had finally grown to the point where it could sustain three fully commercial national networks.

ABC had managed to create flickers of success throughout the nineteen sixties. Its 1959–60 season, much admired by Silverman's thesis, introduced a violent, hour-long series called "The Untouchables." Little more than a typical Hollywood gangster picture adapted for the small screen, the series soon led the ratings and presaged a wave of violent imitators. Prime-time programming success triggered development of the daytime schedule. In 1959, ABC engineered an arrangement with Young & Rubicam to offer daytime advertising at less than half the rate charged by the competition, just $2,000 a minute as compared to $5,000. While CBS and NBC cried foul, Operation Daybreak, as the advertising price war was named, supplied the ABC network with fifteen additional sponsored daytime hours per week. The programming involved was a mixed bag: Liberace, "Day in Court," "The Verdict Is Yours." Now ABC began to collect new affiliates at an alarming rate, each one bringing with it a new audience. Of the 485 television network affiliates in 1959, only 79, or 15.5 per cent, belonged to ABC, while NBC counted twice as many, 213 (41.8 per cent). Just four years later, however, ABC's affiliate strength was up to 117 (21 per cent), while NBC's had slipped to 203 (36.4 per cent).

Suddenly, network broadcasting was a full-blown three-way race, with the third network, the one originally intended to bring diversity to the airwaves, contributing greatly to the climate of programming conformity. CBS and NBC were more interested in not losing ground than in exploring new programming horizons. Because it grew the fastest over this period, ABC, though the third-place network, actually was the most influential of all three in terms of its effect on the competition. Both NBC with Kintner and CBS with Aubrey had program heads who had received valuable training at ABC. In an industry where rate of growth is the ultimate arbiter of commercial success, ABC could boast of the most impressive growth of all. The last-place network, then, set the pace for all three competitors.

However, ABC's years of travail were hardly over. In the mid-sixties, when cash-rich CBS and RCA set about to devour other companies, ABC was small enough to find itself on the verge of being devoured. The first threat appeared in the person of Norton Simon, the California-based businessman who acquired a taste for television when he appeared on an NBC program in connection with his art collection. Simon began buying up shares of ABC; by July 1965 he owned 400,000, or 9 per cent, far exceeding Goldenson's investment. With nearly $23,000,000 invested in ABC, Simon appeared to be engaged in a take-over maneuver, though he denied that he was. Goldenson did not regard the move with favor. Like Paley and CBS, he had come to regard ABC as his personal domain, an extension of himself.

Next, General Electric, the company from which RCA and therefore NBC and ABC originally sprang, tried to bring history full circle and considered a merger with the network, but in light of antitrust considerations backed away. Now the word was out. It appeared that ABC would wind up in someone's arms, and it was merely a question of whose. International Telephone and Telegraph, the multinational conglomerate, appeared to be the next suitor. Under the direction of Harold Geneen, the company hoped to broaden its base of influence in the United States, and owning a national network seemed as good a way as any to do it. ITT first approached CBS, where Stanton was intrigued by the idea, but Paley, not very surprisingly, would have none of it. Goldenson, however, preferred rescue at the hands of ITT, since it appeared the company would allow his management team to stay in place, to vanquishment at the hands of Simon, who might drive Goldenson out of the company. In the parlance of Wall Street, ITT became ABC's White Knight.

A merger with ITT could turn out to be satisfactory all around. The network was about to undertake a vastly expensive conversion to color broadcasting. When CBS and NBC finally announced that they would begin broadcasting in color in the mid-nineteen sixties, ABC, to remain commercially competitive, would have to follow suit, even though it lacked the mammoth resources of either competitor. ITT could function as ABC's RCA, so to speak, a wealthy parent company with enough cash to back the conversion to color. Goldenson dispatched his closest aide, company bookkeeper Simon Siegel, to work out a merger agreement. Meanwhile, ITT lent the company $25,000,000 to go ahead with conversion. It was a satisfactory dowry, but would the FCC give its blessing to the marriage?

At the very end of 1966, the commission barely approved the merger, with a four-to-three vote. The reasoning of those in favor was that a financially strengthened ABC would be better able to compete against its older brothers. The merger was now breathtakingly close to becoming a reality, but the Justice Department had other ideas. Its lawyers went to court to argue that ABC's news programming would be compromised if the network's parent company were a multinational enterprise, not entirely subject to the laws of the land. However, Justice's choice of arguments mattered little compared to its timing. The merger plan specified that if consummation did not occur by January 1, 1968, the marriage was off. The Justice Department's suit slowed the progress of the merger sufficiently to allow the deadline to pass. ITT withdrew its suit. Soon after, Simon sold off nearly all his ABC shares. ABC stock swooped from 80 to 45. The demoralized network still found itself vulnerable to take-over bids, however, and the next one to materialize was the most disturbing to date, for the man who now sought control of ABC was the billionaire recluse of Las Vegas, Howard Hughes.

Early in 1968, Goldenson refused an invitation to sit down with Hughes, who had once owned RKO Pictures and now hoped to acquire ABC through the Hughes Tool Company. The most frightening aspect of the bid was its timing, coming just at the moment when ABC, trying to raise some cash, announced a plan to sell debentures and to mortgage, in effect, its film library to the Hanover Bank. ABC went to court to fight the Hughes take-over bid, and lost. Again, the company appeared to be tottering on the edge of a merger, this one replete with hidden implications.

There remained, however, one small problem. Howard Hughes would have to appear in public and testify before the FCC and perhaps a congressional subcommittee. The last time Hughes had appeared in such surroundings was 1947, to answer questions about the enormous Spruce Goose aircraft he had constructed. The mere thought of appearing again was enough to cause the recluse to ditch his carefully formulated plans.

Now that it was apparent he would have to go it alone, Goldenson took steps to strengthen his network, appointing Elton Rule, former manager of ABC's lucrative Los Angeles affiliate, to the presidency of the television network. From a California background, Rule had begun as a salesman for a West Coast radio station after World War II and moved up the company ranks in the sales department. This, then, was the ABC Silverman found.

At last the *wunderkind* was really in his element, in charge of programming the network whose problems and strategies he had studied with such devotion as a graduate student. The ABC he found was, in his words, "like a high school football team" that had developed "spirit in adversity." With its youthful, urban orientation, with an emphasis on entertainment, pure and simple, rather than a yearning for prestige or other distractions afflicting its older rivals, ABC was a network made for Silverman, and Silverman, with his athletic hunger for competition, his restlessness, narrow tastes, and drive, was made for ABC. He would make a fine head coach for the team.

For the second time in a row, he had taken on a position with extremely good potential. At CBS, the daytime schedule had been so secure that all Silverman was required to do was maintain its strength. Similarly, ABC's entertainment division provided him with strong ammunition. In 1974, the network had hit upon the idea of adapting novels for limited series which contained both the prestige of a special and the habit-forming characteristic of a continuing program. The first miniseries, "QBVII," adapted from the Leon Uris novel, had been broadcast in 1974. Now, Silverman found two more waiting in the wings, "Rich Man, Poor Man," from the Irwin Shaw novel, and "Roots," from Alex Haley's historical novel. Silverman displayed finesse by scheduling the "Roots" episodes on eight consecutive nights, thus endowing the miniseries with a ferocious power to involve—indeed, obsess—the audience, and as a result it received the highest rating ever achieved by an entertainment program. By carefully juggling popular sitcoms and cops-and-robbers series, Silverman led ABC to a finish but a hair behind CBS in 1976. More significantly, most ABC programs such as "Laverne and Shirley" and "Happy Days" appealed to the eighteen-to-thirty-four age group favored by advertisers. In this category, eight of the top ten programs belonged to ABC. As Silverman continued to schedule still more programming in the same mold, "Charlie's Angels" (succinctly described by one publication as a "voyeuristic crime drama with sadomasochistic overtones"), "Three's Company," and "Soap," he began to acquire a reputation unequaled since the heyday of James Aubrey at CBS. Silverman's taste in programming displayed many of the same traits, an abundance of puerile sexuality, a reliance on the habit theory of viewing, and a general tenor of escapism. The primary difference lay in the emphasis on urban rather than rural settings, but the urban setting did not guarantee an exploration of social issues. The Lear brand of satire was fast becoming passé. This new breed of programming merely exploited the loosening of restraints he had pioneered.

Building on ABC's strength, Silverman employed the miniseries again in the 1977–78 season. Using a multipart adaptation of a novel written by convicted Watergate figure John Ehrlichman, Silverman drove a powerful wedge through the competition. By scheduling "Washington: Behind Closed Doors" two weeks in advance of the other networks' fall seasons, he forced them to dig deep into programming budgets to splurge on last-minute attention-getting programming. Their goal was to prevent audiences from being lured away to ABC before the season even began. Silverman had, in effect, rediscovered the effectiveness of Weaver's spectacular, a disproportionately expensive program designed to attract attention to the network as a whole. The ploy not only helped ABC but hurt the competition and guided the network into a secure ratings lead, good for several seasons at the very least.

The momentum bred still more success. During the 1975–78 period, seventeen CBS and nine NBC affiliates switched to ABC, bringing with them their audiences, which instantly meant higher ratings at the expense of the competition. ABC bolstered its lead with a risky but ultimately profitable contract with the National Football League to broadcast games on Monday evenings. By hiring away Barbara Walters from NBC's "Today" for a highly touted $1,000,000-a-year salary, the network attracted priceless publicity and turned a competitor into an asset.

In addition to pluck, ABC also had luck.

In 1970, the FCC, concerned about network domination of the airwaves, promulgated a prime-time access rule. This had the effect of restricting network evening programming to the hours of eight to eleven only. The preceding half hour was now meant to be open to new programming sources. Far from creating a democratization of the airwaves, the rule only served to intensify the concentration of network influence. Affiliates followed the letter, if not the spirit, of the rule by scheduling game shows or reruns of syndicated situation comedies. All networks, in fact, profited from the lifting of the burden of programming for this less lucrative time period. Furthermore, the removal of the half hour increased the demand for the remaining network advertising minutes, thus allowing networks to raise their rates and spend less at the same time. Of all the networks, ABC gained the most from this new wrinkle in programming because it could cancel seven clinkers. Time and again, the FCC, in its zeal to preserve the spirit of free enterprise, proved to be the best friend a network, and especially ABC, ever had.

ABC's pretax profits from its television network hovered around the $25,000,000 mark in 1975, then increased dramatically to more than $75,000,000 a year later, $165,000,000 the following year, and for 1979 topped the $200,000,000 mark. Here was an eightfold increase in network profits in the space of just four years. Over the same period, CBS profits increased by about one third, going from $100,000,000 in 1975

to $150,000,000 in 1979. Finally, NBC's profits during this period actu-
ally skittered downward, but still revealed a lucrative operation.

Though ABC could boast of a growth rate unequaled in network
broadcasting since CBS first came into Paley's control, the economics
were such that all enjoyed huge profits. With the demand for advertising time so high, a ratings lead did not have the decisive quality it
might have had twenty years before. Everyone was coming out ahead;
it was only a question of degree. The demand for advertising ex-
ceeded what all networks combined could handle. While ABC made
the most dramatic increase in its share of advertising revenue, some of
it coming at the expense of the competition, that network, too, was
merely expanding until it reached its limit of growth. The approaching boundary reinforced the vigor of the competition. Profits were
soaring. Each rating point a network earned over the course of a season translated into an extra $30,000,000. But this frenzy concealed a
lack of confidence about the future. The time to cash in, the thinking
ran, was now, because in ten years the system could be drastically
different.

Increased head-to-head competition forced networks, regardless of
the historical circumstances of their origins, into the same mold. Each
offered—and still does—an early morning live news program; afternoon
soap operas; three hours of prime-time filmed series, often pitting the
same genre of programs against each other; and a precious half hour
of evening news headlines. Each commands the loyalty of approximately two hundred affiliates. For all their differences, they have
achieved a remarkable unanimity of function and purpose.

Silverman's surprise move to the presidency of NBC in early 1978
was a symptom of the interchangeableness afflicting the networks. The
standardization of programming policy and procedures had reached
the point where the same group of Hollywood-based producers supplied programming to all networks. With every move it mattered less
and less where Silverman happened to be at the moment. The rate of
turnover accelerated. None of the programmers responsible for scheduling the 1975–76 season, for example, were still in place by the time
the programs began to air in September. The frenzy reflected both the
endemic insecurity afflicting the networks and the standardization of
programming procedures and theories. Only in an era when all networks shared the same values could Silverman become the first individual to program in turn for CBS, ABC, and NBC. Rapid shifting of
key players now has little effect on the course of the game.

Though its announcement came as a shock, Silverman's move to
NBC actually concluded several months of delicate and secret negotiations, for NBC was not just hiring another executive, but a star, a

public personality whose very presence had dollar value independent of his actions. Installed at 30 Rockefeller Plaza, Silverman had even more prestige and power than he had enjoyed at ABC. His salary and bonuses came to $1,000,000 a year, and he was in charge of the entire network, including news and sports, and not just an entertainment division.

Yet for the first time in his career Silverman found himself in an unenviable position, for he had to program against the formidable ABC schedule he had helped to build. And at NBC, he found no "Roots," no "Charlie's Angels" waiting in the wings. It became readily apparent that Silverman had inherited a position with very poor prospects. If NBC was to have any ratings successes, Silverman would have to initiate them. He had proven his ability to schedule pre-existing programs, but his ability to concoct new ones was unknown. The network was weakest in the area in which he was strongest—situation comedies—and was suffering the consequences of years of reliance on specials, thus depriving the network of a roster of regular series returning season after season.

Silverman began by asking himself how he might go about building a schedule of one hit series after another, capture the public's fancy, launch a few unknowns into overnight stardom. In this respect, he subscribed to the Aubrey theory of programming, relying on habit to hold the viewer to the network. Whatever Silverman may have thought of Aubrey as a person, he admired him as a programmer. But Silverman, powerful as he now was, could not go out and write, direct, and cast series himself. He had to find them. He remembered that no one at CBS had planned on "All in the Family." Through a series of lucky accidents, the network had nervously selected the series since it appeared to fit into the new mold. In the hope of bringing about similar lucky accidents, ones which would bring the programming momentum to NBC, Silverman ordered no fewer than thirty pilots to be made. He canceled every new program his predecessors had scheduled. The expense was enormous; series cost about half a million dollars an hour to produce by this time.

Still no lucky accidents were in the offing at NBC.

Silverman pondered the situation in his light-toned, low-ceilinged office. Behind stood an array of awards and a reproduction of his face on the cover of *Time*. In front, a signed photograph from one of his ABC hits, "Laverne and Shirley." He was chain-smoking. His contract with NBC lasted but three years, affording him barely enough time to see the fruits of his labors, and the chances of his turning NBC around grew slimmer with every passing month. As he labored on a seven-day-a-week schedule, unsettling news trickled in. NBC's parent company, RCA, planned to sell channels on its communications satellite to potential competitors. It appeared that RCA, in its wish to remain on the technological frontier, was willing to undercut—even to sacrifice— NBC, in the name of profit. To aggravate matters further, he received news that the network's premiere performer, Johnny Carson, wished to end his participation on "The Tonight Show." Over the course of its twenty-five years, "Tonight" had been a stellar attraction, a magnet for affiliates and a contributor of an astonishing 17 per cent of the network's pretax profits. Carson's departure spelled disaster for any programmer, even Silverman.

As NBC gives signs of becoming the very first network to become obsolete, Silverman, best known of all programmers, may well be the last of the breed.

Part IV

SIGNS OF OBSOLESCENCE

A Problem of Succession

ON DECEMBER 12, 1971, DAVID SARNOFF DIED AT HIS HOME, a thirty-room townhouse at 44 East Seventy-first Street, of complications relating to a mastoid infection. He was eighty years old and had spent sixty-five of those years with the Radio Corporation and its predecessor, American Marconi. He had presided over the development of the company from cable and wireless transmission service to the nation's largest communications complex, embracing virtually every facet of the industry from invention to production, from broadcasting to station ownership, from color television to cable to satellite.

The death came on a Sunday morning, and NBC broke into a weekly public-affairs program, "Meet the Press," to announce the General's passing, then devoted a half-hour memorial program to him. It had been a marathon journey from Uzlian, where he was born, to the lower East Side of New York, where he had spent his childhood, to Siasconset, where he learned his first trade as a telegraph operator, and then to the Wanamaker store where he tallied the survivors of the *Titanic* sinking, the New York World's Fair, where he announced the commercial introduction of television, and, finally, to the fifty-third floor of 30 Rockefeller Plaza, where he ruled over his empire. In an industry in which the entrepreneur took pride of place over all other participants, Sarnoff came first. "Not money, but the opportunity to express the forces within me is my motivation," he said, "and will be till I die."

Sarnoff's most significant legacy turned out to be not radio or television, those complex inventions he packaged and promoted, but the Radio Corporation of America itself, a nucleus of communications power. And though Sarnoff identified with RCA in a profound manner, his efforts to bequeath a mandate and a free rein to a successor were muddled and halfhearted. He left three sons, Robert, Edward, and Thomas, all of whom were involved with RCA at some level at one time or another, but none of whom were granted or claimed an unambiguous role in the company's future. In time, it was left to the eldest, Bobby, to assume his father's mantle, if he, or anyone, could.

With the General's tacit consent, Bobby leaped from one corporate pinnacle to the next. He found himself president of NBC at age thirty-seven, president of RCA ten years later, in 1966, and two years after that, the company's chief executive officer, as his father retreated into retirement. Despite the obvious pattern of nepotism, Sarnoff and son did not always coexist on the most cordial of terms: long periods passed when they did not speak directly but communicated through memos and third parties. To aggravate the situation Bobby stirred more than his share of discontent throughout the company by assuming an attitude others interpreted as diffidence and arrogance.

When Bobby took command of RCA, the pressure to keep the company moving forward at its habitual breakneck pace was enormous. However, by now the mammoth, fifty-year-old organization was nearing the top of its curve of development. Seeking new worlds to conquer, Bobby moved the company heavily into diversification, buying up service companies in unrelated fields. Such was the trend of the times. However, the reorientation of the company contributed to a lessening of the importance of NBC within the overall structure. As RCA's attitude toward NBC changed, the network became merely another profit center within the conglomerate.

RCA broke out of the electronics field in a big way in 1967 when, under Bobby's direction, it bought Hertz, the car-rental company, and later, a frozen-food company, F. M. Stamper, a real-estate management concern, Cushman & Wakefield, and even a carpet company, Coronet Industries. Costing a staggering $578,000,000 in stock, these investments initially did well by RCA, certainly better than CBS's clumsy diversification efforts, but Bobby wanted still more: he wanted to emulate his father's achievements. This was a yardstick neither he nor anyone else should have judged him by, but it was inevitable that he would be judged by it. In retrospect, he would have been better off accepting the relatively modest role of caretaker of RCA's wealth and power rather than trying to add glittering, expensive additions to the corporate edifice his father had erected, but he preferred spending money to counting it.

Bobby's radio music box, his color television, was to be the computer. However, the computer industry is at least as specialized as electronic communications. Bobby moved RCA into the field nonetheless, planning to capture perhaps 10 per cent of a market destined to grow even faster than broadcasting. However, RCA found itself consistently outmaneuvered by a computer specialist, IBM, which was to business machines what RCA was to broadcasting. RCA's computer losses ran so high that by 1972, a year after the General died, Bobby was forced to write off the computer operation at a loss of no less than $490,000,000—one of the largest in the history of American business.

Big as it was, RCA reeled under the blow. Bobby's philosophy—to move RCA out of manufacturing and into service-oriented companies, as he believed the entire economy was moving—boomeranged. If he had wished to concentrate on a service company, one that RCA would have been eminently qualified to manage, he need not have looked any further than NBC. But Bobby actually wished to *reduce* NBC's importance to the company. At the time he came to power, NBC was earning about half of RCA's profits, but in Bobby's opinion it made little sense to allow half the company profits to come from a business that might take a nosedive at any time. Despite its reputation as risky, mystical, impenetrable business, the by now thoroughly commercial NBC was in fact a steady earner whose annual profits had been rising for years at an impressive rate, along with the industry's. Indeed, the network had not lost money since the early years of the Depression. The losses RCA had sustained came rather from the hideous expense of introducing innovations like color television.

Sarnoff had miscalculated and the deed was done. RCA's net worth was reduced by 25 per cent. RCA stock tumbled from 39 to a dismal 10. The newly acquired rent-a-car company was now bringing in more revenue than NBC.

The computer debacle catalyzed discontent among the company's board of directors. One of Bobby's most vocal critics on the board turned out to be the owner of the carpet-manufacturing Coronet Industries, Martin Seretean. Along with two other RCA executives, Anthony Conrad, president, and Edgar Griffiths, executive vice-president, he formed an axis of new leadership. Bobby's five-year contract ran until 1975, when he was fifty-seven. At the November board meeting, he took his customary seat at the head of the table, beneath a portrait of the General, and while he looked on, the board unanimously voted not to extend his contract. For the first time since the nineteen twenties, a Sarnoff was not at the helm of RCA, and RCA was in trouble.

Conrad, who had assumed Sarnoff's title, had to resign less than twelve months later when it was revealed that he had neglected to pay his income tax for the previous five years. Hastily, the board settled on Griffiths to replace him. Under the direction of the former credit analyst, RCA regained some of its momentum. This thoroughly self-effacing man, to whom Conrad had served as mentor, proved to be the caretaker RCA so badly needed. It was Griffiths who hired Silverman away from ABC to run NBC. With his round face, short, upturned nose, and porcine expression, he bears a striking resemblance to the late General.

With its chain of influence ranging from patents to affiliates, the RCA system is inherently stable and self-perpetuating. Not so CBS, whose reliance on the more volatile aspects of the business places it in a constant state of flux. As the company never tires of pointing out, CBS's primary resources are people and their ideas. If this is so, then the company has squandered its resources with a profligacy surpassing even RCA's disastrous investments. In the space of six years the company lost the services of Frank Stanton, who bore the burden of the responsibility of running the company for nearly thirty years; Fred Silverman, who was instantly transformed into the network's nemesis; Richard Salant, the head of CBS News who joined the top echelon of NBC management the day after a mandatory policy at CBS forced him to retire; another vice-president in charge of programming; and *four* company presidents, including several more heirs apparent to Paley. The flight of talent took its toll on most levels of the company's management and programming. Inevitably, CBS's ratings fell. The network found itself lagging far behind ABC and, at times, even NBC. In 1979, the network announced a 50 per cent drop in profits, the first decrease in eight years. In 1971, the network could point to the abolition of cigarette advertising as the cause, but this time there was no such convenient scapegoat. CBS was still getting rich, of course, but in the network business, merely maintaining ground is to lose ground, to cease to grow is to begin to die.

These damaging leavetakings shared a common source: chairman Paley's contradictory attitude towards the network, alternating between the extremes of exerting absolute control over the company and retiring completely from its day-to-day operations to devote his attention to his family, art patronage, and leisure pursuits. As a result of these gyrations, the company has suffered for over a decade from the insecurity of having no known successor to an often ambivalent Paley.

The current succession problem at CBS first erupted in 1966, when Paley, then sixty-five, decided only the day before the board was to name Stanton as his successor not to retire but to continue as chairman, thus forcing Stanton out of the company. Stanton himself had instituted the retirement-at-sixty-five policy. Did he believe that in so doing he would one day hasten Paley's departure from the company and ensure himself at least seven years in the top spot? If so, his strategy backfired, for even as Paley became the sole exception in the company to the rule, Stanton found that upon reaching sixty-five he had to retire.

Paley's maneuver, which Stanton now denies came as a surprise or a disappointment, in spite of several published accounts to the contrary, effectively stood the company's management on its ear. When Paley so abruptly changed his mind, Stanton still had seven years at CBS until his mandatory retirement, ample time for the man to select and groom a successor. Astonishingly, Paley found a dearth of candidates within the company ranks. Members of the Paley family were out. He maintained that he had always rigidly segregated his family life from the network. Yet, in the old days, things had been quite different. His father, Samuel, had brought him into the family tobacco business, and when Paley went off on his own, Samuel, Uncle Jay, and brother-in-law Leon Levy all sat on the CBS board. Throughout the nineteen forties CBS had the aura of a family business, as Fly's Report on Chain Broadcasting had noted. But now, it suited Paley's whim to exclude any potential successor from the family.

Paley avoided personal commitment to a solution by hiring an executive search firm to find a successor from outside the company. The chairman now admitted he was too remote from the day-to-day operations of the company to choose a worthy successor himself. The headhunters Heidrick & Struggles settled on one Charles Ireland, who had been ITT's manager of European Operations. Ireland was installed. Personable, hard-driving "Chick" Ireland began making friends within the company ranks. Stanton retired in 1973, taking with him CBS stock worth about $13,000,000 and a retirement contract lasting until 1987. He became chairman of the American Red Cross and took similarly striking offices in the immaculate Corning Glass Building on Fifth Avenue. Then Ireland, only ten months into the job, dropped dead of a heart attack.

Paley compounded the problem by returning to the same headhunters, who this time turned up Arthur Taylor, an aggressive businessman with an enviable career in investment banking and later at International Paper. Broadcasting or any electronic communications background were noticeably absent from his résumé, but he had studied

Renaissance history at Brown. Perhaps that experience would help. Taylor was young, thirty-seven, and, with the knowledge that he was Paley's chosen successor, intruded on the sensitive and specialized domain of programming. Stanton had had the common sense to leave this area be. Under Taylor's strong-arm guidance, CBS earnings increased handsomely, but in the process he irritated no end of producers by campaigning on behalf of a family viewing hour, an hour of prime time in which the off-color or controversial reference was to be banned. Worse, he allowed Silverman to escape the CBS fold. "I would have done everything possible to keep Silverman at the network," Stanton remarked. Silverman's departure triggered a wave of resignations, decimating the all-important programming department. The pace of executive departures increased. Network president Robert Wood resigned a year after Silverman left. His successor, Robert Wussler, was in and out of the job in less than a year. "I wasn't prepared for the network presidency," he later reflected. "I had never been in programming. But I was the only one around." It was the era of revolving doors at CBS. The financial community sensed real signs of alarm when Paley's heir apparent Taylor resigned, a casualty of the network's having ceded first place in the ratings to ABC.

Paley acted to soothe the turmoil, this time reaching down the company ranks to pluck a new heir apparent. He selected a company vice-president, it is true, but he was neither experienced nor a broadcaster. John Backe had been at General Electric before joining CBS's publishing division. Paley had an opportunity to observe Backe in action when CBS moved to purchase Fawcett Books, a paperback publishing company, and he professed to like what he saw. At the stockholders' meeting of April 20, 1977, Paley announced with great fanfare that he would, at last, step aside in favor of a younger man. Backe was to assume the title of chief executive officer. Little by little Paley was yielding his power, but only as a way of avoiding an embarrassing appearance that he was not prepared to let CBS go its own way.

The performance turned out to be a charade. The following fall, Paley thrust himself back into the limelight. Keeping Backe on a short leash, he assumed the role of CBS's de facto programmer.

The problem shows no sign of resolution in the immediate future. Born in the second year of this century, Paley hails from long-lived stock. His father, Samuel, was active until 1963, when he passed away at age eighty-seven, and his mother, Goldie, lived to be ninety-five. The spectacle of Paley fretting over who will inherit his empire calls to mind the tragedy of *King Lear*. Like Shakespeare's monarch, he appears to be ignorant of his most worthy successor. The Kestens and Klaubers of yesteryear and expert and cunning men like them are absent from the court, as is the vaunted commitment to prestige and public-service programming. CBS now yearns to emulate the success of its younger, more vigorous rival, ABC, copying not only its programs but also its management structure. CBS will have difficulty making progress as long as it chases its own tail.

"I do not like the idea of depending on others," Paley wrote in a recent memoir. "I don't feel safe." Never hesitating to drop valuable associates when they no longer suited his needs—Murrow, Stanton, and Silverman are examples that spring instantly to mind—Paley now finds himself painfully isolated in the business of running the network he purchased more than fifty years ago.

19

Resurrection of an Ideal

FOR YEARS A RESERVOIR OF FRUSTRATION, even rage, had been growing in the face of the complete commercialization of the nation's three major broadcasting networks:

> Believing that potentially the commercial system of broadcasting as practiced in this country is the best and freest yet devised, I have decided to express my concern about what I believe to be happening to radio and television. These instruments have been good to me beyond my due. There exist in my mind no reasonable grounds for personal complaint. I have no feud, either, with my employers, any sponsors, or with the professional critics of radio and television. But I am seized with an abiding fear regarding what these two instruments are doing to our society, or culture, and our heritage.

The speaker was Edward R. Murrow, addressing an October 1958 meeting of the Radio-Television News Directors Association. He continued:

> Our history will be what we make it. And if there are any historians about fifty or a hundred years from now, and there should be preserved kinescopes for one week of all three networks, they will find there recorded in black-and-white, or color, evidence of decadence, es-

capism, and insulation from the realities of the world in which we
live.

By now the audience had caught Murrow's drift, and it made them
feel acutely uncomfortable. Later, some would decide that this time
Murrow had gone too far. He had, in fact, merely trained his resolutely
moral point of view on a target very close to home:

> I invite your attention to the television schedules of all networks be-
> tween the hours of eight and eleven P.M. Eastern Time. Here you will
> find only fleeting and spasmodic reference to the fact that this nation is
> in mortal danger. There are, it is true, occasional informative programs
> presented in that intellectual ghetto on Sunday afternoons. But during
> the daily peak viewing periods, television in the main insulates us from
> the realities of the world in which we live. If this state of affairs con-
> tinues, we may alter an advertising slogan to read: "Look Now, Pay
> Later." For surely we shall pay for using this most powerful instrument
> of communication to insulate the citizenry from the hard and demand-
> ing realities which must be faced if we are to survive. I mean the word
> "survive" literally.

Murrow delivered the most bitter and pessimistic commentary of
his career not against an abstract or hidden menace, but against his
own employer. Now, in his view, the networks themselves posed a
threat to the national well-being. The genesis of his outrage lay less
in his own transformation over the years than in the networks' subtle
but profound mutation. The CBS Murrow found as a young man, for
example, had a commitment to public-service programming, to keeping the "citizenry" informed. But now commercial pressures—competition, the expense of developing new technology—had come to obsess
networks, ending their sporadic commitment to these ideals. Murrow
felt the loss keenly. This was not the industry he had grown up with.
Perhaps other powerful men in the network system, Kintner, Paley,
or Sarnoff, could in good conscience accommodate themselves to the
realities of their networks' daily programming, but Murrow could not.
He felt betrayed. The sponsors had run off with the networks:

> The top management of the networks, with a few notable exceptions,
> has been trained in advertising, sales, or show business. But by the na-
> ture of the corporate structure, they also make the final and critical de-
> cisions having to do with news and public affairs. Frequently they
> have neither the time nor the competence to do this. It is not easy for
> the same small group of men to decide whether to buy a new station
> for millions of dollars, build a new building, alter the rate card, buy a
> new Western, sell a soap opera, decide what defensive line to take in

connection with the latest Congressional inquiry, how much money to spend on promoting a new program, what additions or deletions should be made in the existing covey or clutch of vice-presidents, and at the same time—frequently on the same long day—to give mature, thoughtful consideration to the manifold problems that confront those who are charged with the responsibility for news and public affairs.

Now Murrow was drawing real blood. Surely he could not have expected to return to his desk at CBS after giving such a speech and expect to continue as before. His position, indeed, was so extreme that it demanded some kind of response, some action:

There is no suggestion here that networks or individual stations should operate as philanthropies. But I can find nothing in the Bill of Rights or the Communications Act which says they must increase their net profits each year, lest the Republic collapse.

How would Murrow propose to rectify this lamentable state of affairs? "I would like television to produce some itching pills rather than this endless outpouring of tranquilizers," he recommended, and toward that end he proposed this policy:

Let us have a little competition. Not only in selling soap, cigarettes, and automobiles, but in informing a troubled, apprehensive, but receptive public. Why should not each of the twenty or thirty big corporations which dominate radio and television decide that they will give up one or two of their regularly scheduled programs each year, turn the time over to the networks, and say in effect: "This is a tiny tithe, just a little bit of our profits. On this particular night we aren't going to try to sell cigarettes or automobiles; this is merely a gesture to indicate our belief in the importance of ideas." The networks should, and I think would, pay for the cost of producing the program. The advertiser, the sponsor, would get name credit, but would have nothing to do with the content of the program.

Neither Murrow nor anyone else could think of a name to give this unusual plan, but without realizing the foresightedness of his idea, he had just succeeded in outlining some of the fundamental tenets of a new, fourth network, the Public Broadcasting System. At the time, Murrow was still hoping that some accommodation for public-service programming could be made within the existing three-network structure, but he would live long enough to change his mind and propose an entirely new network to undertake the mission.

It was over two years before Murrow's call for help received an answer. In the interim, he had undergone a falling out with Paley and

Stanton, resigned from CBS, and accepted an appointment President-elect Kennedy offered him as director of the United States Information Agency. Government service had become inevitable for Murrow once he no longer had a home in the world of commercial broadcasting. The change in administrations had also brought a new atmosphere to the FCC, where Kennedy's appointee for chairman, a lawyer and former campaign assistant for Adlai Stevenson named Newton Minow, was nervously eyed by the industry's old guard. They wondered if the crew-cut young man from Chicago would play along as most chairmen in the past had done, or if he would make quixotic gestures recalling the deeds of James Fly.

The industry found out at the thirty-ninth annual convention of the National Association of Broadcasters in 1961. Addressing the same body Fly had taken to task, Minow sent ripples of apprehension through his audience as he stated, "Your license lets you use the public's airwaves as trustees for a hundred and eighty million Americans. The public is your beneficiary. If you want to stay on as trustees, you must deliver a decent return to the public—not only your stockholders." Well, Minow was still young, he would learn. But then he went a step further, deliberately provoking an industry he viewed as introverted and complacent:

> I invite you to sit down in front of your television set when your station goes on the air and stay there without a book, magazine, newspaper, profit and loss sheet or rating book to distract you—and keep your eyes glued to that set until the station signs off. I can assure you that you will observe a vast wasteland.

Minow, then, shared Murrow's indignation about commercial television. Here was Minow's way of describing the phenomenon Murrow had noted:

> You will see a procession of game shows, violence, audience participation shows, formula comedies about totally unbelievable families, blood and thunder, mayhem, violence, sadism, murder, western badmen, western good men, private eyes, gangsters, more violence, and cartoons. And, endlessly, commercials—many screaming, cajoling, and offending. And most of all, boredom. Sure, you will see a few things you will enjoy. But they will be very, very few. And if you think I exaggerate, try it.

Minow was not here to engage in a business-as-usual exchange of favors. The phrase "a vast wasteland" entered the language, denoting the entire range of commercial effluvia polluting the media and society.

Later in his speech Minow promised, "If there is not a nationwide educational television system in this country, it will not be the fault of the FCC." This lesser-known declaration proved to be Minow's real source of concern. The frustration and rage at the irresponsibility of commercial network programming had finally made the transition from being the opinion of one man, Murrow, to the status of an official policy. As a result, public television was a giant step closer to becoming a reality. The change in FCC strategy marked a new despair and a new hope—a despair over the commission's ability to regulate effectively the networks through the limited means of licensing stations, and a hope that Congress would create its own broadcasting system to fill the long-felt need for public-service programming. Thus public broadcasting came to represent nothing less than the resurrection of the ideal of public-service programming originally championed by NBC's Blue network, and later CBS. Once before, the FCC had moved to correct the commercial imbalance, forcing RCA to divest itself of a network. This order had led to the demise of the Blue and the rise of thoroughly commercial ABC. Now Minow proposed an even more extreme measure, one without precedent in the history of the networks.

He laid the groundwork for a "nationwide educational television system" by initiating legislation specifying that all television sets be capable of receiving UHF stations. RCA, it will be recalled, had set an industry standard by manufacturing and flooding the market with television sets equipped with VHF only as a way of staving off the threat of a competing CBS color system, which would have operated on UHF frequencies. Now all three networks monopolized stations on the VHF band, the only one most sets in use could receive. By employing the FCC's uncontested authority to assign frequencies and set standards, Minow circumvented this closed system and forced a widening of the spectrum, allowing new choices for the viewer. The move did not immediately put UHF on a par with VHF. At first, the UHF tuning system was primitive, inexact. It was in the interests of the industry to keep the number of competing stations to a minimum. Even subsequent legislation to rectify the problem still had to contend with the fact that UHF requires a stronger signal to reach the same area as a VHF station. The government move to establish a public-service network received additional momentum in 1962 when the Department of Health, Education, and Welfare was empowered to make matching grants for the construction of "educational" stations.

As Minow cleared the way for a public debate focusing on the rapaciousness and inadequacy of broadcasting services provided by the commercial networks, the Ford Foundation, which had previously demonstrated its commitment to public-service programming within the system through its nurturing of "Omnibus," now actively campaigned for a fourth network. Ford went to the obvious choice for a first head of such a network, Murrow. Could he be lured away from the USIA? As a preliminary step, Murrow drafted a tantalizing proposal for a "competitive alternative" to conventional networks. To staff the organization, he proposed hiring away people who had become "disillusioned with network practices" but "remain in their employ due to the absence of any alternative." As an example, he singled out his old friend and associate from "See It Now," Fred Friendly. Murrow went on to describe a network in his own image. He saw it as fulfilling the role he had played during his glory days at CBS, "The mature, discerning gadfly to all mass media," and "the conscience of communications." As a final twist, one that could have more serious repercussions than many of his other carefully considered recommendations, Murrow suggested that the term *educational* should never be used in connection with the new network, because "anything tagged educational in this country is handicapped at the outset."

Here Murrow broke with the existing concept of noncommercial broadcasting. Ever since radio's inception, a substratum of largely independent, noncommercial programming had existed, fostered by stations affiliated with educational or religious organizations. When assigning television frequencies after the freeze was lifted in 1952, the FCC had set aside as many as 242 places for "educational" stations. The first to begin broadcasting was KUHT, affiliated with the University of Houston. But where commercial television thrived, "educational" television starved. By 1960, there were but forty-four "educational" stations operating, many for only a few hours a day. In comparison with 573 commercial stations going full blast, their impact was negligible. Murrow perceived that for a program or a network to qualify as a public service, it could have human-interest and entertainment value as well as "educational" content. This approach, not to be confused with the escapism cultivated by the commercial network, proved to be the breath of life for the entire system, lifting it out of narrow concerns and endowing it with a public appeal and commitment.

In the time it took for public television as envisioned by Murrow to gestate in the bureaucratic womb, its leader-to-be fell ill. When Murrow resigned from the USIA at the beginning of 1964, it was not to head a fourth network but to retire to La Jolla, California. He died of lung cancer the following year. A younger man, Fred Friendly, would have to pick up where he left off.

The Public Broadcasting System which finally came into being in 1967, nineteen years after Murrow had first sounded the alarm, had its genesis in Lyndon Johnson's Great Society. In its haste to adopt Johnson's legislative agenda, Congress formally created the bureaucracy necessary to administer the fourth network. In so doing, it adopted most of the recommendations of a report prepared under the auspices of the Carnegie Foundation. Ten members of the Carnegie Commission were Johnson appointees, and an illustrious body it was, including James Conant, former president of Harvard; author Ralph Ellison, inventor and businessman Edwin Land; Robert Saudek; and the pianist Rudolf Serkin. The Carnegie Commission prefaced its report, which appeared in January 1967, with an eloquent appeal by the essayist E. B. White:

> Non-commercial television should address itself to the idea of excellence, not the idea of acceptability, which is what keeps commercial television from climbing the staircase. I think television should be the visual counterpart of the literary essay, should arouse our dreams, satisfy our hunger for beauty, take us on journeys, enable us to participate in events, present great drama and music, explore the seas and the sky and the woods and the hills. It should be our Lyceum, our Chautauqua, our Minsky's, and our Camelot.

Here was a skillful restatement not only of Murrow's notion that the new network should avoid the narrow confines of "education," but also of that by now age-old hope expressed by an essayist of an earlier era, H. G. Wells. Network broadcasting had been faced with other second chances—FM radio, the introduction of television—and in each case the innovation succumbed to the well-established pattern. This time the hope was that a fourth network could resist the trend toward assimilation in the commercial morass.

The Carnegie Commission recommended the creation of a Corporation for Public Television, now known as the Corporation for Public Broadcasting, to administer the fourth network, and the establishment of not fewer than two major national production centers. This proposal marked a distinct departure from the traditionally centralized commercial network. This new network would have no such concentration of power. Each region was to be equally represented. As the commercial networks, for all their technical sophistication, were basically modern adaptations of the technology of the nineteen twenties, when they began, so this new network reflected the more advanced technology of the nineteen sixties, which permitted greater decentralization. Months in advance of the Carnegie Commission, the Ford Foundation had recommended that the network be linked by communications satellites rather than the traditional AT&T landlines (or microwaves). In time—1978—the Public Broadcasting System became the first network to use satellite transmission for distributing programs to local stations for broadcast. By the standards of the commercial network, the system was open-ended, lacking in a clear-cut chain of command, and that is just what the Carnegie Commission wished. In this network, the individual station would count for more than the conventional commercial affiliate, and the headquarters count for less. In one crucial area Congress did not adopt the report's recommendation. The Carnegie Commission had advocated funding based on the British system of issuing licenses to television-set owners. This revenue would pay for the network's expenses. Congress instead decided that funding should come from three distinct sources: congressional appropriations, members of the public, and corporations.

It was in the glow of expectations kindled by the swift adoption of the report's recommendations that Fred Friendly, armed with a $10,000,000 grant from the Ford Foundation, oversaw the development of the new network's first major offering, "Public Broadcasting Laboratory." PBL threatened to do for the war in Vietnam what "See It Now" had done for McCarthyism; i.e., provide an outlet for dissent and possibly tilt the balance of public opinion against it. The series, in the format of a two-hour-long news magazine, made its debut in November 1967. (It was more than just a coincidence that the following year CBS launched its news magazine, "60 Minutes.")

Political turmoil now seriously affected the course of public broadcasting's development. LBJ, whose Great Society had made it possible, decided not to seek re-election, and the newly installed Nixon administration could not comprehend or countenance a federally funded broadcasting network that appeared to defy its policies, especially those concerning Vietnam. Though congressional appropriations for the network increased appreciably between 1969 and 1973—from $5,000,000 to $45,000,000—the administration tried to direct funds away from the major production centers, WETA in Washington, D.C., WNET in New York, KQED in San Francisco, and WGBH in Boston, which it feared would create anti-administration programming, and toward smaller, more locally-oriented public television stations around the country. Grateful to receive money, the thinking ran, they would be less eager to criticize the status quo. In addition, Friendly's confrontation tactics generated ill will. The Brilliant Monster's abrasiveness itself became an issue. "Public TV's Most Powerful Friend," ran the title of one assessment, "May Also Qualify As Its Worst Enemy."

Despite the Nixon administration's efforts to hobble the network, public television survived. Congress had given it just enough momentum to survive the Nixon years. The number of affiliates increased, reaching 277 by 1978, more than any commercial network could claim. The fifty-three days of Watergate hearings PBS broadcast during 1973 helped the network in the way the Army-McCarthy hearings had come to the rescue of a struggling ABC nineteen years earlier. The hearings provided cheap public-affairs programming about an issue of consuming national interest, incidentally attracting attention to the network carrying them. PBS reaped a harvest of over $1,000,000 in viewer donations as a by-product of carrying the hearings.

When PBS finally began to present its own programming, lo and behold the network did attract a significant audience, still miniscule in comparison with the 100,000,000 or so who tuned into the commercial networks each evening, but large enough to receive greater attention in the industry and press. Those who did tune in found programming which bore strong resemblances to the late, great days of early television. As the French Chef, Julia Child added new spice to televised cooking lessons. PBS's answer to "Kukla, Fran, and Ollie," and "Romper Room" turned out to be "Mister Rogers' Neighborhood" and "Sesame Street." Where the commercial networks had earlier discovered the drawing power of blockbuster movies, PBS turned to foreign films. The public-affairs program covered the political spectrum with William F. Buckley's "Firing Line" on the right and "Bill Moyers' Journal" on the left. Moyers' "Essay on Watergate" strongly echoed Murrow-style commentary. There was even a PBS version of that classic commercial genre, the game show. "We Interrupt This Week," in 1978, revived the sophisticated parlor-game atmosphere of "Information Please." "Monty Python's Flying Circus," a comedy series produced by the BBC which began appearing on domestic screens in 1975, contained strong echoes of Ernie Kovacs' surreal manipulation of the medium's conventions. With the addition of "The Dick Cavett Show" and "The Robert MacNeil [later MacNeil/Lehrer] Report," the public television ranks began to swell with cadres of disaffected, principled refugees from the commercial networks, as Murrow once envisioned.

The programming with greatest popular appeal, however, was not produced by PBS at all, but rather imported from Great Britain. In 1969, WGBH acquired twenty-six episodes of the BBC's adaptation of John Galsworthy's *The Forsyte Saga*. Here was a new kind of programming, combining elements of sociology and soap opera, sophistication and that elusive quality called showmanship. Public television imported one visually sumptuous British series after another, historical dramas such as "Elizabeth R" and "The Six Wives of Henry VIII," as well as original dramatic series which had been commercially produced, "Upstairs/Downstairs" and "The Duchess of Duke Street," all hewing to standards of craftsmanship in both performance and design far higher than those of American commercial television.

The commercial networks took note, though not because they feared that PBS would steal audiences. At the moment PBS's ratings hovered at an average level of 1 per cent of sets in use, as compared to almost 19 per cent for the average commercial program broadcast in prime time. They took note because PBS was coming up with new programming ideas at a time when they had gone profitably stale. In addition to providing the impetus for a news magazine like "60 Minutes" and the miniseries, PBS's success with "Upstairs/Downstairs" induced CBS to attempt an American version, "Beacon Hill," which did not last the season. The prevalence of British imports also returned to haunt PBS, for its domestically produced programming looked thin, even amateurish by comparison. Attempting to emulate the British success with historical re-creation in "Elizabeth R" and "The Pallisers," WNET undertook to produce "The Adams Chronicles," and WGBH to adapt Hawthorne's *The Scarlet Letter,* neither of which measured up to the British standard.

The commercial networks tended to disparage PBS. Stanton said he thought the network was fine, "but you have to get a search warrant to find the audience." Nevertheless, the network was making its presence felt; its unadmitted rivals were already beginning to lift ideas from it. Yet the imitation so characteristic of network existence worked the other way as well. As PBS became more popular, it began to mirror the practices of the commercial networks in an alarming fashion. PBS began to draw on heavy financial support from major corporations to present its most popular programming. While no one employed the term *advertising,* Mobil Oil Corporation, believing itself to have been unduly criticized by the networks' news divisions, embarked on an aggressive public relations campaign which involved the company's "underwriting" of "Masterpiece Theatre," the catch-all title PBS employed for its Sunday evening presentations of British imports. Mobil received a brief mention of its support on the air and proceeded to trumpet its relationship with PBS in newspaper advertisements. By 1978, Mobil's financial commitment reached $12,000,000, and the company certainly expected some return on this sizable investment in public goodwill. The strategy recalled advertising in the early days of television, when companies departed from rigid cost-per-thousand formulas in favor of association with prestigious programming, especially live drama.

In the early nineteen seventies a host of oil companies followed closely on Mobil's heels. Exxon, Gulf Oil, and Atlantic Richfield all wished to bask in the reflected glory of PBS's prestigious programming, but Mobil succeeded in making the greatest impact on the public, creating more goodwill through its connection with PBS than it could ever have through conventional broadcast advertising. Now corporations such as Mobil could call themselves not merely advertisers but patrons. In the process, however, PBS earned the nickname Petroleum Broadcasting System.

PBS officials strenuously denied that the tastes or political leanings of their corporate underwriters in any way affected the selection of programming, though suspicions were constantly aroused that the corporate presence created a tacit form of censorship. Nearly half a century before, RCA had inaugurated NBC as a public service, then admitted some sponsorship to share the burden of bringing programs to the public. Finally, that network and all networks became hopelessly addicted to advertising revenue. Now, Congress is weighing the possibility of allowing public broadcasting stations to sell a limited amount of advertising time as a means of supporting themselves. It is entirely possible that a small but influential bit of history might repeat itself as a consequence. For the moment, however, public broadcasting survives on a precarious balance consisting of corporate underwriting, congressional appropriations, and viewer donations, often stimulated through on-the-air solicitations.

In addition to its financial quandaries, public television has suffered from the effects of a bureaucratic tangle created by the Public Broadcasting Act of 1967. While the network itself, the Public Broadcasting System, has moved rapidly into the public eye, its administrative overlord, the Corporation for Public Broadcasting (CPB), still holds the ultimate authority on many vital decisions. The dual bureaucracies have tended to overlap, duplicating one another's functions and hampering production of high-quality programming.

In response to widespread frustration, another Carnegie Commission, coming twelve years after the original, undertook to redress these bureaucratic wrongs. Though greeted as the long-awaited solution, Carnegie II's report only asked for more of the same—more money and more bureaucracy. Seeking to emulate the polish and prophecy which characterized Carnegie I, the rewrite offered little more than a conventional pious denunciation of the television wasteland. In reviewing the lengthy report, the normally moderate industry observer

Martin Mayer was moved to reflect on Talleyrand's observation that man invented language to conceal his thoughts.

Among its proposals, Carnegie II proposed to replace CPB with a new body, the Public Telecommunications Trust, a solution perpetuating the folly of dual bureaucracy. Carnegie II also asked for increased funding, over $1,000,000,000 by 1985, or about twice PBS's present level of funding, half of which would come from the government, and another part from a tax on use of the airwaves. In the face of inflation, this apparently impressive sum would do little to increase PBS's relative financial health. Carnegie II's attempt to correct the errors of the past threatened to create new problems of equal magnitude.

In 1978, President Carter appointed Newton Minow, the former FCC chairman who once vowed to create a noncommercial television system, to the unsalaried chairmanship of PBS. "We've inherited a system based more on history than on logic," Minow said, appraising PBS's bureaucratic tangle. The youngest network now seeks to avoid the entanglements of Washington-style bureaucracy on the one hand and creeping commercialization on the other. In light of present difficulties, Carnegie I's original recommendation to fund the network through a tax on sets retains a commonsense appeal.

For all its newness, public broadcasting represents but one of an array of challenges to the traditional commercial network system. Others, revolving around the use of cable and satellite technology, are still embryonic. Awaiting their Sarnoffs, Paleys, and Weavers, these burgeoning industries cannot yet lay claim to being networks. Over the course of the next decade, however, the four existing networks—the one intended as a public service to promote the sale of radios (NBC), the one designed as an advertising medium (CBS), the one the FCC hoped would add diversity to the marketplace (ABC), and the one Congress created to fill the public-service void left by all the others (PBS)—will find they are sharing a vastly widened broadcast spectrum with a host of new distribution systems catering to an overlapping patchwork of minority groups and subcultures that comprise our pluralistic society. The name of this phenomenon is narrowcasting. In place of broadcasting, or programming designed to reach the greatest possible audience, narrowcasting will be distinguished not by its universal appeal or acceptance but by its specialization.

From Broadcasting
to Narrowcasting

"NETWORKS CANNOT GROW IN SIZE OR SCOPE," said Eric Sevareid, the veteran CBS commentator, in a recent speech. "They can own only so many stations; they cannot seriously increase their affiliates. They cannot expand the hours in the day." They have, in short, reached the limit. If they have always thrived on a rate of growth which has outstripped that of the national economy, going from good in a time of national depression to better in periods of robust economic health, then they are now trying to get along without that vital condition.

In the meantime, a variety of new technological alternatives have sprung up and are now making the arduous transition from marvel of the future to potent commercial force. Beginning with the establishment of RCA and NBC, network power over the airwaves was originally based on control over technology, ownership of patents, and manufacture of equipment. With the technology deployed, a secondary center of broadcasting power grew up, the use of network broadcasting as an advertising medium. Here CBS made its contribution. Now, an arsenal of new technology has entered the marketplace, technology over which the networks have little control, and which has all the makings of creating rival advertising mediums. No matter what the manifold variations on the new technology happen to be—and they vary considerably—nearly all revolve around a combination of satellite and cable transmission. While they cannot expand time either, they can divide it, a process which amounts to a form of expansion. What these new systems of transmission engage in cannot exactly be termed broadcasting. No, that phenomenon of widespread distribution of a signal belongs in the network domain. Rather, they use satellites to go over and cable to go around the conventional broadcasting spectrum, offering a bewildering array of new possibilities and a real threat to the network domination of the airwaves. The current situation—three commercially successful networks each battling for a share of the mass audience with programs indistinguishable in content—only appears to be stagnant. Vast but still unseen changes promise to make the networks antiques.

Curiously, cable television, a form of narrowcasting, is not only the newest of the alternatives to the conventional network structure but also the oldest. As we have seen, cable transmission preceded both networks and wireless transmission. In the nineteen twenties, AT&T considered the possibility of creating a system of toll broadcasting, running a wire into the home carrying programs for which the listener would be charged, just as he was charged for the telephone. A monopoly, AT&T withdrew from the field when it realized that it would be facing stiff competition from the likes of RCA, to whom it sold its flagship station, WEAF. In the vacuum left by AT&T, three monolithic commercial networks eventually grew and flourished. However, cable transmission—whether it goes by the name of narrowcasting or point-to-point communication—did not die out; it merely lay dormant for about half a century. There was not much in the way of commercial imperative for its use. The networks absorbed all the advertising. But, as the demand for their services exceeds the supply, cable transmission is on the verge of a revival. Unwittingly, the networks helped it along.

With the coming of television after World War II and a four-year-long freeze on building stations, early television stations were few and far between. To enhance reception, communities in remote areas employed communal antennas which then relayed clear pictures to individual users. New York City, with its transmission-blurring skyscrapers, resorted to a similar tactic. This arrangement, known as community antenna television (CATV), was at first but an extension of the conventional network system. As its use spread, entrepreneurs realized that local systems could also serve as programming sources providing specialized services to subscribing homes.

By the early sixties, when cable television in one form or another appeared to be on the verge of capturing a mass audience, both the networks and the FCC moved to control the boom. The networks, for their part, launched a two-pronged attack, reminiscent of the movie

industry's campaign to woo the audience away from the television
tube. On the one hand they mounted a publicity campaign based on a
simple theme: Why pay for what you already enjoy for free? On the
other hand, they aggressively snapped up cable companies in the
United States and Canada as part of their diversification drives. The
FCC did not help much, either. In 1966, Congress gave the commission power to regulate cable; the FCC tried to kill it off. At one point
it forbade cable systems from showing one of their most popular attractions, new movies, for a full two years after their release. Cable
appeared to shrivel. However, the FCC also ordered the networks to
divest themselves of their cable interests. It did not wish them to increase their already formidable monopoly, especially in an area where
FCC regulation was, at best, uncertain.

Existing on the fringes of network activity and government regulation, cable grew in bits and pieces, not as a unilateral movement like
the networks, but as a grass-roots movement resembling pre-network
radio stations. The spectrum of programming ran the gamut from the
educational to the pornographic. By the end of the nineteen sixties,
however, cable was a widespread phenomenon, reaching 1,000,000
homes. As network advertising time became ever scarcer and rates
soared, advertising agencies began to take note of this maverick alternative. An executive at Young & Rubicam, William Donnelly, set an
informal industry standard by declaring that when cable reached
about a third of television-equipped homes, it would become a mass
advertising medium capable of rivaling the networks. Cable will reach
this point of critical mass sometime in the early eighties. This patchwork system of transmission received a further encouragement in 1977
when the District of Columbia Court of Appeals struck down remaining FCC programming restrictions on cable. Since cable does not use
the public's limited fund of airwaves, it seems that the FCC will exert
much less control over it than it has over the networks.

Slowly, cable's biggest drawback, that it existed in a no-man's-land,
has become its greatest asset, for it can grow in ways the networks
cannot. Currently, broadcasting is limited to but seven channels in any
one market. In practice, few enjoy as many as that. Despite a generous allocation of UHF channels, most of these are empty even today,
as UHF finds itself swamped by the audience the networks attract to
VHF, and further hindered by inherent technical limitations. The
cable, however, frees the viewer from a limited selection of television
fare, a limitation that has for a quarter of a century protected network
domination of the airwaves. Instead of receiving the legal limit of
seven stations, a cable-equipped set can receive twenty additional stations and, in some cases, up to sixty. And new technology promises to

increase the number of available stations to a thousand, all enjoying a uniform level of reception. This new, high-capacity cable will not be made of copper or other metals but rather of glass, and the signals will be transmitted not by electronic impulses but by light emitted from a laser. Fiber optics, as this system of transmission is known, possesses several advantages over the conventional cable. Since the raw material for glass is sand, it is cheap. It cannot corrode. Signals can travel farther through it without amplification than they can through metal. In fact, it is possible that homes will one day receive television and telephone signals through a single fiber optic tube.

On one level, the cable presence is local, specialized, but, joined by communications satellites, cable systems become mega-networks, distribution systems that can be done and undone in an instant and reconnected in a variety of ways to suit the needs of viewers and advertisers. The satellite, then, maximizes the cable threat, providing it with the attention-getting programming that a local system would not usually have and, at the same time, supplying an advertiser with a far-flung audience. In a field replete with historical ironies and a recurring sense of *déjà vu,* it is worth noting that the vanguard of the satellite movement happens to be none other than RCA. It is possible that this company, which launched the first broadcasting network, will control the dominant transmission system of the twenty-first century. It is also possible to speculate that it will inadvertently hinder NBC in favor of new satellite-oriented networks. Desperately in need of programming, local cable systems receive a great deal of nourishment from communications satellites such as RCA's Satcom I, which supplies movies, sports, children's programming, continuous news, and the proceedings of the House of Representatives to subscribing systems. All these channels compete for the viewer with NBC and the other networks.

The implications of communications satellites extend as well to local broadcasting stations, not just cable systems. With a satellite supplying programming, a local station need not be subservient to an established network as its primary source of programming. With equal ease it could siphon off a movie or other popular events from the satellite (for a fee, of course), and transmit the program to viewers in the area. Thus the communications satellite threatens to steal viewers not only from the network but from affiliate stations as well. The net result will be a serious erosion of the network audience, an end, in fact, to television as it has existed over the past thirty-odd years. In place of the monolith of network broadcasting, a variety of systems—the conventional networks, cable systems (both local and satellite-connected) and independent stations drawing on the satellite—will compete for

the audience. There will be room not for just two or three or four networks, but for unlimited programming sources. Narrowcasting will be
limited only by what its practitioners are capable of conceiving.

The networks, needless to say, do not see things the same way.

They view the coming of alternative distribution systems with a
mixture of disdain and suspicion. A 1977 study conducted by NBC, for
example, predicted little change in the status quo. "We see cable
growing, but we do not see it competing with television as a basic national mass medium," concluded the report, entitled "Broadcasting:
The Next Ten Years." All commercial networks, in fact, pin their
hopes for future profits on the knowledge that they will remain major
suppliers of programming. Furthermore, they each own the regulation
limit of five stations, located in the most lucrative markets. With these
guaranteed outlets, the networks have access to the population centers
advertisers most want to reach, and today these network owned and
operated stations can be counted on to provide the lion's share of network revenues.

However, high profits, elements of a monopoly, and confident statements about the future mask a profound unease. As cable and sat-
ellite-based systems of distribution continue to penetrate the marketplace, the networks' growth rate, feeling the pressure of competition,
will slow. Even today, before the advent of cable, only a single network, ABC, displays an indisputably robust financial condition. The
coming of cable and satellite promises to do to the networks what television did to radio nearly thirty years before: relegate them to an inferior role. Then, the networks survived the heavy losses radio sustained because they controlled its successor, television, but the
successor to network television eludes their grasp. The FCC has seen
to that. In fact, the transition from radio to television offers some clues
as to what the networks can expect from the coming transition from
networks to cable.

As with cable, early television pundits predicted that once 30 per
cent of homes were equipped with a television set, radio would be in
for a serious decline. Sometime in the early nineteen fifties this figure
was attained. Because of the spread of television, for example, Jack
Benny's rating on radio in the New York area plummeted from 26.5
per cent in 1948 to less than 5 per cent in 1951. Similarly, "Amos 'n'
Andy" slipped from over 13 per cent to less than 6, Bob Hope's
from 26 per cent to nearly 3, and that old standby Arthur Godfrey's from over 20 per cent to under 6. In response to this massive
audience shift away from radio to television, the radio networks were
forced to cut their advertising rates by as much as a fifth.

Furthermore, the financial decline happened all at once, without warning. In 1951, CBS's radio profits stood at an all-time high. The following year the network lost money for the first time since 1928 and, beginning in 1956, lost money for seven years in a row. As late as 1960, radio sales were only a fraction of what they had been in 1948. And it was all due to television, a new, often disparaged, and often postponed medium. The networks have shown themselves over the years to be remarkably impervious to the ups and downs of the national economy, as their performance during the Depression proves. Here was the spectacle of that same radio network withering in a time of economic health. The decline, then, should properly be laid at the feet of the new technology which had finally, after many years of postponement, gained widespread acceptance. And what television did to radio in the midst of its glory cable and satellite can do to *all* of network broadcasting.

As the networks adapt to this challenge, their programming strategy will have to undergo some profound alterations. It will no longer make sense to concentrate exclusively on the traditional goal of how to defeat the other network. Instead, all the networks will have to work together to keep audiences away from alternative programming coming into their homes. And what an array of programming they will have to face. Television will have wriggled free of the networks' grasp, where it has languished since its birth, and bloom into diversity and plurality. In its coming diversity, it will resemble a more sophisticated version of the prenetwork radio boom in the early twenties. Then, chaos in the air and the high cost of talent combined to deliver the industry to the networks. Now, technology will liberate it from them. This evolution hardly means that the networks will fold their tents and steal out of town after more than fifty years, but they will be forced to make an accommodation.

Examining the future of network fare by type, it appears that sports programming is the most vulnerable to other distribution systems. As cable systems continue to reach greater audiences and, as a result, have more money to spend to keep those audiences, they will be able to afford the broadcast rights to key events, a Super Bowl, a World Series, a boxing match. Remember that it was with sports programming (Dempsey v. Carpentier) that David Sarnoff first attracted attention to his system. Entertainment programming—those three hours of prime time—may well remain stable, however. The networks, unlike cable, which fragments the audience into specialized markets, have always been predicated on reaching the largest possible audience, and entertainment programming has always been based on mass appeal.

Finally, the fate of one crucial area remains in doubt: news. Faced with the challenge of a growing cable audience, the networks may elect to take one of two courses. They may decide they no longer can afford the burden of maintaining a news department, in spite of the prestige they engender. Losing audiences to cable and faced with declining profits, they may cut back network news to a bare minimum and rely instead on lucrative local news. Following the other course, they may decide to emphasize news to a degree that appears to be wildly extravagant by present standards. There is an economic justification for this plan as well. Because news programming tends to appeal to a more affluent audience, often predominantly male, the networks may decide to cultivate an audience that many advertisers would want to reach.

A last possibility is that networks, following the pattern of radio's adaptation to television, will become decentralized, not really networks at all.

The FCC, too, has heard and believes in the coming of cable and satellite as major communications forces. Since their widespread application has the effect of eliminating the chronically short supply of airwaves on which the FCC's regulation has been posited all these years, a House subcommittee has been preparing a revolutionary new set of provisions for the Communications Act, provisions calculated to tear down the superstructure of regulation the FCC has erected over the years. Since cable, the most rudimentary of electronic communications systems, and satellite, the most sophisticated, have combined to provide a practically infinite number of places on the spectrum, the FCC, having less of a reason for being, would lapse into a caretaker role, treating every facet of the communications industry, from telephone to television, with equal restraint, throwing the new, expanded communications industry open to untrammeled free enterprise in a way not seen since the early nineteen twenties.

Overseen by California representative Lionel Van Deerlin, a former broadcaster, the deregulation promises to affect every level of the industry. Television-station licenses, for example, which are now the primary source of FCC authority, would be completely deregulated, except for technical considerations. The controversial Fairness Doctrine and Equal Time laws, which are in fact well-intended abridgments of the First Amendment, would at last become obsolete. Under the new plan, even the hallowed FCC would become obsolete, replaced by a new five-member commission with relatively limited powers.

For fifty years and more, electronic communications have been synonymous with broadcasting, and broadcasting with networks, but the rapid, unstoppable spread of new technology and new distribution systems taking place right now promises to bring an end to network dominance. The industry will be stirred from its lucrative torpor as if waking from a spell. Electronic life after the networks promises to be awesome and varied, both regional and global. And then, if he were alive to see it, even as harsh a critic as H. G. Wells might be pleased.

Notes on Sources

Chapter 1   High Hopes

3 The Wells article appeared in the New York *Times*, April 3, 1927.
4 The replies by De Forest and Kent appeared in the New York *Times*, May 8, 1978.
4 Sarnoff made his remarks in a speech at Syracuse University, reprinted in the New York *Times*, April 29, 1927.
6 Broadcasting's bone: author's interview with Robert Saudek, 1978.
8 advertising agencies: *Television/Radio Age*, September 12, 1977.

Chapter 2   Making Waves

11 his works: Carl Dreher, *Sarnoff*, New York, Quadrangle, 1977, p. 7.
11 ff. For conventional accounts of the role of wireless communications in the *Titanic* sinking, see *Fortune*, December 1930, and Erik Barnouw, *A Tower in Babel*, New York, Oxford University Press, 1966, p. 77.
12 bulletin boards: David Sarnoff, *Looking Ahead*, New York, McGraw-Hill, 1968, pp. 22–23.
12 incidentally me: Eugene Lyons, *Sarnoff: A Biography*, New York, Harper, 1966, p. 60.
12 Dreher insists: Dreher, p. 28.
13 a publisher: Lyons, p. 37.
17 an engineer: Dreher, p. 31.
17 AC current: Robert Conot, *A Streak of Luck*, New York, Seaview Books, 1979, p. 253.

17   their earphones: Barnouw, *Babel*, p. 20.
18   human voice: David Sarnoff, et al., *The Radio Industry*, Chicago, A. W. Shaw, 1928, pp. 3–4.
18   Opera House: New York *Times*, December 28, 1978.
19   Invisible Empire: Lee De Forest, *Father of Radio*, Chicago, Wilcox and Follett, 1950, p. 4.
19   wireless telephones: New York *Times*, November 8, 1916.
20   The radio music box memo is reproduced in Sarnoff, pp. 31–33.
21   Sarnoff backdated: *American Film*, October 1977.
22   She spoke: Lyons, p. 77.
22   I realized: *Atlantic Monthly*, February 1966.

Chapter 3   Cats' Whiskers

25   two thousand: Robert Landry, *This Fascinating Radio Business*, Indianapolis, Bobbs-Merrill, 1946, p. 39.
26   execution chamber: *American Heritage*, August 1965.
26   crowded ether: New York *Times*, November 11, 1926.
27 ff.   For a detailed account of AT&T's involvement in broadcasting, see William Peck Banning, *Commercial Broadcasting Pioneer*, Cambridge, Harvard University Press, 1946.
28   of $150,000: *Atlantic Monthly*, February 1966.
28   incalculable importance: *Printer's Ink*, April 27, 1922.
28   advertising paprika: *Radio Broadcast*, November 1922.
28–29   advertising chatter: Herbert Hoover, *The Memoirs of Herbert Hoover*, New York, Macmillan, 1952, p. 140.
29   electric money: Abel Green and Joe Laurie, Jr., *Show Biz from Vaude to Video*, New York, Holt, 1951, p. 233.
30   musicians' fees: ibid., p. 237.
30   George Gershwin: Frank Buxton and Bill Owen, *The Big Broadcast*, New York, Viking, 1972, p. 79.

Chapter 4   E Pluribus Unum

33   Langmuir application: Report of the Federal Trade Commission on the Radio Industry, p. 27, reprinted in Hiram Jome, *Economics of the Radio Industry*, Chicago, A. W. Shaw, 1925, pp. 52–53.
35   blocks of stock: Landry, p. 33.
35   the saddle: Dreher, p. 60.
35   the third: Sarnoff, pp. 33–34.
36   than fifteen hundred: *Reader's Digest*, December 1955.
37   made history: Lyons, p. 101.
37   in 1924: Sarnoff, pp. 33–34.
37   amusement company: *Fortune*, February 1930.
37 ff.   This memo is reproduced in Sarnoff, pp. 41–44.
38   of business: Archer, *Big Business and Radio*, New York, American Historical Society, 1939, p. 112.

39    $800,000 for goodwill: Landry, p. 53.
40   engineers plotted: Paul White, *News on the Air*, New York, Harcourt,
         Brace, 1947, p. 59.
41   the masses: *Fortune*, September 1932.
42   President Coolidge: Archer, p. 292.
42   to come: New York *Times*, November 17, 1926.
42   per hour: *Broadcasting*, June 21, 1976.
43   the sandwich: *Radio Broadcast*, December 1924.

Chapter 5   Shoestring

44 ff.   For accounts of the earliest days of the network, see *American Herit-*
            age, August 1955 (from which Judson's words are taken); Landry; and
            Archer, pp. 307–18.
45   ends nowhere: *Fortune*, June 1935.
46   mere shoestring: ibid.
46   the wires: *American Heritage*, August 1955.
47   New York studios: J. Andrew White, General Order No. 3.
48   male quartet: see "Highlights in the History of the Columbia Broad-
            casting System," CBS.
48   Accounts of the opening broadcasts draw on "Opening Day on the New
            CBS Network" and "The First Day at CBS—September 18, 1927,"
            CBS.
49   violent names: *American Heritage*, August 1955.
49   the pen: ibid.
50   Steinway Hall: ibid.
50   For accounts of the development of CBS's relations with affiliates, see
            Fortune, June 1935, and William S. Paley, *As It Happened*, Garden
            City, New York, Doubleday, 1979, pp. 42–43.
50 ff.   For information about Paley and his family, see *Fortune*, June 1935;
            Paley; Robert Metz, *Reflections in a Bloodshot Eye*, New York, Play-
            boy Press, 1975; and Archer, p. 319.
51   For accounts of Paley's first involvement with broadcast through WCAU,
            see Archer, p. 319, Metz, pp. 16–21, and Paley, pp. 35–36.
52   forty-seven stations: New York *Times*, January 9, 1929.
53   sponsored broadcasts: Paley, pp. 35–36.
53   Trust Company: Landry, p. 64.
53   serious intentions: Metz, p. 27.
54   public image: Edward L. Bernays, *Biography of an Idea*, New York,
            Simon and Schuster, 1965, p. 428.
54   a plunge: Paley, pp. 54–60.
54   hustling ability: *American Heritage*, August 1955.
55   of 50,000,000: *Fortune*, December 1930.
55   broadcasting programs: letter from George Washington Hill to Merlin
            Aylesworth, 1928.
56   of cigarettes: *Fortune*, September 1932.
56   bodily functions: "New Policies," CBS, 1935.

56   his shoes: Peter Goldmark, *Maverick Inventor*, New York, Dutton, 1973, p. 39.
57   they're told: "You Do What You're Told," CBS, 1935.
57   the lion's share: *Fortune*, September 1932.
57   it all: *Fortune*, June 1935.
57   American firesides: New York *Times*, January 26, 1930.
58   of entertainment: *The Radio Industry*, pp. 240–41.
59   a prostitute: Erik Barnouw, *The Sponsor*, New York, Oxford University Press, 1979, pp. 32–33.
60   balance sheet: *Atlantic Monthly*, February 1966.
60 ff. For accounts of the first Crossleys and the Price, Waterhouse survey, see *Fortune*, June 1935, and Paley, p. 104.
62   twenty-six: Metz, p. 38.
62   to ribbons: author's interview with Dr. Frank Stanton, 1978.
62   its license: Barnouw, *Babel*, p. 273.
63   by 1933: *Fortune*, June 1935.
64   well-to-do: *Atlantic Monthly*, September 1977.
65   American leaders: *Fortune*, June 1935.

Chapter 6   Dialogue

69   Amos 'n' Andy: John Dunning, *Tune in Yesterday*, Englewood Cliffs, N.J., Prentice-Hall, 1976, p. 36.
70   John Dunning, ibid., p. 33.
71 ff. Information about Gosden's career has been drawn primarily from the author's interviews with Freeman Gosden, 1978–79. See also Barnouw, *Babel*, pp. 225–31.
75   of tobacco: Mary Frances Rhymer, ed., *Vic and Sade*, New York, The Seabury Press, 1976, p. 11.
75   three years: Dunning, p. 177.
76   at home: Mary Livingston and Hilliard Marks, *Jack Benny: A Biography*, Garden City, N.Y., Doubleday, 1978, p. 65.
77   or simile: Steve Allen, *The Funny Men*, New York, Simon and Schuster, 1956, p. 55.
78   a conference: ibid., p. 54.
78   soon followed: Ben Gross, *I Looked and I Listened*, New York, Random House, 1954, p. 124.
78   substantially higher: *Fortune*, September 1932.
79 ff. For a financial analysis of CBS at this time, see ibid.

Chapter 7   Exhibit A

81 ff. For accounts of how Lewis came to CBS, see *Westways*, June 1975, and Erik Barnouw, *The Golden Web*, New York, Oxford University Press, 1968, pp. 62–65.
82   for entertainment: *Printer's Ink*, May 16, 1935.
82   rehearsal time: *Westways*, June 1975.

82 · from sale: Barnouw, *Web*, p. 69.
82 workshop's popularity: author's interview with Norman Corwin, 1978.
83 the eye: New York *Times*, October 30, 1938.
83 For the text of MacLeish's play, see Archibald MacLeish, *The Fall of the City*, New York, Farrar and Rinehart, 1937.
83 and simplicity: New York *Times*, October 13, 1938.
83 sound effects: ibid.
84 earning $169,097: *Fortune*, June 1935.
84 For a review of Welles's early career, see Dunning, pp. 407–8.
85 prestigious program: ibid., p. 409.
85 thirty-eight changes: Metz, p. 5.
86 on radios: Hadley Cantril, *The Invasion from Mars*, Princeton, Princeton University Press, p. 5.
86 New York: ibid.
86 in CBS: Dunning, p. 410.
86 saying 'Boo!': ibid., p. 40.
86 For the reaction of the press, see New York *Times*, October 31, 1938.
87 ff. Information about Corwin's career has been derived from the author's interview with Norman Corwin, 1978, from which the following quotations come. Some of Corwin's plays have been collected into Norman Corwin, *Thirteen by Corwin*, New York, Holt, 1942.
90 network broadcasting: John F. Royal interview with William Hedges, August 24, 1964, Broadcast Pioneers Library, Washington, D.C.
90 University Theatre: *Newsweek*, July 3, 1937.
91 ff. Royal's remarks are from the transcript of the interview with Hedges.
91 higher offer: ibid.
92 ff. For accounts of Toscanini's involvement with CBS and NBC, see Lyons, pp. 195–97; Samuel Chotzinoff, *Toscanini*, New York, Knopf, 1956; and Harold Sachs, *Toscanini*, New York, Lippincott, 1978.
92 ten concerts: Lyons, p. 197.
93 domestic broadcasting, *Fortune*, May 1938, Archer, p. 397.
93 ff. For biographical information about Murrow, see Alexander Kendrick, *Prime Time*, Boston, Little, Brown, 1969.
95 old boobs: New York *Times*, October 12, 1931.
95 per week: White, p. 38.
95 for days: ibid., p. 39.
96 the participants: ibid., p. 41.
96 he for it: Kendrick, p. 137.
97 before him: *Saturday Review*, October 26, 1957.
97 the company: II. V. Kaltenborn, *Fifty Fabulous Years*, New York, Putnam, 1950, p. 111.
97 to participate: Barnouw, *Web*, p. 82.
98 debatable question: *Broadcasting*, December 15, 1937.
98 William Lewis: Kendrick, p. 252.
98 was accepted: Kendrick, p. 139.
99 not announcers: New York *Times*, April 28, 1965.
99 goal line: Barnouw, *Web*, p. 77.

99   radio engineers: Kaltenborn, p. 208.

100 one minute: ibid., p. 209.

100 out of place: Edward Bliss, Jr., *In Search of Light*, New York, Knopf,
     1967, pp. 35–36.

101 shall live: Bliss, p. 47.

101 the professor: New York *Times*, April 28, 1965.

101 language survives: Bliss, p. 31.

101 it originally: ibid.

102 go home: ibid., pp. 34–35.

103 done at all: New York *Times*, December 3 and 7, 1941.

104 First Amendment: New York *Times*, May 9, 1978.

Chapter 8   My Way

106 broadcast station: David Sarnoff, "Radio Broadcasting Activities," mem-
     orandum to directors of RCA, April 5, 1923.

107 mechanical system: New York *Times*, November 18, 1928.

107 ff. Information about Zworykin's career has been drawn from the au-
     thor's interview with Dr. Vladimir Zworykin, 1978, from which the
     following quotations come.

108 business purposes: Conot, p. 424.

109 poor definition: *Television Quarterly*, November 1962.

110 For a good description of the electronics of television circa 1939, see
     Fortune, April 1939.

110 for the company: Lyons, p. 209.

111 his honor: ibid., p. 162.

112 Machine Company: Landry, p. 55.

112 RCA et al.: Lyons, p. 162.

112 Sarnoff boasted: Lyons, p. 167.

113 For a detailed account of the consent decree, see Archer, *Big Business
     and Radio*, pp. 378–79.

113 and reformed: Landry, p. 57.

114 and energy: Bernays, p. 437.

114 ff. For a technical account of the early electronic television systems, see
     P. K. Werner, "A Historical Review of the Development of Television
     Pickup Devices (1930–1976)," IEEE Transactions on Electron De-
     vices, July 1976. For more information on Farnsworth, see George
     Everson, *The Story of Television*, New York, Norton, 1949.

115 a distillery: Barnouw, *Web*, p. 39.

115 300 lines: New York *Times*, December 4, 1930.

115 3.5 per cent: *Fortune*, April 1939.

116 patent attorney: Everson, p. 246.

116 in his set: *Fortune*, April 1939.

116 ff. For more information about Armstrong, see Dreher; Laurence Les-
     sing, *Man of High Fidelity*, New York, Lippincott, 1954; *Fortune*,
     February 1948; *Scientific American*, April 1954; *Radio Broadcast*,
     July 1924; and New York *Times*, May 21, 1978.

117   so fast: *Fortune*, February 1948.
117   urgently required: ibid.
118   largest stockholder: ibid.
118   of 549: Lessing, p. 149.
118   became all-important: *Fortune*, February 1948.
118   I can find: ibid.
119   engineering community: ibid.
120   be with us: *Fortune*, February 1948.
120   October 1935: *Fortune*, February 1948.
121   last ditch: Dreher, p. 203.
121   For a description of the evolution of the broadcasting spectrum, see
       Christopher H. Sterling and John M. Kittross, *Stay Tuned*, Belmont,
       Calif., Wadsworth, 1978, p. 229.
122   to manufacture sets: Dreher, p. 205.
122   RCA lawyers: Lessing, pp. 280–81.
123   kill Armstrong: Dreher, p. 207.
123   troubled world: Sarnoff, p. 101.
125   other communities: New York *Times*, March 20, 1940.
125   before publication: Lyons, p. 219.
126   goodwill luncheon: ibid., p. 220.
126   first commercial: Les Brown, *The New York Times Encyclopedia of
       Television*, New York, Quadrangle, 1977, p. 150.

Chapter 9   Monopoly

129 ff.   See Report on Chain Broadcasting, Washington, Federal Communi-
          cations Commission, May 1941, from which all quotations have been
          drawn.
134   of the air: New York *Times*, May 5, 1941.
134   impotent vassals: New York *Times*, May 4, 1941.
134   two networks: *National Broadcasting Co., Inc., et al.* v. *United States
       et al.*, 319 U.S. 190, May 10, 1943. See Frank J. Kahn, *Documents of
       American Broadcasting*, Englewood Cliffs, N.J., Prentice-Hall, 1978,
       p. 99.
134   shines and stinks: Landry, pp. 225–26.
135   time sold: Ned Midgley, *The Advertising and Business Side of Radio*,
       New York, Prentice-Hall, 1948, pp. 112–13.
135   Edward J. Noble: Tide, August 15, 1943, *Advertising Age*, November
       1, 1948.
135   American people: Barnouw, *Web*, p. 189.
136   want to hear: *Advertising Age*, November 1, 1948.

Chapter 10   Color War

137   my own career: Goldmark, p. 50.
138   benevolent marketing: ibid., p. 51.
138   color to television: ibid., p. 55.

138   champion of color: ibid., p. 62.
138   color system: St. Louis *Post-Dispatch,* September 22, 1940.
139   two weeks' time: Goldmark, p. 64.
142   TV outlets: Goldmark, p. 94.
142   our plea: ibid., p. 104.
143   off the scent: ibid., p. 107.
143   to play with: Sarnoff, p. 133.
143   good laugh: Dreher, p. 210.
143   win the war: *Variety,* December 13, 1971.
144   first place: Goldmark, pp. 113–14.
144   way of life: *Time,* December 4, 1950.
144   color adeptness: Goldmark, p. 114.
146   was worth it: ibid., p. 112.

Chapter 11   War and Peace at CBS

147   For an account of Paley's war years, see Paley and *From D-Day
      Through Victory in Europe,* New York, Columbia Broadcasting Sys-
      tem, 1945.
149   to fly again: Bliss, pp. 70–76.
149   good as that: ibid., p. 263.
150   Corwin resigned: author's interview with Norman Corwin, 1978.
151   For an assessment of Kesten's career, see *Variety,* December 12, 1956.
151   minority-oriented network: Paley, p. 173.
152   well-ordered mind: *Fortune,* May 1968.
153   him at all: author's interview with Dr. Frank Stanton, 1978.
153   for my grinder: *Time,* December 4, 1950.
153   enthusiastic a reception: Paley, p. 83.
153 ff.   For assessments of Stanton's career, see *Broadcasting,* March 26,
      1973, and *The New Yorker,* January 18 and 25, 1947. For a first-person
      account, see *Broadcasting,* October 18, 1971.
154   color television: *The New Yorker,* January 25, 1947.
155   Joseph Ream: Metz, p. 281.
155   corporate enterprise: Fred Friendly, *Due to Circumstances Beyond
      Our Control . . .* New York, Random House, 1968, p. 161.

Chapter 12   Prelude: Rise of the Programmer

160   our left hands: *Fortune,* December 1958.
161   to like them: author's interview with Dr. Frank Stanton, 1978.
161   total earnings: Metz, p. 176.
161   the audience: author's interview with Dr. Frank Stanton, 1978.
161   very contemptuous: ibid.
161   the responsibility: Allen, p. 197.
162 ff.   This conversation has been drawn from the author's interviews with
      Freeman Gosden, 1978–79.

163   Gosden, Correll, and Benny: Paley, pp. 193–94.
164   48,000,000: *Fortune*, December 1958.

Chapter 13   Operation Frontal Lobes

167 ff.   Much information about Robert Sarnoff's career has been drawn from the author's interviews with him, 1979.
167   for Bobby: Erik Barnouw, *The Image Empire*, New York, Oxford University Press, 1970, p. 59.
168   for a rhapsody: Martin Mayer, *About Television*, New York, Harper and Row, 1972, p. 381.
168   on people: *The New Yorker*, October 16, 1954.
169   pleasure product: ibid.
171   class man: ibid.
175   mother or father: Barnouw, *Empire*, p. 33.
177   about $5,500,000: Barnouw, *Empire*, p. 70.

Chapter 14   Quiz Kids

181   28.7 to 11.2: Barnouw, *Web*, p. 287.
183   civil war: *Red Channels*, New York, American Business Consultants, 1955, p. 1.
183   HUAC report: ibid., pp. 155–57.
183   as possible: John Cogley, *Report on Blacklisting*, New York, Fund for the Republic, 1956.
184   right connections: ibid.
186   another boy: New York *Times*, April 28, 1965.
186   tomorrow as well: Kendrick, p. 49.
188   national security: Friendly, p. 50; William F. Buckley, Jr., and Brent L. Bozell, *McCarthy and His Enemies*, Chicago, Regnery, 1954.
188   eyebrow pencil: Friendly, p. 54.
190   land scandal: ibid., p. 76.
190   with the job: ibid., p. 92.
191   Now and Then: ibid.
191   period now: Friendly, p. 77.
193   committed perjury: Metz, p. 209.
194   their schedules: New York *Times*, October 17, 1959.
194   bothering him: Kendrick, p. 43.
195 ff.   Van Doren's testimony appeared in the New York *Times*, November 3, 1959.
196   any irregularity: Friendly, p. 101.
196   your forte: New York *Times*, December 9, 1959.
197   For a detailed account of the editing of *The Selling of the Pentagon*, see Mayer, pp. 254–64.
198   the source: For the Fairness Doctrine, 13 FCC 1246, June 1, 1949, see Kahn, p. 271 ff.; for the Mayflower Doctrine, 8 FCC 333, 338, January 16, 1941, see ibid., 95 ff.

Chapter 15   CBS Plus Thirty

201   joined ABC: New York *Times,* October 24, 1965.
202   Century-Fox: ibid.
202   regular basis: For accounts of ABC's early financial difficulties, see
        Fortune, April 1957; Bob Shanks, *The Cool Fire,* New York, Norton,
        1976, pp. 68–69; and *Business Week,* May 9, 1959.
202   95 per cent: Sterling and Kittross, p. 512, and White, p. 58.
203   of the stock: *Fortune,* April 1957.
204   Army-McCarthy hearings: New York *Times,* October 24, 1965.
205   three sponsors: *Fortune,* April 1957.
205   before taxes: ibid.
206   by 1958: *Business Week,* May 9, 1959.
206   severance pay: *Fortune,* April 1957.
207   General himself: New York *Times,* October 4, 1965.
207   on camera: ibid.
208   your life: *The New Yorker,* August 3, 1968.
208   Least Objectionable Program: Mayer, p. 98.
208   before taxes: Brown, *Encyclopedia,* p. 301.
209   criticize the senator: Cogley.
209   Brinkley complained: *The New Yorker,* August 3, 1968.
209   Kintner rubbed: Friendly, p. 160.
210   the week: *The New Yorker,* August 3, 1968.
210   For an account of the rivalry from the point of view of CBS, see
        Friendly; the men's-room incident appears on p. 93.
211   including entertainment: *The New Yorker,* August 3, 1968.

Chapter 16   The Aubrey Dictum

213   to New York: Shanks, p. 68.
213   programs at ABC: *Life,* September 10, 1965.
213   president of CBS: author's interview with Dr. Frank Stanton, 1978.
215   bring us prestige: Friendly, pp. xi–xii.
215   of news: ibid.
215   and fun: Barnouw, *Empire,* pp. 153–54.
215   "Bus Stop": *Broadcasting,* February 13, 1978.
216   each night: *Life,* September 10, 1965.
216   trade report: *Television/Radio Age,* April 29, 1963.
216   *My Fair Lady:* Paley, p. 336.
217   shares of CBS: Gallagher Report, May 6, 1964.
218   what you want: Friendly, p. 167.
218   corporate cliché: ibid.
219   placed sensors: Goldmark, p. 53.
219   For reviews of CBS acquisitions, see *Forbes,* May 1, 1975, and *Fortune,*
        May 1968.

222   Stanton summoned: *Life*, September 10, 1965; author's interview with
       Dr. Frank Stanton, 1978.

Chapter 17   A Student of Television

224 ff. Silverman, Fred, "An Analysis of ABC Television Network Pro-
         gramming from February 1953 to October 1959," Ohio State Univer-
         sity, 1959, unpublished, CBS.
226   were unbelievable: Les Brown, *Television*, New York, Harcourt Brace
       Jovanovich, 1971, p. 247.
228   network's demographics: author's interview with Fred Silverman, 1979.
228   leading it: Brown, *Television*, p. 56.
228 ff. For a penetrating analysis of the 1970–71 season, see Brown,
         Television.
229   schedule the program: ibid., p. 138.
230   continued to increase: Brown, *Encyclopedia*, p. 301.
230   future plans: author's interview with Fred Silverman, 1979.
231   36.4 per cent: Sterling and Kittross, p. 515.
232   takeover maneuver: New York *Times*, July 19, 1965.
232   none of it: *Fortune*, March 1969.
233   was off: ibid.
233   Goldenson refused: ibid.
233   Hanover Bank: *Variety*, July 3, 1968.
234   in adversity: author's interview with Fred Silverman, 1979.
234   one publication: Charles Moritz, ed., *Current Biography Yearbook:
       1978*, New York, Wilson, 1978.
236   lucrative operation: *Fortune*, January 29, 1979.
236   in September: New York *Times*, September 7, 1975.

Chapter 18   A Problem of Succession

242   till I die: New York *Times*, December 31, 1971.
242   third parties: *Fortune*, September 1972.
242   these investments: ibid.
243   American business: ibid.
243   than NBC: ibid.
244   five years: *Fortune*, December 31, 1978.
245   forcing Stanton: Metz, p. 402.
245   now denies: author's interview with Dr. Frank Stanton, 1978.
245   until 1987: *Broadcasting*, March 26, 1973.
246   Stanton remarked: author's interview with Dr. Frank Stanton, 1978.
246   one around: *Fortune*, January 29, 1979.
247   feel safe: Paley, p. 2.

Chapter 19   Resurrection of an Ideal

248 ff.   The full text of Murrow's speech appeared in *The Reporter*, November 13, 1958.
251 ff.   The text of Minow's speech appeared in *Broadcasting*, May 15, 1961.
253   the outset: Kendrick, p. 488.
253   was negligible: Broadcasting Yearbook, 1977, p. A7.
254   our Camelot: *Public Television: A Program for Action:* New York, Harper and Row, 1967.
256   worst enemy: *TV Guide*, September 15, 1971.
257   the audience: author's interview with Dr. Frank Stanton, 1978.
257   public goodwill: New York *Times*, July 2, 1978.
259   his thoughts: *American Film*, April 1979.
259   on logic: *TV Guide*, November 4, 1978.

Chapter 20   From Broadcasting to Narrowcasting

260   in the day: New York *Times*, May 9, 1978.
262   William Donnelly: New York *Times*, July 31, 1978.
264   as a fifth: New York *Times*, June 27, 1951.
265   in 1948: Paley, pp. 227–28.
266   the deregulation: *Broadcasting*, June 12, 1978.

Bibliography

I. Books

A Public Trust: The Report of the Carnegie Commission on the Future of Public Broadcasting. New York: Bantam Books, 1979.

Allen, Fred. *Treadmill to Oblivion.* Boston: Little, Brown, 1954.

Allen, Steve. *The Funny Men.* New York: Simon and Schuster, 1956.

Archer, Gleason. *History of Radio: to 1926.* New York: American Historical Society, 1938.

———. *Big Business and Radio.* New York: American Historical Society, 1939.

Baker, W. J. *A History of the Marconi Company.* New York: St. Martin, 1971.

Banning, William Peck. *Commercial Broadcasting Pioneer: The WEAF Experiment, 1922–1926.* Cambridge, Mass.: Harvard University Press, 1946.

Barnouw, Erik. *A Tower in Babel: A History of Broadcasting in the United States to 1933.* New York: Oxford University Press, 1966.

———. *The Golden Web: A History of Broadcasting in the United States, 1933–1953.* New York: Oxford University Press, 1968.

———. *The Image Empire: A History of Broadcasting in the United States from 1953.* New York: Oxford University Press, 1970.

———. *Tube of Plenty: The Evolution of American Television.* New York: Oxford University Press, 1975.

——. *The Sponsor: Notes on an American Potentate.* New York: Oxford University Press, 1978.

Bernays, Edward L. *Biography of an Idea: Memoirs of Public Relations Counsel Edward L. Bernays.* New York: Simon and Schuster, 1965.

Bliss, Edward J., ed. *In Search of Light: The Broadcasts of Edward R. Murrow, 1938–1961.* New York: Knopf, 1967.

Brown, Les. *Television: The Business Behind the Box.* New York: Harcourt Brace Jovanovich, 1971.

——. *The New York Times Encyclopedia of Television.* New York: Quadrangle, 1977.

Bucher, E. E. "Radio and David Sarnoff." RCA (unpublished).

Buckley, William F., Jr., and Bozell, Brent L. *McCarthy and His Enemies.* Chicago: Regnery, 1954.

Burns, David. *Herbert Hoover: A Public Life.* New York: Knopf, 1978.

Buxton, Frank, and Owen, Bill. *The Big Broadcast: 1920–1950.* New York: Viking, 1972.

Cantril, Hadley. *The Invasion from Mars.* Princeton, N.J.: Princeton University Press, 1947.

Chase, Francis, Jr. *Sound and Fury: An Informal History of Broadcasting.* New York: Harper, 1942.

Chayefsky, Paddy. *Television Plays.* New York: Simon and Schuster, 1955.

Chotzinoff, Samuel. *Toscanini: An Intimate Portrait.* New York: Knopf, 1956.

Cogley, John. *Report on Blacklisting II: Radio-Television.* Fund for the Republic, 1956.

Conot, Robert. *A Streak of Luck: The Life and Legend of Thomas Alva Edison.* New York: Seaview Books, 1979.

Correll, Charles J., and Gosden, Freeman F. *All About Amos 'n' Andy.* New York: Rand McNally, 1929.

Corwin, Norman. *Thirteen by Corwin.* New York: Holt, 1942.

——. *More by Corwin: 16 Radio Dramas.* New York: Holt, 1944.

——. *On a Note of Triumph.* New York: Simon and Schuster, 1945.

——. *Untitled and Other Radio Dramas.* New York: Holt, 1945.

De Forest, Lee. *Father of Radio: The Autobiography of Lee De Forest.* Chicago: Wilcox and Follett, 1950.

Dreher, Carl. *Sarnoff: An American Success.* New York: Quadrangle, 1977.

Dunlap, Orrin E., Jr. *The Story of Radio.* New York: Dial Press, 1935.

Dunning, John. *Tune in Yesterday: The Ultimate Encyclopedia of Old-Time Radio 1925–1976.* Englewood Cliffs, N.J.: Prentice-Hall, 1976.

Everson, George. *The Story of Television: The Life of Philo T. Farnsworth.* New York: Norton, 1949.

Faulk, John Henry. *Fear on Trial.* New York: Simon and Schuster, 1964.

Friendly, Fred. *Due to Circumstances Beyond Our Control. . . .* New York: Random House, 1967.

——. *The Good Guys, the Bad Guys, and the First Amendment: Freedom of Speech vs. Fairness in Broadcasting.* New York: Random House, 1976.

From D-Day through Victory in Europe. New York: Columbia Broadcasting System, 1945.

Gates, Gary Paul. *Air Time: The Inside Story of CBS News.* New York: Harper and Row, 1978.

Goldmark, Peter. *Maverick Inventor: My Turbulent Years at CBS.* New York: Dutton, 1973.

Green, Abel, and Laurie, Joe, Jr. *Show Biz from Vaude to Video.* New York: Holt, 1951.

Gross, Ben. *I Looked and I Listened: Informal Recollections of Radio and TV.* New York: Random House, 1954.

Head, Sydney W. *Broadcasting in America: A Survey of Television and Radio.* Boston: Houghton Mifflin, 1956.

Heighton, Elizabeth J., and Cunningham, Don R. *Advertising in the Broadcast Media.* Belmont, Calif.: Wadsworth, 1977.

Hoover, Herbert. *The Memoirs of Herbert Hoover: The Cabinet and the Presidency 1920–1933.* New York: Macmillan, 1952.

Johnson, Nicholas. *How to Talk Back to Your Television Set.* Boston: Little, Brown, 1970.

Jome, Hiram L. *Economics of the Radio Industry.* Chicago: A. W. Shaw, 1925.

Kahn, Frank J. *Documents of American Broadcasting.* Englewood Cliffs, N.J.: Prentice-Hall, 1978.

Kaltenborn, H. V. *Fifty Fabulous Years: 1900–1950.* New York: Putnam, 1950.

Kendrick, Alexander. *Prime Time: The Life of Edward R. Murrow.* Boston: Little, Brown, 1969.

Landry, Robert. *This Fascinating Radio Business.* Indianapolis: Bobbs-Merrill, 1946.

Lazarsfeld, Paul F., and Stanton, Frank N., eds. *Communications Research 1948–1949.* New York: Harper, 1949.

Lessing, Laurence. *Man of High Fidelity: Edwin Howard Armstrong.* Philadelphia: Lippincott, 1956.

Lichty, Lawrence W., and Topping, Malachi C. *American Broadcasting: A Source Book on the History of Radio and Television.* New York: Hastings House, 1975.

Livingston, Mary, and Marks, Hilliard. *Jack Benny: A Biography.* Garden City, N.Y.: Doubleday, 1978.

Lyons, Eugene. *David Sarnoff: A Biography.* New York: Harper and Row, 1966.

MacLeish, Archibald. *The Fall of the City: A Verse Play for Radio.* New York: Farrar and Rinehart, 1937.

Mayer, Martin. *About Television.* New York: Harper and Row, 1972.

Metz, Robert. *CBS: Reflections in a Bloodshot Eye.* New York: Playboy Press, 1975.

Midgley, Ned. *The Advertising and Business Side of Radio*. New York: Prentice-Hall, 1948.

Paley, William S. *As It Happened; A Memoir*. Garden City, N.Y.: Doubleday, 1979.

Public Television: A Program for Action. New York: Harper and Row, 1967.

Red Channels: The Report of Communist Influence in Radio and Television. New York: American Business Consultants, 1950.

Rhymer, Mary Frances, ed. *Vic and Sade: The Best Radio Plays of Paul Rhymer*. New York: The Seabury Press, 1976.

Rose, Reginald. *Six Television Plays*. New York: Simon and Schuster, 1956.

Ryan, Milo. *History in Sound*. Seattle: Washington University Press, 1963.

Sachs, Harold. *Toscanini*. New York: Lippincott, 1978.

Sampson, Anthony. *The Sovereign State of ITT*. New York: Stein and Day, 1973.

Sarnoff, David. *Looking Ahead: The Papers of David Sarnoff*. New York: McGraw-Hill, 1968.

——, et al. *The Radio Industry: The Story of Its Development*. Chicago: A. W. Shaw, 1928.

Schechter, A. A. *I Live on Air*. New York: Stokes, 1941.

Schickel, Richard. *The Disney Version: The Life, Times, Art and Commerce of Walt Disney*. New York: Simon and Schuster, 1968.

Shanks, Bob. *The Cool Fire: How to Make It in Television*. New York: Norton, 1976.

Silverman, Fred. "An Analysis of ABC Television Network Programming from February 1953 to October 1959." Ohio State University, 1959 (unpublished).

Sterling, Christopher H., and Kittross, John M. *Stay Tuned*. Belmont, Calif.: Wadsworth, 1978.

Subject Guide to the Radio and Television Collection of the Museum of Broadcasting. New York, 1979.

Thurber, James. *The Beast in Me and Other Animals*. New York: Harcourt, Brace, 1948.

White, Paul. *News on the Air*. New York: Harcourt, Brace, 1947.

II. Periodicals

Advertising Age, Chicago, weekly, 1930– .

American Film, Washington, D.C., monthly, 1975– .

Annual Report of the Federal Radio Commission, annual, 1927–34.

Aware, New York, 1954–56.

Billboard, Cincinnati, monthly, then weekly, 1894– .

Broadcasting, Washington, semimonthly, weekly, 1931– .

Columbia Broadcasting System annual report, New York, annual, 1933– .

Columbia Journalism Review, New York, quarterly, bimonthly, 1962– .
Counterattack: The Newsletter of Facts on Communism, New York, monthly, 1947–55.
FCC Reports, Washington, 1935– .
Fortune, New York, monthly, then biweekly, 1930– .
Radio Broadcast, Garden City, N.Y., Doubleday, Page, monthly, 1922–30.
RCA annual report, New York, annual, 1921– .
RCA Review, Princeton, N.J., quarterly, 1936– .
Sponsor, New York, monthly, 1948–68.
Television Quarterly, Syracuse, N.Y., quarterly, 1962– .
Television/Radio Age, New York, biweekly, 1953– .
TV Guide, Philadelphia, weekly, 1948– .
Variety, New York, weekly, 1905– .

III. Programming

Examples of most of the programming discussed in the text are available for public replay on the premises of the Museum of Broadcasting in New York.

Index